AF661306

CITIES AND HOUSING

PERSPECTIVES IN URBAN GEOGRAPHY
VOLUME ELEVEN

Concept's International Series in Geography

1. Perspectives in Agricultural Geography (In Five Volumes)
   Edited by Noor Mohammad
2. Perspectives in Geomorphology (In Four Volumes) *Edited by H.S. Sharma*
3. Perspectives in Urban Geography *Edited by C.S. Yadav*
   1. New Directions in Urban Geography
   2. Comparative Urban Research
   3. Comparative Urbanization: City Growth and Change
   4A. Models in Urban Geography (Theoretical)
   4B. Models in Urban Geography (Mathematical)
   5. Urban Research Methods: Central Place, Hierarchical and City Size Models
   6. Contemporary City Ecology
   7. Slums, Urban Decline and Revitalization
   8. Contemporary Urban Issues
   9. Rural-Urban Fringe
   10. Morphology of Towns
   11. Cities and Housing
   12. Perceptual and Cognitive Image of the City
   13. Urban Economics
   14. City Planning: Problems and Prospects
   15. City Planning: Administration and Participation
   16A. Urban Planning and Policies: Reorientation of Policy Norms
   16B. Urban Planning and Policies: Cross-cultural Urban Policies

---

About the Editor

C.S. Yadav received his post-graduate and doctoral degrees from the Delhi School of Economics. He had participated in the UNESCO seminar on The Teaching of Geography in South-East Asia held in December 1974 and has also contributed a paper on "Uneven Development of The World" for a UNESCO publication. He has attended and presented papers in International Conferences. He has been invited to attend an international symposium on urban modeling held in Waterloo University (Canada) in 1982. He had also attended and International Conference on Asian Urbanisation held in Akron University (U.S.A.) in 1985 and presented a paper on "Process of Migration and Urbanisation in India". He is keenly interested in urban problems and is at present engaged in studies on slums and cognitive image of The Delhi City. He taught geography at Shaheed Bhagat Singh College, University of Delhi.

PERSPECTIVES IN URBAN GEOGRAPHY

VOLUME ELEVEN

CITIES AND HOUSING

Edited by

C.S. YADAV

CONCEPT PUBLISHING COMPANY PVT. LTD.
NEW DELHI-110059

© 1987, Editor

All rights reserved. No part of this work may be reproduced, stored, adapted, or transmitted in any form or by any means, electronic, mechanical, photocopying, micro-filming recording or otherwise, or translated in any language, without the prior written permission of the copyright owner and the publisher. The book is sold subject to the condition that it shall not, by way of trade or otherwise, be lent, resold, hired out, or otherwise circulated without the prior publisher's written consent in any form of binding or cover other than that in which it is published.

The views and opinions expressed in this book are editor(s) own and the facts reported by him/her have been verified to the extent possible, and the publishers are not in any way liable for the same.

ISBN: 978-81-7022-080-0 (Set)
ISBN: 978-81-7022-030-5 (Volume 11)

Edition 2025

Published and Printed by

Since 1974

Concept Publishing Company Pvt. Ltd.
A/15-16, Commercial Block, Mohan Garden,
New Delhi-110059 (India)
T : 91-11-41101460
E : publishing@conceptpub.com, *W*: www.conceptpub.com

Preface

NATURE OF URBAN GEOGRAPHY

There are several studies on urban geography which reveal that, as a major sub-discipline, it has a long tail but a short body. However, the spectrum is so vast and broad that researchers are able to make general statements in defence of its conception, philosophy, nature and orientation. Urban geography today encompasses and interfaces with various disciplines which are interested in urban studies. As an introduction to this series, our task here is to make an attempt to briefly review the development of geographical interest in various aspects of cities.

There are several reviews of the early development of urban geography which have been dealt with by Berry and Harton (1970)[1] and Carter (1974).[2] Berry and Harton in their book, **Geographical Perspective on Urban System**, have made an attempt to introduce readers to its present-day status. They have clearly resolved that "the formative years of the social science in the late nineteenth century and early twentieth century were also the years in which urban studies first developed,"[3] thus providing the context for geography's emerging interest in cities. However, the emergence of urban studies dates back to the writing of Greek scholars, but as a sub-discipline, it has reached its present-day status only in the past 30 years.

In their historical perspective the works on urban geography show that the pre-20th century studies primarily concerned themselves with themes of location, size and shape of the cities. The initial findings were strongly subjective, descriptive and dependent more on observation such as the works of Hassert (1907)[4] and Blanchard (1911).[5] In the succeeding years the conceptual framework of site and situation was criticized by Aurousseau (1924)[6] and Crowe (1938)[7], their conception being that cities were not inanimate objects in landscape, but also organic elements which involved people and their movements. The morphologist, later in 1960, truly brought the indigenous line of evolution in the sphere of urban geography and studies on the build-up fabric of cities (Conzone, 1960).[8] Smails (1955)[9] constituted the prime base of urban geography, which remained articulated without any major conceptual change till early 1960s. The studies on the morphological aspects of the urban system were influenced by external forces, consequently the methodological frameworks got impetus within the discipline. At this juncture the evolution of concepts was not based on environment but took shelter under the umbrella of economics of location, and incorporated analysis of land values and rents, and the concept of nodality and accessibility. These concepts were derived from the economic theories of Cooley (1894)[10], Weber (1899),[11] and Hurd (1903).[12]

The Chicago School of Urban Ecology hastened the evolution of urban geography. In his monumental work Park (1925)[13] developed the idea of order and analysis of towns. Further, a powerful thrust and much of the rationale was provided to the studies of urban geography by the Central Place Theory of Christallar (1933).[14]

The impact of the statistical method was powerful and it brought rapid and enormous changes in the field of urban geography. It also brought new insights intc the development and application of urban geography towards increased quantification. Brian J. Berry, a pioneer in the field, analysed the spatial order, size and location of towns and cities. There was widespread use of innovative techniques to explore the nature of urban problems, hypotheses were tested, new theories propounded and old theories remodelled. The statistical methods were put to a variety of uses. Smith (1965)[15] evaluated the classification of settlements; Berry and Garrison (1956)[16] examined the utility of the rank-size rule for urban populations. The models of Park and Burgess (1925),[17] Harris and Ullman (1945)[18] and Homar Hoyt (1939)[19] were tested and re-examined by various geographers.

A new impetus to urban geography came from social area analysis which was initially propounded by Shevky and Bell (1955)[20] and later on this provided a basis for factorial ecology. The collaboration of this stream in urban geography was offered by Berry (1971)[21], Herbert (1972)[22] and Johnston

(1971).[23] As a consequence of these thrusts in geography after 1960, the techniques of investigation were sharpened and this has provided the basis for a scientific explanation of cities. Attempts were made to introduce new theories and frame laws to make the explanation of events more rational and logical. Sophisticated models were propounded as urban geography entered a new era of rationalizing the subject matter of urban studies on the basis of new philosophies, new concepts, new theories, new methodologies and applications.

However, the status of contemporary urban geography has been elevated only recently by the behavioural approach. The studies of perception and cognition which have a long tradition in physiology were first introduced into the field of geography by Lynch (1960)[24] Dowson and Stea (1973)[25], Gould and White (1974).[26] At present there is a sudden spurt in the studies on the subject with a new paradigm. But the full impact of behavioural approaches upon urban geography has yet to be realized.

The aim of this series is to seek reorientation of the discipline strengthened by new philosophies, methodologies, subject matters or application. The series has been arranged in such a way that all contemporary viewpoints are covered comprehensively. Hopefully, this series will inspire researchers to appreciate the work already done by geographers in studying cities. Geography by nature seems to be a synthesizing field of inquiry. As such we have made an endeavour to combine some of the otherwise disparate facts garnered by other disciplines in such a manner that we can gain a better understanding of the urban system. The study of urban geography is essential if we are to analyse the human consequences of the settlements in which we live. It is useful to planners, decision makers in government and corporations and also to each one of us as citizens. Finally, it gives us a perspective on what may be happening to our cities and to the nature.

To achieve the above goal only those contributions with originality and contrasting viewpoints were selected for inclusion in this series. In doing so the editor does not wish to compete with the journals in the field in which innovative research and methodological aspects are presented. But he does wish to convey, and convey with conviction, that significant researches are being undertaken in the different branches of urban geography and in other allied disciplines. The present series is an attempt to provide a selective reappraisal and rigorous examination of the assumptions and the urge to disseminate new knowledge created by the mutual interaction. Emphasis is also placed on the conceptualization and theorization of the subject matter so that general laws may emerge. A conscious effort has been made to organize the series in such a way that it reflects the philosophical approach parallel to that of the behavioural school. Finally, a vigorous attempt has been made to demonstrate throughout the series how geographers are basically involved in solving the urban problems.

C. S. YADAV

REFERENCES

1. Berry and Harton, **Geographic Perspectives on Urban Systems: With Integrated Readings**, New Jersey, Prentice Hall, Inc, Englewood Cliffs, 1970.
2. Carter, **The Study of Urban Geography**, Edward Arnold, London, 1974.
3. Berry and Harton, 1970.
4. Hassert, K., **Die Stadte Geographisch Betrachect**, Leipzig, 1907.
5. Blanchard, R., **Grenoble: Etude de Geographic Urbanine**, Paris, 1911.
6. Aurousseau, M., "Recent Contributions to Geography: A Review," **Geographical Review**, 1924, 14, p.444.
7. Crowe, P.R., "On Progress in Geography," **Scottish Geographical Magazine**, 1938, 54, 1-19.
8. Conzone, M.R.G., "The Plan Analysis of an English City Centre," In Norkorg (Ed), **Proceedings of I.G.U. Symposium on Urban Geography**, C.W.K. Gleerup, Lund, 1962.
9. Smails, A.E., "The Urban Mess of England and Wales," **Transactions and Papers**, Institute of British Geographers, 1946, 11, 85, p.101.
10. Cooley, C.H., "The Theory of Transportation," **Publications of the American Economic Association**, 1894, 9, p.5-7.
11. Weber, A.F., **The Growth of Cities in the Nineteenth Century: A Study in Statistics**, New York, 1899.
12. Hurd, R., **Principles of City Land Values: New York Record and Guide**, 1903, p. 19-21.
13. Park, R.E., "Suggestions for the Investigation of Human Behaviour in an Urban Environment," in R.E. Park, E.W. Burgess, R.D. Mackenzie (eds), **The City**, University of Chicago Press, 1925.
14. Christallar, W., **Central Place in Southern Germany**,

Gustar Fischer, Teno, 1933.

15. Smith, R.M.T., "Method and Purpose in Functional Town Classification," **Annals of the Association of American Geographers**, 1965, 55, pp.539-548.
16. Garrison, W.L., "Applicability of Statistical Inference to Geographical Research," **Geographical Review**, 1956, 46, 427, 429.
17. Burgess, E.W., "The Growth of City," in R.E. Park, E.W. Burgess and R.D. Mackenzie (eds), **The City**, University of Chicago Press, 1925.
18. Ullman, E.L., "The Nature of Cities," **Annals, American Academy of Political and Social Science**, 1945, 242, 7-17.
19. Hoyt, H., **The Structure and Growth of Residential Neighbourhoods in American Cities**, Washington, Federal Housing Administration, 1939.
20. Shevky, E. and Bell, W., **Social Area Analysis**, Stamford University Press, Stamford, 1955.
21. Berry, B.J.L. (ed), "Comparative Factorial Ecology," **Economic Geographic (Supplement)**, 1971, 47.
22. Herbert, D.T., **Urban Geography: A Social Perspective**, David and Charles, Newton Abbot, 1972.
23. Johnston, **Urban Residential Pattern**, Bell, London, 1971.
24. Lynch, **Image of the City**, Massachusetts, Cambridge, 1960.
25. Dowson and Stea, "Image and Environment", Chicago and London, 1973.
26. Gould and White, R., **Mental Maps**, London, 1974.

Acknowledgements

We are highly thankful to Prof. David G. Dickason Western lMichigan University Kalamazoo (U.S.A.) who guided us whole heartedly during the initial stage of the Project. We regret that his name was not acknowledged in earlier volumes.

We also thank Editors Gerd-Michael Hellstern, Frithjof Spreer Hellmut Wollmann, Heft 2, Vol. II and Vol. III for their permission to use material from "Applied Urban Research", Proceedings of the European Meeting on Applied Urban Research, Essen, 2-4, Oct. 1981.

Contents

List of Contributors

Arza Churchman: Faculty of Architecture and Town Planning, Technion, Israel Institute of Technology, Haifa, Israel

Christina R. Victor: Research Team for the care of the Elderly, Welsh National School of Medicine, St. David's Hospital, Cardiff

David C. Thorns: Department of Sociology, University of anterbury, Christchurch 1, New Zealand

Dieter Frick: Institut fur Stadt-und Regionalplanung, Der Technische Universitat, Dovestr, 1-5, D-1000, Berlin 10

Eberhard Muhlick: Institut Wohnen Und Umwelt, Annastr. 15, D-6100, Darmstadt

Erwin Zimmermann: Swiss Federal Institute of Technology, Lausanne, Switzerland

Frederick A. Lazin: Humphrey Center, Ben-Gurion University of the Negev, University of California, Los Angeles California-90024, U S A

Gary Sands: Associate Professor, Department of Urban Planning, Wayne State University, Detroit 2, Michigan

Glenn Yago: Department of Sociology, State University of New York at Stony Brook, NY 11794, U S A

Helmut Kromrey: Ruhr-universitat, Friederikastr.111, 4630, Bochum

Hermann Zinn: Institut Wohnen und Umwelt, Darmstadt, Federal Republic of Germany

Horst-Juergen Wienen: Amt Fuer Statistik and Stadt forschung, City of Bochum, Department of Statistics and Urban Research, Federal Republic of Germany

Jan Van Weesep: Department of Geography and Planning, Vrise Universitit, P.O. Box 7161, NI-1007, Amsterdam

John C. Weaver: Associate Professor of History, Department of History, McMaster University, 1280, Main Street West, Hamilton, Ontario, L854L9, Canada

Hazimiers Z. Sowa: Assistant Professor, Cooperative Research Institute, Krakow, Poland

Michael Harloe: Professor, Department of Sociology, University of Essex, Wivenhoe park, GBCOLCHESTERCOY 3SQ

Nandeshwar Sharma: Reader and Head, Department of Geography, L.N. Mithila University, Darbhanga - 846004, Bihar, (India)

Roderick J. Lawrence: Departement D'Architecture, EcoLe Polytechnique federale de Lausanna, 12,av del' Eglise-Anglaise Case 1020, CH-1001 Lausanna, Switzerland

Sam Aroni: School of Architecture and Urban Planning, University of California, Los Angels, California 90024, U.S.A.

Tor Bysveen: Norwegian Institute of Urban and Regional Research, Postboks 15 Grefsen, N - Oslo 4

Yona Ginsberg: Center for Urban and Regional Studies, Tel-Aviv University, Ramat-Aviv, Israel

Zbigniew Pucek:

ONE

C.S.YADAV

Introduction

TWENTIETH CENTURY HOUSING

Shelter, which is the basic human need and is the traditional definition of housing, is the highest and finest product of civilization. Undoubtedly, every human being requires shelter a roof over his head, and for most of the individuals, it means a home, a permanent "base" where a greater part of one's life is spent. Obviously then, housing is an important phenomenon in most people's lives. It is a great force moulding the mind, character, attitude and behaviour of the people. In its essence the physical character of dwellings affects the myriad daily activities necessary for normal personal care and family life. Undeniably, in poor housing there is a high incidence of illness and death high rates of mental illness, and adult delinquency. Thus housing plays an important role in the life of each individual. Its physical condition may facilitate or restrict every-day activities and may affect physical and mental health (Marzoric Branin Keizer).[1] The location of housing determines social and economic development of the citizens. Some past studies have argued that housing industry plays a crucial role in the political, economic and social order. It contributes nearly one-fourth of our national wealth, it provides employment for hundreds of thousands of people who are involved in the construction of new houses, the manufacturing of the components and supplies, the maintenance of homes. Further it is also identified that housing in an urban setting plays an important role in the use of energy, the design of transportation networks and communication system. Indeed, then, housing is an important factor in the life of urban citizens and this importance is assumed in its social and political significance. The significance of housing can be evaluated by this fact that it is a major issue in every party's platform at all elections, and there are various pressure groups who have seen housing deficiencies at the core of society's problems. Furthermore, various sections of many of the United Nations agencies have considered housing as the World's major problem. These organizations are the FAO, WHO, PAHO, UNCTAD, IBRD, IDA and IFC. Besides, there are some centres of the United Nations which carry out feasibility studies on housing, provide training and advisory services, technical assistance and specialized documentation in support of codings and norms to be adopted for good housing facilities. Planning projects have been carried out in the field of national physical planning, regional and urban planning, legislation and management. The United Nations Centre for Housing, Building and Planning provides information about sites and services, policy formation, land development, squatter settlement, low cost housing, co-operative housing, and institutional support. In the housing field, material and methods, prefabrication, architectural design and material substitution have been the areas of concern. Another organization, United Nation's International Habitat and Human Settlements Foundation (IHHSF) undertakes those activities which seek provision of capital, identification of innovative approaches to investment and financial strategies and mobilization of local resources.

Thus these institutions and their activities, as would be seen from the foregoing, represent a range of concerns and experience which sufficiently clearly reflect the problems confronted by all nations in the drawing up of housing programmes. A wide range of these institutions and organizations are :

Housing Related Organizations and Addresses

Office of Housing Agency for International Development
Washington, D.C.20528
Overseas Private Investment Corporation
1129 20th Street, N.W., Washington, D.C. 20548
Peace Corps
806 Connecticut Avenue, N.W., Washington, D.C. 20525
Economic Commission for Europe
Palais des Nations, Geneva, Switzerland
Economic Commission for Africa
Addis Ababa, Ethiopia
Economic and Social Commission for Asia and the Pacific
Bangkok, Thailand
International Council for Building Research Studies
and Documentation (CIB)

Weena 704, P.O. Box 20704
Rotterdam, The Netherlands (International)
National Academy of Sciences
2101 Constitution Avenue, NW
Washington, D.C. 20027 (US Secretariat CIB)
International Association for Housing Science
P.O. Box 340254, Coral Gables, Miami, Fla. 33134
Bouwcentrum
P.O. Box 229, Rotterdam, The Netherlands
International Cooperative Housing Development Association
5159 Kerpen, Burgstrasse 47, Germany
Union International des Architects
4, Impasse d'Antin, Paris VIII, France
International Union of Local Authorities
5 Paleisstraat, The Hague, The Netherlands
International Union of Testing and Research Laboratories for Materials and Structures (RILEM)
12 rue Rancion, 75 Paris-15, France
Federal National Mortgage Association
1133 15th Street, N.W., Washington, D.C. 20005
National Savings and Loan League
1101 15th Street, N.W., Washington, D.C. 20005
Foundation for Cooperative Housing
2101 L Street, N.W., Suite 409, Washington, D.C 20037
World Bank
(International Bank for Reconstruction and Development)
1818 H Street, N.W., Washington, D.C. 20433
UN Centre for Housing, Building and Planning
United Nations, New York, N.Y. 10017
United Nations Environment Programme
P.O. Box 30552, Nairobi, Kenya
United Nations Habitat and Human Settlements Foundation
P.O. Box 30552, Nairobi, Kenya
International Referral Service (IRS)
U.S. International Environmental Referral Center, PM-213
c/o U.S. Environment Protection Agency
401 M Street, S.W., (Room 2902 WSM)
Washington, D.C. 20460 (Focal Point)
Office of International Affairs
U.S. Department of Housing and Urban Development
451 7th Street, S.W. Washington, D.C. 20410
(IRS Subfocal point)
International Labor Organization
Palais des Nations, Geneva, Switzerland

Although the definition of housing varies, majority of scholars define a building or a part of building which is designed to be occupied by a single family or an individual.

R. Neutra 1951[2] broadly described housing as "interior and exterior spaces" and specifically as "the nursery in which a child spends its formative years. the bath in which the essentials of cleanliness are taught. the structure containing the rooms. the streets to which the structure belongs".

The Traditional definition of housing as "Shelter". "a commodity" or "product" is not adequate because housing includes more than just shelter (Stewart. 1979).[3] Housing is more appropriately defined as a process involving the interaction between an organism and its environment. The organism may be single individual. a family or a communal group. The environment refers to natural surrounding along with political. economical. social and cultural environments surrounding the organism. As a matter of fact. the logic behind this definition seems to be based on the principle that for most organisms the environment is a well-defined place in which they grow and reproduce. The longer the organism lives in these surroundings. the more perfectly attuned to them it becomes. Thus human beings like other organisms. evolve their shelter by adapting to the environment. It is a truism that various dwelling forms result from a complex phenomenon which defies any single explanation (Rapoport. 1969)[4] but respond to the environment of people holding different attitudes and ideals. Various religious. social. cultural. physical. and economic factors form the base of different house forms which vary from culture to culture and from area to area.

A comprehensive definition of housing is provided by Samuel Aroni (1978)[5] who postulates that "Every society. developed or developing. has a basic need for housing. For every individual. alone or as a part of a family unit. a house. be it a cave or castle. is hopefully more than just physical shelter. It should be a home. a residing place in which to try to fulfill the fundamental purpose of human society. namely. a scheme. rewarding. happy or at least livable life. In our society. still based on the family as its fundamental unit. a house and home also represent an extended womb for the young during the formative years. during their physical. psychological. educational and emotional development. so vital both to the person and to the community. Through its nature. physical location and characteristics. a house provides the enabling or constraining influence on a variety of important services. These include physical services such as power. water. transportation or sewage; social services such as health. education or recreation; and economic services such as opportunities for work and income. For the individual or the family, the house is both, shelter and symbol, physical protection and physiological identity of economic value and a foundation for security and self-respect".

Ecology and Housing Design

It is a general belief that human desires change in their societal context, so must the design of shelter change. Housing form in an urban setting is a direct consequence of a whole range of socio-cultural factors which take shape in a broad ecological context. Due to technological innovations, the methods of planning and housing codes have changed considerably, so the basic form of most of the houses has also changed. The change in the design of housing is the consequence of a whole range of social, cultural and environmental factors, which occur in a broad ecological framework. One of the basic principles of human ecology is the conception of life as a continuous struggle for adjustment of aggregates of organism to their environment. A population adjusts to its physical world through the coordination and organization of individual actions to form a functional unit. Thus it is emphasized that technological innovations influence population distribution and the spatial arrangements of physical structures which are designed to cater to the requirements of the organisms within communities. The adoption of technological innovations is always influenced by the social values of the group in which an individual resides. Housing designs, then, are influenced not only by the natural environment, the size and characteristic of population, and the available technology, but also by the social organizations within society, economic and political activities and cultural values (Stewart, 1979)[6]. A given culture has a symbolic image and meaning of housing. Rapoport 1969[7] has rightly remarked that housing design changes as the social image of "right" and "adequate" housing changes. As a matter of fact, changes in design occur as a result of reactions to symbol and fashion that occur within the limits of available materials and technology.

The Influence of Industrial Revolution

It is an obvious fact that the industrial revolution in the 19th century has greatly shaped the technological innovations, which in turn, have influenced the design and location of housing. Prior to the industrial revolution, family had been considered the major social institution and thus society was centred around a family which was believed to be a closely knit, largely self-sufficient unit and played a crucial role in the social organization. In colonial society families were large and the home was the centre for the industry and family. Activities and comforts were largely confined in and around the home. Colonial homes were designed with kitchens and work areas with smaller rooms. Homes were built by the occupants, usually with the assistance of neighbours. Housing design reflected both climate and heritage. Housing in urban areas varied according to the physical setting of the city, available transportation, period of construction and heritage of local areas.

The industrial revolution, in its wake, had also influenced the form and quality of human environment, population, city growth, social organization, family patterns and housing. As a matter of fact industrialization was followed by new inventions, new machinery, new techniques and new forms of production and distribution that largely produce an influence on the design and arrangement of housing. The whole infrastructure of the housing was changed accordingly. By 1820, wood or coal-burning cast iron stoves began to replace the fireplace. Gas and electric stoves and steam-heating system became popular by the beginning of the 20th century. Water supply, plumbing and sanitation had developed slowly during the 19th century. However, at the turn of the century the houses were big with large kitchens and pantries, separate dining rooms, a number of bedrooms, spacious attics, large collars, verandahs and the back stoops.

Thus it is evident that the industrial revolution, with the population growth and a redistribution which accompanied it, was a strong agent of change in the city community structure. It had a direct impact on the design of housing through new techniques, better material and mechanization of household equipment.

Impact of family structure

The industrial revolution with its two attendants, the increasing specialization and high level of technology, brought changes in the social and family values and family structures which in turn influenced the design of houses (Stewart, 1979)[8]. The traditional families in the developed countries performed a variety of functions including education, protection, recreation, economic support and affection (Ogburn, 1968)[9]. Thus the entire family had to co-operate in order to survive but gradually in the industrialized countries, the family lost many of these functions or transferred them to other organizations. This change in the family functions influenced the house design. The family size was reduced which meant that less inside space in the house was required. This led to homes being designed for maximum comfort and convenience rather than as show places. The spacious drawing rooms of former years were replaced by open plans with flexible spaces that could be adapted to the families changing needs. And, in course of time, more open plans and multipurpose family rooms developed in response to the informal living patterns.

Families differ from each other in terms of choice of location and capacity to pay for housing, and the "structure and location of family is changing constantly which, in turn, influences the housing design.[9] As a matter of fact family size and stage in the life-cycle have greatly influenced the type of housing that is needed at a given point in time. For example, a young newly married couple wishes to live in or near an urban area so that they are close to the work-place and recreation facilities. With this in view they try to select an apartment on rent which demands less in terms of time and maintenance. Increase in the size of family with the addition of children demands more space within the house, and also the demand for ownership of a single-family home increases. This demand reaches the peak at about the age of 35-54 and then declines slightly as families in the contracting stage of life-cycle begin to reduce the size of their homes in response to the decreasing family size (Stewart, 1979).[10]

Family values

Families not only differ in their lifestyle but also in terms of values that they hold, and these values influence a family's decision about the design of its home. Beyer and Montgomery (1955)[11] have thrown some light on the relationship between family values and housing design. They have identified four basic value groups : economy, family-centred, personal and prestige. The families which were economy-oriented were supposed to be highly conservative and conventional who placed highest value on price and durability of home. The family-centred one viewed the housing design to enhance the well-being and security of the family members. The family which paid more attention to personal values put more emphasis on personal enjoyment and privacy of individual family members. The fourth group attached more value to prestige and considered their house as a symbol of their success, so they emphasized impressiveness more than convenience or efficiency. These distinct variations in value orientation stressed the need for a variety in housing alternatives within any market, so that families could have choice in the selection of the type of housing that related to their value orientation.

Different families view a home in different ways. One family may view the home as primarily a place for family interaction and the nurturing of children, while another may emphasize individual development....(Dean, 1966).[12] The style of the exterior and interior of a home reflects the personality of the resident. Many people while considering purchase of a house give first priority to its capacity to bolster the image of self since the house is a symbolic statement of the status of the family in society (Cooper, 1974).[13]

So it is envisaged that as human needs change due to technological innovations, population growth and change in family life-style, so must the design of shelter change. Housing form is a consequence of various socio-cultural factors which take place in a broad illogical context. The evaluation of housing as a process occurring within an ecological system justifies that there is deep interrelatedness between the individual or family unit, the natural and manmade environment and the level of technology available at any point in time.

Influence of standards, codes and zoning

It is a paradox to state that in practice residential design is not determined by trained architects and designers but by the forces of circumstances operating at any given time. In a real situation builders are constrained by consumer acceptance attitudes of the lenders, cost factors, location, building codes and zoning ordinances. At the national level, government institutions and health agencies influence design and construction - "from the kinds of materials and products that go into a house to structural design to mechanical equipment and water supply and sewage disposal requirements" (Beyer, 1955).[14] As a matter of fact the minimum housing standard as determined by the Government obviously becomes maximum and results in housing development of identical dwellings. These standards as laid down by Government of a country are very important because through their influence on the building industry, they virtually dictate the size of millions of dwelling units.

Building codes are laid down to regulate new construction and to bring changes in existing buildings by means of remodelling. This is necessary in order to ensure quality of housing to be rented out or purchased. Although building codes serve the housing consumer they have also been used to "serve the self-interest of some parts of the housing industry by protecting certain traditional materials and work methods and by impeding technological innovations" (Hartman, 1975).[15] Thus it can be concluded that building codes have served as a constraint to innovations in building techniques that would naturally have occurred given the technological changes within the environmental system (Stewart, 1979)[16]

Zoning laws have been established to control haphazard development of housing and place emphasis on an orderly development of housing design. As a matter of fact in our cities the pressure of population growth has resulted in more houses being built each year and land is increasingly subdivided at the edges of urban concentrations. The environmentalist has questioned and countered this and the elite citizen has raised objection to the way in which land is subdivided and developed. In order to resolve this zoning was considered as a most appropriate and effocting tool for checking haphazard growth of the city and restricting entry of apartments and low income housing into suburbs. Thus standards, zoning, codes and regulations have all been responses against haphazard development of the city housing. Moreover, each of these regulations was an attempt by the social organization to control conditions unfavourable to desired city housing.

World urban housing situation

The technological innovations have started a new era in the field of transportation and communication and as a result of which today man is living in an age of awareness of global problems. Never before have people of different nations, with cross-cultural differences in terms of history, religion, economic means and political set-ups faced such common problems as today and shown an urgent need to share solutions. And it is a fact that many problems have been solved and conditions have improved tremendously with the passage of time. Yet, some of the most crucial problems basic to existence and well-being pose big questions which have to be answered. The foremost among these problems is shelter. The world housing situation is grave; it has worsened considerably in less developed countries (United Nations, 1974).[17] The dismal picture of world housing is portrayed by the estimates between now and the year 2000. It is estimated that in the year 2000, the urban population of developing nations will triple, and 65 per cent of their citizens will live an urban life. It is further highlighted that the present-day urban infrastructure was proposed to handle a 2 to 4 per cent increase in the annual shelter need. However, now they will require 12 per cent annual increase. To meet this situation some 8 to 10 per cent units per year per 1000 population would have to be built in most of the so-called developing nations. The situation is quite contrary for most of four billion people because it is estimated that only 2 to 4 units per 1,000 population are actually being built. This then indicates that, in urban areas alone, the worldwide housing deficit is growing at a rate of some 4 to 5 million units per year. It is also concluded that while 37 per cent of the world population is now urban, at the end of the century approximately 50 per cent of all people will be living in urban centres. This shows that, by all means, the housing production now caters to the needs of only one-third of the population. The nations of the world are cautioned if this situation continues up to the end of the century. The world will face an uphill task. One important question which time and again is asked is, "where the two-thirds of these people go?" and the probable answer is that most are accommodated by squatters and slums, the remaining are absorbed by existing dwellings, often the densities allowing only floor space for sleeping. People agree to live in congestion, with no facilities, in unhygienic surroundings. Thus no matter how disturbing today's figure may be, plans for effective solutions must be considered, taking into account that today's housing needs are only a beginning. In this direction the essential steps for adequate activity include (Callaway).[18]

1. Policy direction and national priority.
2. Recognition that while important, money alone does not solve housing needs, and that there is no single, simple, or quick solution to housing problem.
3. Policy, economic, social and technical institutions, coordinated and suited to local needs.
4. Trained and experienced professionals and subprofessionals who relate to local conditions and capabilities.
5. Technology transfer, national and international with stress on appropriateness and based on adaptation rather than on adoption.
6. Information exchange, national and international to create awareness of existing alternatives.

7. Research programme oriented, directed to fill gaps in knowledge and improve processes but not as an end in itself.
8. Technical assistance, directed to national and local institutional development, and inducement and support of maximum self-help at all levels.

ABOUT THIS VOLUME

ONE cannot deny that housing is an important component of the urban structure because it is the predominant land use. It is a truism that residential land constitutes about half the total area of most of the towns and cities. As a matter of fact urban land is put to various land_uses commercial, industrial, recreational educational and official_nevertheless residential usage is the largest single noteworthy category. Moreover, housing through the role of politics and public conscience, is one of the key problems which links both material and social aspects of the city. The study of housing moreover straddles the boundaries of those traditional academic disciplines which are directly preoccupied with urban problems. In the present-day situation housing assumes complex dimensions in terms of its economic, social, political and legal framework that no single discipline can claim monopoly knowledge of. Moreover, since housing plays a crucial role in the city, no study can hope to do justice to all its facets. In this volume, the editor cannot pretend to deal adequately with every aspect of housing. However, essays in this volume present an attempt by scholars in a number of different disciplines to bring a common, social, psychological perspective to bear on the study of the house and its relation to the self and nature of the social order. The house, it is argued, is an extremely important aspect of the built-up environment, embodying not only personal meaning but expressing and maintaining the ideology of prevailing social orders. The essays draw upon a wide variety of intellectual, cultural and historical ma erial.

The essays in this volume are divided into four sections. Section I deals with those articles which reflect different attributes of housing. Section II includes those articles which reflect on a multinational perspective on housing policies. Section III has those articles which demonstrate the implementation of housing and urban revitalization policies at the local level and Section IV includes those articles which pertain to problems and issues confronting housing policies : Policy inputs and Residential evaluations.

The explicit study of the urban housing stock has only recently been encompassed by geographers. Nevertheless, concern with the distribution of varying types of dwellings and housing environment has formed an integral part of ecological urban studies. More recently research scholars have made an attempt to analyse specifically the nature and mechanisms of the allocation system, the spatial impact of housing policy. However, Christina R. Victor in the article, "The Nature and Pattern of Housing Stress in Nottingham C.B. 1971", tries to explore the physical quality of the urban housing stock and the spatial distribution of housing stress. The author tries to define the concept of deprivation. The paper first presents the analytical procedure, then describes briefly the overall standards of housing in Nottingham C.B. and then presents and evaluates the multivariable analysis of housing stress.

The results of the present article obviously suggest that the present practice of combing census measures of housing quality is erroneous and misleading. The author suggests that the dichotomous nature of the housing problem should be recognized by both researchers and planners concerned with housing and incorporated into a more realistic analysis and definition of housing problems in cities.

The area of space called home is often seen as the centre of human family life and family life is seen as focussed on caring of children. Thus the connections and interrelations between the socio-economic changes in the structure of the household and the situation of the child in the family on the one hand, and the changes in the physical design of the living area, on the other, would appear to be of special interest. Hermann Zinn in his article, "The Influence of Home Environments on the Socialization of Children", feels that in recent years an increasing amount of research has been done on the topic of environment and behaviour. He visualizes that at first this research was limited mainly to laboratory studies, which were designed to discover whether behaviour observed in animals could also be found in human beings. More recent efforts attempt to reduce the theoretical deficiencies which limited the value of the earlier studies. Even now, there exists a dearth of studies aimed at producing concrete suggestions for the design of the built-up environment. In this paper the author wishes, first of all, to take a look at the historical changes in children's living environments in order to challenge somewhat present perspectives concerning the relationship between architectural structure and social needs. This approach seems to have been adopted even in dealing with the problem of crowding. The author does not confine himself to mere observations concerning the socializing effects of architectural environments which must, of necessity, remain abstract. He attempts to translate these into specific planning requirements for shaping children's home environments.

The prolific growth of interest in urban and housing history during the past two decades has meant that architectural, economic and social historians, urban geographers and others have published extensive descriptions of buildings and public spaces and studied those policies and procedures which had led to their construction. Thus, in recent years there has been a growing interest in urban environments including house planning, the layout of residential quarters and daily life therein. Roderick J. Lawrence in his article, "The Ideological Nature of Urban Dwellings in Geneva", illustrates that different groups of people partake of different ideas about the design and use of domestic buildings; just as the landlords and tenants of the 19th century tenement buildings in Switzerland had divergent views about the design and use of space, so this divergence is still evident today with respect to the definition and regulation of public and private domains in rented buildings. The author analyses the ideological nature of building layout and housing plans.

Gary Sands in his article, "Housing Conservation in Detroit's Harmony Village", attempts to explore that in the U.S.A. individual preferences have traditionally favoured new development over conservation. There are a number of government programmes and policies which encourage new housing construction while very little assistance has been provided for the maintenance of the existing housing stock. Through this paper the author conveys that emphasis on production of new housing has resulted in the deterioration of the housing stock. The author reveals that America's housing policy has traditionally relied on filtering strategies, the deliberate creation of a surplus of higher quality housing in order to create housing bargains which are accessible to lower income households also. His evaluation is that persistence of surplus housing may cause a decline in housing quality. He provides an example of the adverse consequences of production oriented housing strategies while explaining the Detroit metropolitan housing market.

Improvement of the living conditions is actually one of the most important problems which face the developing countries. In order to solve this problem some of the countries accept indiscriminate living patterns and related technologies from advanced industrial countries. Their successful adoption depends upon determined social, cultural and economic as well as physical and climatic conditions which are not always obtainable in particular developing countries. One can notice it in connection with the modernizing tendency shown by housing programmes launched in some of the Third World countries. Such a programme was also started in the seventies in Iraq. Zbigriew Pucek, Kazimierz Z. Sowa in his article, "Changes in the Living Habits in Modern Dwelling Houses in Iraq", deals with distinctive features of the adaptation process of Iraqi population to a new and rather alien housing condition. In this paper the author analyses results from research programmes carried out in the late seventies in three largest towns of Iraq, that is, Baghdad, Mosul and Basra. The research programme was a part of the comprehensive governmental housing programme for Iraq. It is based on scores of detailed problem inquires held with families which occupy flats in modern multifamily buildings. In addition to the enquiry with lodgers, some interviews were also carried out with social experts/owners of apartment houses, including contractors, and this led to a more complicated discussion on a number of problems, that is, types of modern houses under analysis, life organizations, flats in the buildings and in the housing estates. The author, in his concluding remarks, strongly recommends that estate projects and preparation of lodging should be accompanied by a correct educational policy both on macro and micro-scales. The author says that it is noteworthy that adaptation problems are reflected not only in the organization of life within flats or a block of flats or in how to live in new housing conditions, but may refer to more primitive aspects of how to use the modern technical facilities present-day multifamily building is equipped with.

The history of housing places Canada squarely in the main stream of advanced capitalism. Moreover, by having a correct understanding of how abundant resources for housing construction and of how certain technological and financing innovations have improved the performance of the private sector, it is possible to explain why the provision of shelter in Canada has differed from that in many Western societies in its limited recourse to government land, banking or public ownership of housing. John C. Weaver in his article, "Capitalism, Land Development and Housing in a New Society : The Case of Urban Canada", while discussing the history and historical geography of housing in urban Canada, focusses his attention on the following themes : the pattern of land tenure and property development; construction practices in the shelter industry, home ownership and tenancy; and the social patterns of residential space. He, however, concludes that Canadian housing issues are not carbon copies of those in the United States. He argues that environment and resources differ; the labour pool and market dimensions always have been made smaller in Canada; the housing crisis in Canada is less evident; housing and financing laws have been distinct. Finally, he indicates that the interest in Marx's guide to urban questions has opened in prospect for research into the study of structural or institutional practices involved in the city building process.

Nandeshwar Sharma in his article, "Urban Housing, Dimension, Complication and Implication", has tried to evaluate the dimensions of the housing as : (i) a numerical dimension, (ii) a compositional dimension, (iii) locational dimension, and (iv) a qualitative and quantitative dimension. The author feels that urban housing has to be geared up (i) not as a concept of technology alone but as that of action, (ii) not as an action of creation alone but as that of infrastructural development also, (iii) not as a responsibility of public institutions and organizations alone but as that of private agency also, (iv) not as developer's operation alone but as a self-help operation, and (v) not as a sector of consumptive nature but as that of productive quality also and (vi) not as a city biased phenomena alone but as one with regional bias also.

In recent years some historians and sociologists have considered the influence of the domestic environment upon household work. It is now apparent from diverse studies that at an international scale from about the last decade of the 19th century the protagonists of public health and home economics based their lessons upon increased efficiency for house work and a higher standard of cleanliness in the home. The development of facilities for the preparation and eating of food is largely mirrored in the history of values and ideas upheld by different groups of people in particular socio-cultural contexts at different times. Given this framework it is possible to explore the interaction between the development of architecture and technology in specific socio-cultural contexts. Roderick J. Lawrence in his third article, "Household Technology and Domestic Space : The

Development of the Domestic Kitchen in Australia", attempts to relate those architectural, technological and socio-cultural factors which have interacted in the development of the Australian domestic kitchen since the early 19th century. From an analysis of historical sources this essay explores : (i) whether the importation of domestic technology into Australia was of equal or of more importance than indigenous developments in household technology; (ii) whether the evolution of the design and use of the kitchen in Australia was influenced by social reforms; (iii) whether the transformation of the domestic kitchen from a separate building into the main structure of the house was influenced by technological and socio-cultural trends during the 19th century; and (iv) whether the subsequent rationalization of the kitchen did not occur in Australia until after the Second World War as the result of the architectural ideas rather than of the doctrine of scientific household management.

There is a general consensus based on the past studies that a general problem with housing policy formulation and implementation was the absence in most countries of a coherent strategy towards urban development. Housing policies are particularly prone to bureaucratic compartmentalization even when it is obvious that a successful housing strategy depends on an integrated planning, land values, employment and transportation approach. There is also a need to link housing supply and locational policies with architectural and aesthetic considerations. In this sense, housing policy graphically illustrates the problems of resource allocation in a mixed economy. Public intervention of one sort or another is universal in every housing sector, in every country, but this intervention interacts with market forces in subtle and complex ways. Neither politicians nor public has come to terms with this complexity which brings with it policy of uncertainty and confusion. Thus it can be inferred that housing policy experience has been broadly similar across countries.

Perhaps the most interesting and ambitious attempt in this direction is provided by Michael Harloc in his article, "Housing and the Market". In this paper Harloc argues that housing in advanced capitalist societies has become "recommodified" or that the spread of owner occupation has returned housing to the market as a consumption good. The author believes that the post-war period, in contrast, was characterized by the socialization of housing public sector burgeoning almost everywhere in response to politically mobilized industrial working classes. With its return to the market, the contradictions and conflicts inherent in market or capitalist transactions have begun to manifest themselves-especially as the coalitions supporting owner occupation also enjoy public or government support. Harloc sees the politically powerful demands placed on scarce investment capital by these coalitions as indirect competition with industrial capital. By implication, at least, he predicts the collapse of the coalitions as the needs of capitalism force out private housing investment in favour of industrial investment.

In this paper the author advocates the development of housing and housing policy in six advanced countries : Britain, France, West Germany, Denmark, the Netherlands and the United States. A central feature of all these housing markets has been the growing dominance of owner occupation. As a matter of fact the author, in this paper, attempts to "Periodize" the development of housing policy historically relating it to political and economic circumstances. He concludes by discussing the present trend back towards market or quasi-market solutions to housing provisions and the problems that they are likely to encounter.

Conventional housing policy is busy ensuring the necessary living space in a spatially, temporally, constructionally and socially acceptable way within the industrialization and urbanization process, at the same time resolving, politically, arising conflicts of interests towards compromise. Eberhard Mublich in his paper, "New Functions in Housing Policy and New Agencies Engaged in Provision of Living Space", wishes to submit considerations as to the future of living, as required by the future of work. Working and living, which were both melted into the domestic economy previous to industrialism, were separated step by step and except for a few remnants were, due to industrialization, subdued to bureaucratic rationality. Only house work remained unnoticed at home. The author is quite justified when he states that today it seems that the peak of this development is reached and there are indications that a proportion of work could return to the vicinity of house and neighbourhood newly evaluated. Apparently a modern informal economy is emerging. The author believes that a growing need for space in the home and vicinity of the home is to be expected. The conventional patterns of compromise will no longer serve to cover this need for space, not to meet the new problems of distribution and segregation conditioned by the development on the labour market. The author firmly believes that conflicts of terests between demand on the one hand and supply on the other cannot, in the face of growing demand and falling income, be worked out with the help of inflation, as was the case until now.

The policies of the state in Western capitalistic societies are shaped by contradictions and conflicts between different fractions of capital and different class interests. The configurations of interests and conflicts are not static but change over time and are shaped by both internal and external social processes. It is important, therefore, in any analysis of state policy to give some consideration to the structure of state organization and allocative mechanism within the arena of policy being considered. David C. Thorns in his paper, "Housing Policies and the Influence of the Growth of Owner Occupation in Social and Political Change", looks at the aspect of development of housing policies at the national level in New Zealand, Australia and the United Kingdom. The objective of this examination is to explore the role played by the State in the housing market and the extent to which housing has been and is viewed as a welfare good, as an investment opportunity and as a base for consumption. The changing role of housing in public policy is related to the arguments regarding the fiscal crisis of the capitalist state and the privatization of resources. The latter process occurs during the period when resources are transferred from the public to the private domain such as has occurred with the sale of public rental housing. The author in this paper explores the character of housing policy changes, access to house ownership, wealth transfer, social and political changes. Finally, the author advocates the promotion of ownership because it improves choice for the consumers of housing and allows for a more effective and natural distribution of housing resources. However, the structure of housing market demonstrates the limitations that all housing opportunities are shaped not by choice but by sets of constraints which relate to the individual's economic capacity and the availability of a range of housing in the region in which the household is located.

Most Western countries aim to provide all their inhabitants with adequate housing and a safe and suitable residential environment at an affordable price. To this end, most countries acknowledge the necessity of some form of public intervention in the housing market. Jan Van Weesep in his article, "Dutch Housing Policies-Problems and Prospects", tries to demonstrate that the housing market in the Netherlands is a good example of a strictly controlled market with substantial government intervention in both the production of new dwellings and in the allocation of available housing units. But the post-war proliferation of policies and huge public expenditures have not solved the persistent housing crisis.

The paper demonstrates that most inhabitants of the Netherlands are well housed, at a reasonable price. Political pressure is continually averted to at least maintain the present level of government involvement in the housing market. Thus in recent years the government has been forced to increase the housing expenditure in spite of its general commitments to drastically cut public spending. For the same reason the government cannot shift its support from presently subsidized groups to others. For economic reasons it cannot afford to expand its activities drastically, in order to subsidize housing for groups not served by current housing programmes. Thus, briefly, the paper sketches the historical development of the public housing intervention system and interprets some aspects of its complex nature. It then outlines some of the current problems and prospects that have emerged in spite of the system and, to certain extent, because of the system.

Swiss national housing policies became quite important during the Second World War. Rent controls like other price stops are intended to prevent a massive monetary inflation in times when housing production levels are low. Progressively, however, other measures were employed to protect tenants against unjustified realizations of leases by landlords. By 1942 housing construction supply declined and unemployment increased. For the first time in the history the Swiss confederation intervened by means of special capital outlays in order to increase the volume of housing construction in general. Erwin Zimmermann in his article, "The Implementation of Public Housing Policy in Switzerland", presents selectively a few findings of an ongoing research project on implementation of Swiss federal public housing policies during the years 1965 to 1976. Theoretical considerations and hypotheses relate to interests and resources of cantons, municipalities and private housing promoters as principal actors of policy implementation. Entries of analysis are cantons and public housing units. The three major findings may be summarized as follows : (i) At the local and regional level, the volume of public housing construction remains unrelated to measurable indicators of "needs" for such housing. Federal and state incentives have, indeed, been most attractive for private promoters in areas where housing shortages were least dramatic and rents rather low; (ii) The principle promoters of housing construction in the "free market" have chosen not to respond to policy incentives. Public housing promoters are found among actors who were able or willing to invest only a minimal of the own financial resources; and (iii) The actors' interests and resources had also quite important consequences for the kind of public housing effectively built. In conclusion, implementation features result, to a large extent, from the failure of the Swiss public housing policy to specify selective incentives depending on local housing market conditions and characteristics of perspective implementors.

By the mid-1970s many American scholars, politicians and government bureaucrats considered the federal low-income public housing programme a dismal effort. The programme failed to build a sufficient number of units to meet the minimum needs of eligible persons and frequently constructing poorly designed high rises which become segregated enclaves of poor socially marginal minorities fostering social malaise. Public support for the programme dissipated and white and black communities, throughout the country increasingly opposed new construction for families outside of unattractive areas of inner cities. Frederick A. Lazin and Sam Aroni in their article, "The Implementation of Low-Income Housing Policy in the United States : The Case of Section 8 Existing Housing", examine the implementation of the federal Section 8 (existing) Rent subsidy programme in Los Angeles from its inception in 1975 through 1985. Its objectives are : (i) To evaluate the statutory goals : does it serve the intended recipients, foster economic integration, reduce concentration in minority and low-income areas, contribute to the upkeep and/or upgrading of buildings and increase the freedom of choice for eligible recipients? (ii) To determine the effects of regulations, market conditions and administrative behaviour of local and federal officials on the programme's output and outcome. (iii) To compare the record of section 8 existing with previous federal low-income housing programmes. Has it been more successful than public housing?

The occupation of abandoned houses for the purpose of rehabilitation in Bochum, the number of new dwelling units decreasing every year, particularly in the agglomeration areas of the Federal Republic of Germany, the poor housing situation of the students of the Ruhr University, the regional asymmetry of housing subsidization which has adverse consequences for agglomeration areas, all call for a correction and underline at an ever increasing rate the necessity to integrate municipal housing policy into the entire economic, legal and social system. Horst-Juergan Wienen in his article, "The Integration of Parameters of Action for the Local Government of a Big City in the Ruhr Area into the Economic, Political and Institutional Environment"; discusses the symptoms and causes of turbulences on the housing markets of agglomeration areas and differentiation of partial housing markets. The paper discusses 12 causes of the turbulences on the separate housing markets with emphasis on those in the agglomeration areas of the Federal Republic of Germany. This is done on the background not only of the rapidly declining production of new dwellings since about five years in these areas and not only on the background of the illegal house using, the so-called "Instandbesetzungen" in Bochum and in other cities; but, too; and more important; because of the wish for evaluation of the local political aim to concentrate housing ("spatial order concept") which has been formulated in 1974 by the local parliament; the "Rat". The great restrictions because of the economic; political and institutional environment and last, but not least the small amount of local parameters of actions are presented.

Tor Bysveen in his article, "Analysing Moving Chains in Oslo"; argues that the conventional programming of housing needs in Norway is based on information and assumptions about housing frequencies. But even at the frequency of 100 when all households in a specified age groups have dwellings on their own, we can experience housing demands. These demand's cause population shifts. In Oslo new-built houses count for 20 per cent of the primary offers and all the subsequent changes that are generated. The data were collected by interviewers. The registered average link of this change multiplier was 1.9. Taking into account interviewing failures; we estimate a multiplier 2.3. Parallel to reports from the countries; the author found that the buildings of large dwellings; high priced dwellings and privately built or produced dwellings generate a strong market impact. But we also found that the houses built by the housing cooperatives generate a strong market impact. The average income of the occupants in the same buildings falls with rising positions in the sequences. This indicates that a process of filtering by income is at work. But data rather suggest an assumption that the poor pay more in the housing market than the assumption that a filtering process secures a reasonable social distribution of housing in the population. By this study we have thrown some light on some structural points of housing demands. We have analysed elements of different housing markets and the shifts between these markets. In order to broaden the knowledge of the structure of the population housing needs further study of the change generated by households moving out of Oslo leaving vacant dwellings behind is under way.

The affluence of the post Second World War housing market has been replaced in recent years by increasing scarcity, run away inflation and declining quality. Historic patterns of home ownership, affordability and increased housing supply have been steadily reversed in recent years. Besides, a variety of federal actions affecting housing location; supply, financing, quality, standards, prices and residential segregation have exacerbated the impact of unhealthy demographic and economic trends on housing shortages and the maldistribution of housing. As other researchers have noted the jigsaw of state policies has been directed not towards resolving the housing crisis; but towards accommodating private financial, construction and real estate interests in the housing market. Glennyago in his article, "Housing Speculation Impact on the Quality and Cost of Housing"; examines problems of housing inflation in the rental housing market. As demographic, economic and federal policy patterns converge to exacerbate the housing crisis, local governments will be increasingly confronted with the issues of the structure of the local housing market. Renters are specially vulnerable as they are a growing part of the US housing market. Their income lags behind rental increases and the availability of rental housing is declining. The study uses heretofore unused local data for studying the housing market. Rapid residential property turnover (housing speculation) is shown to be associated with high annual rates of appreciation, a greater number of building code violations; greater tenement transiency and a rise of absolute ownership.

This study investigates the relationship between housing speculation, housing inflation; tenure; quality and neighbourhood stability. This exploratory research suggests the types of dislocations and market distortions that shift investment behaviour towards the use of housing for speculative investment rather than its service or use value. Further, the study well indicates the relationship between local speculative practices and other local housing problems such as displacement, condominium conversion and the distortion of new production towards luxury housing.

It should be pointed out that the housing market in Israel differs from that in many countries in several respects : (i) a large proportion of the housing construction has been carried out by the Ministry of Construction and Housing for specific population groups; (ii) most apartments are owner-occupied in some form of condominium arrangement; (iii) most of the urban population of Israel lives in apartment buildings. However, in recent years high-rise housing has become a common phenomenon in Israel, and buildings of 8 to 20 storeys with up to 120 apartments have been constructed in the urban centres. Yona Ginsberg and Arza Churchman in their article, "The Future of Housing Quality : Satisfaction with Living Quality in Multistorey Housing", reveal that high-rise housing has been a controversial issue in various Western countries for some time. The common image is a negative one. It is assumed that living in high-rise buildings leads, on the one hand, to anonymity and loneliness and, on the other; to difficulties in achieving privacy. The most negative image relates to the implications for children. Although some studies have supported this negative image, others have arrived at different conclusions. A possible explanation for these differences lies in the fact that most negative findings regarding high-rise living apply to lower class residents, families with young children, and people who have no choice but to live there. A critical question that arises is whether the problems identified are due to the particular attribution of high-rise buildings; for example, the question whether the building type has any effect at all upon residents' behaviour or whether differences in behaviour found between high-rise and low-rise families are due to factors such as self selection, social class; and stage in the life-cycle. Another question is whether the problems found to be associated with high-rise buildings are universal or are dependent upon the specific social and cultural context of the countries concerned. This paper thus is based on three studies conducted in multi-family housing; ranging from 4 to 20 storeys in urban areas in Israel. The findings of the authors do not confirm the negative image of high-rise buildings commonly held in other countries. In the sample there were hardly any problems of isolation from neighbours, feeling of crowding or difficulties in organization for maintaining the building. The only families with any problem seem to be those whose children were all under the age of five.

There is no lack of criticism concerning the social quality of usages of urban residential areas. Dieter Frick in his article, "Evaluation of the Quality of Usage of Urban

Residential Quarters Through the Communicational Behaviour of Inhabitants : Approach to an Empirical Study", aims to develop complementary criteria for the evaluation of the quality of usages of urban residential quarters of low social status, and for the revision of urban design conceptions of measures concerning sanitation, modernization, or reconstruction in such quarters. The author suggests that a contribution should be made towards eliminating the lack of suitable criteria for physical structures in residential quarters, especially for outdoor space structures; that is, to complement existing criteria, which are more oriented towards production and utilization, with such criteria which include everyday usage by the inhabitants of the quarters and the social quality of the physical structures and thereby facilitate a more precise definition of the experimental field and measures in the area of urban design. He suggests that our approach proceed from the usage for appropriation potential existing in the physical and social structures. Moreover, its relation with communicational behaviour that can be observed be examined as an indicator of the presence of or the degree to which these potentials can be exhausted familiarity with the social relation inherent in the physical structure which manifests itself in communicational behaviour is assessed as the degree of participation in the social terrain of interaction relating to outdoor spaces.

Any research aiming at an empirical assessment of the quality of residential environments, or at results of the effects of residential surroundings on behaviour, cannot, according to the present standard of knowledge, be content with gathering questionnaire data. What is even more important is that it is no sufficient to ascertain the information by asking direct questions concerning the subject to be examined. Helmut Kromrey in his article, "Evaluating the Quality of Residential Environments", points towards the problem. In its first part he argues against simple, only questionnaire-based research when evaluating such complex subjects as residential environments. In the second part some results of an empirical analysis of multi-level data on 21 urban; suburban and ex-urban residential quarters are reported. The refined analysis proves that living in urban environments does not by far appear as negative as conventional research on housing aspirations and housing satisfaction seems to indicate.

NOTES

1 Keizer, Marzorie Branin, **Housing : An Environment for Living**; MacMillan Publishing Co. Inc.; New York.
2 Neutra, R. **Survival Through Design**, Oxford University Press; New York. 1951.
3 Stewart; K. Kay, "Twentieth Century Housing Design from an Ecological Perspective" in Gertrudes, Fish (Ed.), **The Story of Housing**; MacMillan Publishing Co. Inc.; New York, 1979; p.449.
4 Rapoport, Amos; **House Form and Culture**, Prentice Hall; Englewood Cliffs; N.J., 1969; p.46.
5 Samuel, Aroni, "Housing Policies : A Developing World Perspective"; **Housing Science**; 1978; Vol.2, N4., pp. 299-334.
6 Stewart; K. Kay, op. cit, pp.453.
7 Rapoport; op. cit. pp.130-135.
8 Stewart; op. cit., p.476.
9 Ogburn; William F., "The Changing Functions of the Family" in Robert F. Winch and Lonis Goodman (Eds.). **Selected Studies in Marriage and the Family**, Holt, Rinehart and Winston, 1968; p.27.
10 Stewart; op. cit., p.478.
11 Beyer, Glen H., and Montgomery; James E., **Houses are for People**, Cornell University Press, Ithaca, N.Y. 1955.
12 Dean, John P., "Housing Design and Family Value" in William Wheaton; et.al. (Eds.); **Urban Housing**, New York Free Press, pp. 127-138.
13 Cooper Clare, "The House as a Symbol of Self" in Jon Lang et.al. (Eds.); **Designing for Human Behaviour**, Stroudsburg, Pa : Hutchingson and Ross; 1974. p.132.
14 Beyer, Glen H. and Montgomery, James E. op. cit., p.497.
15 Hartman, Chester, 1975 **Housing and Social Policy**, Prentice Hall, Englewood Cliffs, N.J., p.26.
16 Stewart; K. Kay, op. cit., p.480.
17 United Nations World Housing Survey, 1974.
18 Callaway, Thomas R., "World Housing Today" in Gestrudes S. Fish (Ed.) **The Story of Housing**.

SECTION ONE
ATTRIBUTES OF URBAN HOUSING

TWO

Christina R. Victor

The Nature and Pattern of Housing Stress in Nottingham C.B., 1971

INTRODUCTION

The explicit study of the urban housing stock has only recently been encompassed by geographers. Concern with the distribution of varying types of dwellings and housing environment has formed an integral part of ecological urban studies. However, the emphasis placed upon housing in such work has been indirect and descriptive in nature. More recent research has specifically stressed housing, especially the nature and mechanisms of the allocation system (Duncan, 1976), the spatial impact of housing policy (McDonald, 1974) and the quality of the housing environment (Kirby, 1971).

The physical quality of the urban housing stock and the spatial distribution of housing stress has attracted considerable research (Victor, 1980). This research interest has been stimulated by two inter-related trends. Firstly the extensive slum clearance schemes characteristic of British cities in the post war and their aftermath, provided a massive stimulus to the study of urban housing quality differentials. A further impetus was provided by the recent concern with the concept of deprivation and the identified links between housing problems and social malaise. However, despite the growth of housing stress studies there have been few attempts to define the concepts involved. Indeed this comment is not restricted to housing studies but applies equally to the majority of spatial work concerned with deprivation (Victor, 1980).

British housing stress studies have usually defined

their topic of investigation in terms of the dwelling quality measures derived from the decennial census. These indices provide information, in terms of households, about the provision of amenities (e.g. hot water, fixed bath/shower, inside/outside w.c.), occupation densities (i.e. the number of persons per dwelling room) and the multiple occupation of dwellings. The usual practice is then to construct an indicator based upon some combination of these indices. This procedure has resulted in an implicit tendency to define housing quality in terms of 'plumbing standards' or overcrowding rather than more appropriate, but less readily available measures, which identify standards in terms defined by the consumers of housing.

Integral to these housing stress studies has been the assumption that the two aspects of housing stress combined (i.e. the amenity provision and occupancy characteristics measures) are both statistically and spatially interrelated. Given the lack of an alternative data, it is inevitable that the practice of combining census variables to define and measure housing stress will persist. This paper, therefore, examines the assumption implicit in this procedure within the context of the former County Borough of Nottingham. The paper first presents the analytical procedure, then describes briefly the overall standards of housing in the study area and then presents and evaluates the multivariate analysis of housing stress.

ANALYTICAL PROCEDURE

Six indices measuring housing stress were extracted from the small area tabulations of the 1971 enumeration (Table 2.1). These variables summarised each of the aspects of dwelling quality measured by the census. Each variable was calculated for the 99 planning zones of the County Borough. These areas were amalgams of the 596 enumeration districts defined in 1971. The data were then analysed by multivariate statistical technique. Factor analysis was considered the most appropriate tool for identifying the nature of housing stress. A standard principal axes method with an oblique rotation was the technical procedure employed.

HOUSING QUALITY IN NOTTINGHAM C.B.

The population was enumerated in 1971 and the town functioned as the regional capital of the East Midlands. The area, with its economic base of manufacturing and consumer goods industries, was relatively prosperous. However despite this appearance of material prosperity, overall housing standards were poor (Table 2.1). With the exception of the non-exclusive use of a w.c. index, Nottingham recorded levels of amenity provision well below the national average. In addition, levels of dwelling multiple occupancy in Nottingham were also well below the national norm.

TABLE 2.1

Housing quality in Nottingham, 1971

% Households	Nottingham C.B.	G.B.
Share/Lack hot water	12.5	9.7
Share/Lack fixed bath	21.1	14.4
Share/Lack inside w.c.	16.5	26.5
Density of 1.5 p.p.r*	4.4	4.4
Shared dwellings	4.7	2.8

* Persons Per Room
Source : Victor (1980)

THE STRUCTURE OF HOUSING STRESS

Analysis of the six variables data matrix by the methods described previously produced two factors with eigenvalues in excess of unity (Table 2.2). These two dimensions represented 87% of the estimated common variance suggesting a meaningful solution at least in statistical terms.

TABLE 2.2

Housing deprivation: Factor analysis summary table

Factor	Eigenvalue	Variance (%)	Cumulative variance (%)
1	3.55	59.3	59.3
2	1.65	27.6	87.0

Interpretation of the nature of these two dimensions was based upon the factor pattern matrix listed as Table 2.3. All variables with a loading of ±0.29 were taken as diagnostic of the factor structure. From this two retained dimensions were described as representing amenity provision levels (factor 1) and dwelling occupancy characteristics (factor 2). This complex statistical analysis therefore suggests that within the study area, housing stress could be

THREE

Hermann Zinn

The Influence of Home Environments on the Socialization of Children

THE LIVING CONDITIONS OF CHILDREN IN HISTORICAL PERSPECTIVE

The area of space called home is often seen as the centre of human family life, and family life is seen as focussed on caring for children. This appears to many people to be a quasi-natural condition, pertaining to all people at all times. This impression is, however, false. I would like below to correct this picture by making reference to several far-reaching processes of change in the last two centuries. The connections and interrelations between the socio-economic changes in the structure of the household and the situation of the child in the family on the one hand, and the changes in the physical design of the living area on the other hand would appear to be of special interest. Characteristic living behaviour patterns have developed at different epochs. The origin of these patterns and the way they have changed can be seen to be the result of socio-spatial socialization processes (Aries 1975, De Mause 1976, Elias 1969, Zinn 1979).

Medieval Household and Living Structures

Living and working were not spatially separated from one another during the Middle Ages. The predominant unit then was not the family, but rather the household. It often included a great many servants, day labourers and craftsmen. It is probable that the majority of the lower estates never achieved their own households. In these working and living communities, rooms were usually shared by everybody : master, mistress, family, servants and workers. Household terized by a high score on both factors were assigned to category A - few areas were so classified. The mutual exclusiveness of groups B (overcrowding) and C (low levels of amenity provision) confirm that these two dimensions of housing stress were spatially independent.

Figure 2.1 Nottingham C. B : Housing Stress Factor Analysis : Factor One

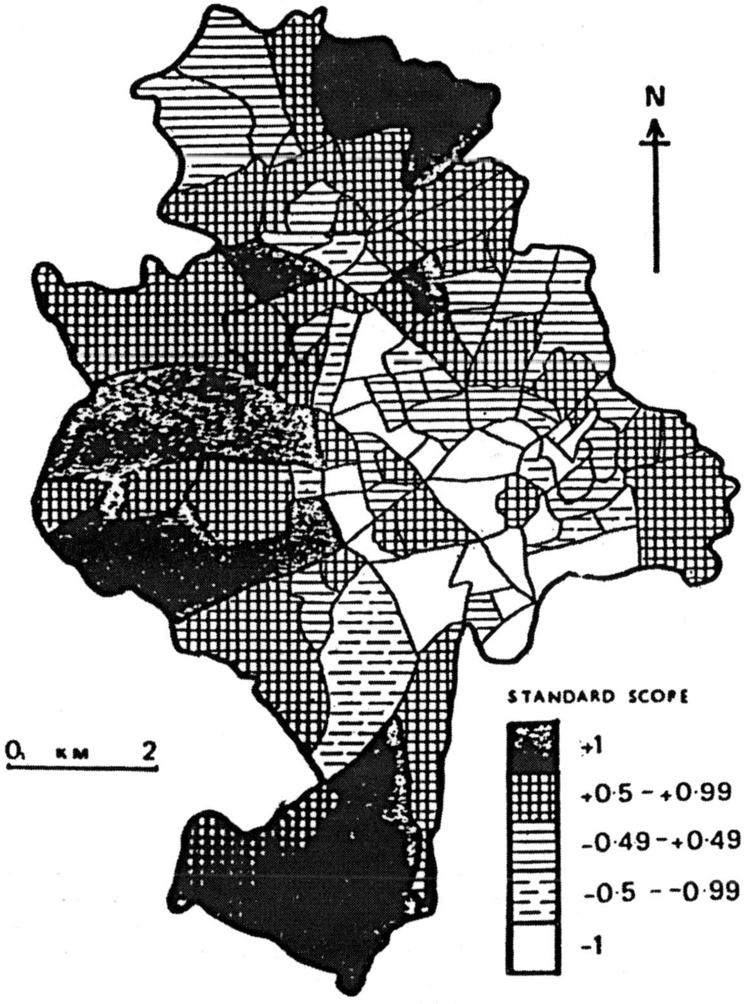

Figure 2.2 Nottingham C. B : Housing Stress Factor Analysis : Factor Two

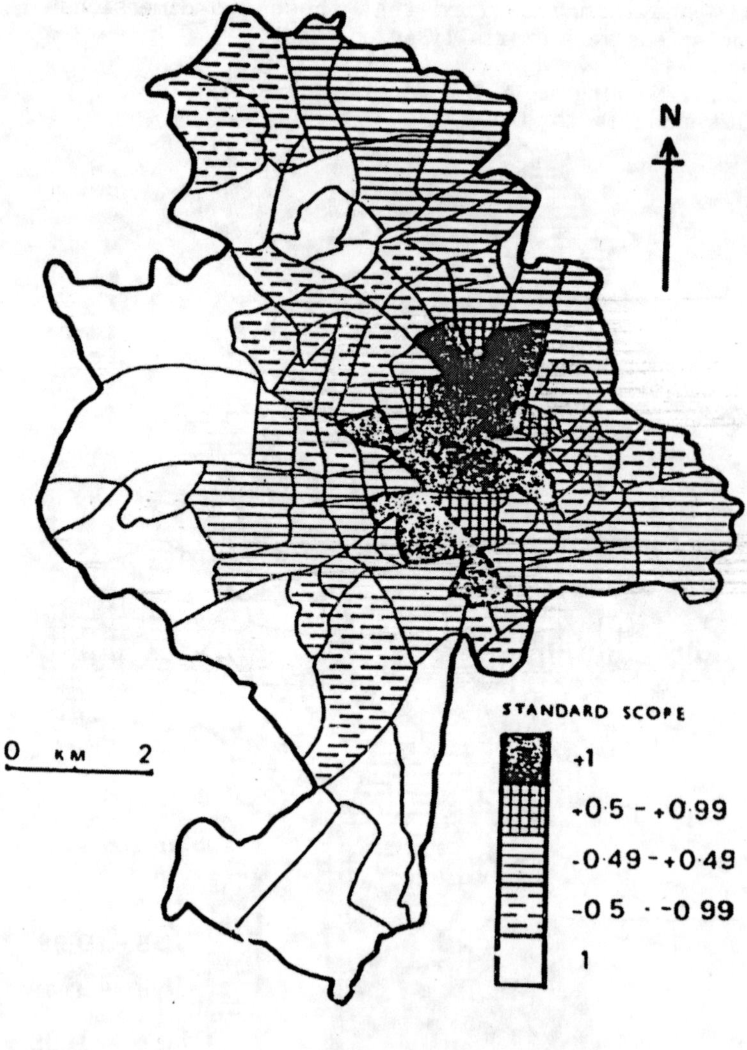

DISCUSSION

The above results show that, within Nottingham, housing disadvantage as traditionally defined, was composed of two separate concepts. These were shown to be both spatially and statistically independent and confirm the earlier statistical analysis of Harrison and Webber (1977).

Figure 2.3 Nottingham C. B : Spatial Comparison of Housing Stress Factor

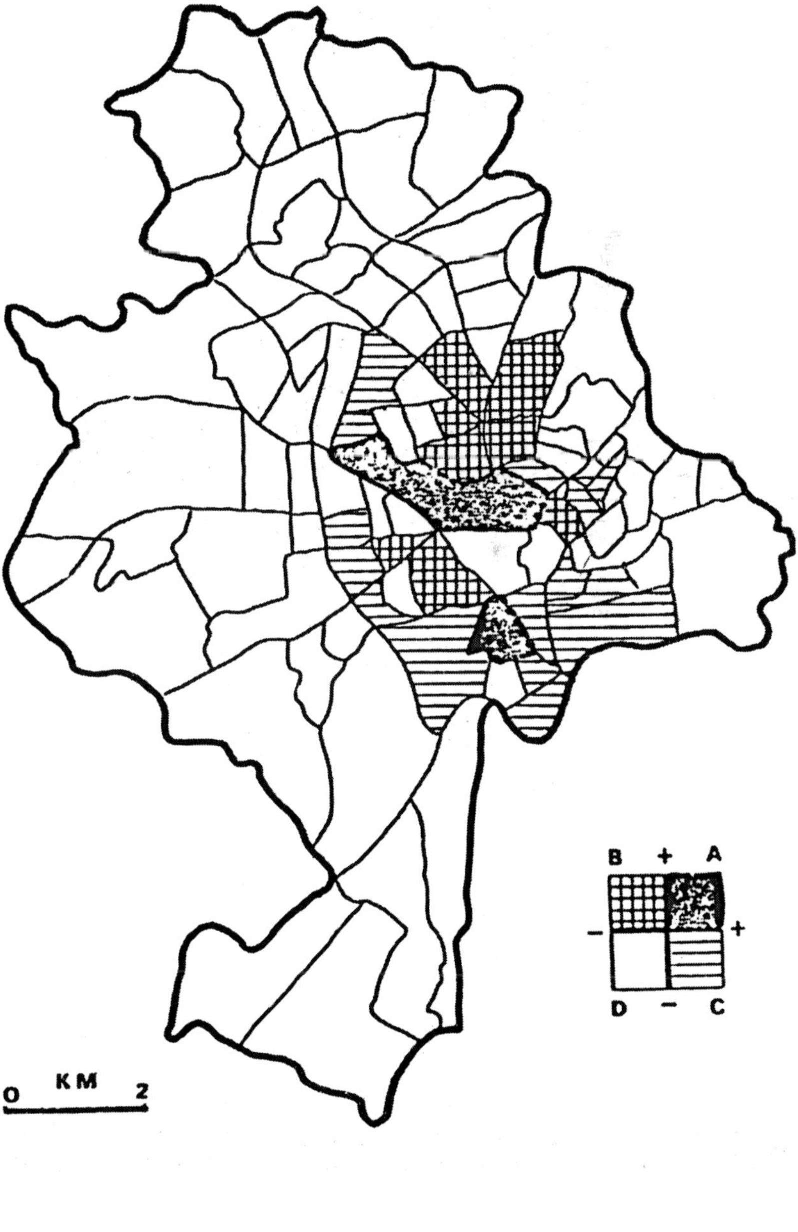

Explanation for the mutually exclusive nature of these two types of housing problem is provided by the nature of the housing stock in the study area. The low levels of amenity provision, shown to be concentrated in the inner city, were characteristic of the Victorian terraced dwellings constructed originally for the working class. However, as these dwellings were small in size, few have been subdivided into multiple unit accommodation. In contrast, the areas characterized by the dwelling occupancy aspect of housing stress illustrate a different type of housing stock. These areas were characterized by large high status dwellings of Victorian origin which were constructed to high standards. However, both functional and technological obsolescence, in conjunction with changing social values, combined to make these dwellings less popular as single family dwelling units. Hence these dwellings have been subdivided into multiple unit accommodation as they have filtered down the housing market. As a result of their high standard of original construction, amenity provision was not an extreme problem in such dwellings. Therefore, within the study area, housing problems were largely confined to dwellings of Victorian origin. However, the type of problem varied with the nature of the older housing.

These results obviously suggest that the present practice of combining census measures of housing quality is erroneous and misleading. The dichotomous nature of the housing problem should be recognized by both researchers and planners concerned with housing and incorporated into a more realistic analysis and definition of housing problems in cities.

REFERENCES

Duncan, S.S., Research directions in social geography : housing opportunities and constraints, **Transactions Institute of British Geographers**, New Series, 1 (1), 1976, pp. 10-19.

Harrison, A. and Webber, R., Capital spending on housing. **C.E.S. Review**, 1, 1977, pp. 31-6.

Kirby, D.A., The inter war council dwelling : A study of residential obsolescence and decay. **Town Planning Review**, 42, 1971, pp. 250-268.

McDonald, G., Metropolitan housing policy and the stress area. **Urban Studies**, 2, 1974, pp. 27-37.

Victor, C.R., Social structure and social malaise : A geography of Greater Nottingham - unpublished M.Phil. thesis, University of Nottingham 1980.

THREE

Hermann Zinn

The Influence of Home Environments on the Socialization of Children

THE LIVING CONDITIONS OF CHILDREN IN HISTORICAL PERSPECTIVE

The area of space called home is often seen as the centre of human family life, and family life is seen as focussed on caring for children. This appears to many people to be a quasi-natural condition, pertaining to all people at all times. This impression is, however, false. I would like below to correct this picture by making reference to several far-reaching processes of change in the last two centuries. The connections and interrelations between the socio-economic changes in the structure of the household and the situation of the child in the family on the one hand, and the changes in the physical design of the living area on the other hand would appear to be of special interest. Characteristic living behaviour patterns have developed at different epochs. The origin of these patterns and the way they have changed can be seen to be the result of socio-spatial socialization processes (Aries 1975, De Mause 1976, Elias 1969, Zinn 1979).

Medieval Household and Living Structures

Living and working were not spatially separated from one another during the Middle Ages. The predominant unit then was not the family, but rather the household. It often included a great many servants, day labourers and craftsmen. It is probable that the majority of the lower estates never achieved their own households. In these working and living communities, rooms were usually shared by everybody : master, mistress, family, servants and workers. Household members of all classes were, as a rule, together for meals, work, play and festivities, as well as when sleeping; this state of affairs was not considered a social problem.

Children were seen first and foremost as workers and potential inheritants. To regard children as emotional beings with specific corresponding needs was quite unknown at a time when a high death rate in children was normal. An upper class infant was typically given to a nurse to be raised. Children were in their parents' homes, if at all, only between 2 and 7 years of age. After this, children of all classes went into apprenticeship. For this period, the child usually moved to another household. Medieval daily life united people of all ages in every form of activity; no space was set aside as particularly for children's needs.

The rooms in which people lived in those times could be called all-purpose rooms. They were rarely specialized for different, specific purposes; they usually joined each other immediately without corridors or halls in between so that, in order to go into most rooms, it was necessary to go through other rooms. This spatial organization made the seclusion of one person or family and thus, aspects of life that we know such as privacy, individuality and intimacy, impossible. People in those days, however, did not feel the need for individual or family privacy, just as there were no places especially reserved for the public.

Until the 16th century, beds were often made to be disassembled, and were put together again in the evenings. The change in the 17th century to beds as solid pieces of furniture can be seen as a sign for the growing need for intimacy. This announced the movement towards privacy in the bourgeois family which brought the separation of the sleeping areas of family and servants and which later led to the separation of sleeping and living rooms.

The Development of the Nuclear Family and Bourgeois Living Structures

With industrialization and the rise of the bourgeois middle classes, household and place of work gradually ceased to be identical. The function of the home became limited to harboring the immediate members of the family. It now became possible for the lower classes to establish their own families and households, although for a long time a great number of them remained as servants in the households of the middle and upper classes.

The bourgeois family household saw itself as a "private" household. The family withdrew from the public gaze - a totally new way of thinking - and went into the seclusion of the home. Visiting friends or business partners without having previously arranged to do so was suddenly "not done". Modern etiquette, which was intended to protect the individual and family freedom from societal pressures, emerged. The urge of the family to cocoon itself away from society called for new forms of spatial organization. The layout of the bourgeois home changed after the 18th century. The principle of private space for the individual penetrated into the family household. Single rooms were no longer planned as connected, all-purpose rooms, but went off separately from a hall. They thus obtained for their users a measure of independence and acted as shields against unwelcome or unexpected intrusion. At the same time, private areas were expanded at the cost of the rooms with representational functions.

The relationship between family and servants changed together with the emergence of specific bourgeois or middle-class dwelling and living conditions. The family living area was separated from that of the servants. Symbolically, the family now had a bell-rope in the living room. This was an indicator of the breakdown of the hierarchical society of the Middle Ages. As long as that social order had retained a high degree of legitimacy, physical barriers had been unnecessary. As the middle-class ideology of equal rights for all was asserting itself, any inequality still existing lost its legitimacy. Thus arose the need to demonstrate differences of class with symbols. Living in close proximity with servants was inconsistent with this need, so the middle classes reacted to the advance of the lower classes with spatial segregation.

The increased spatial isolation of the middle-class family automatically strengthened the ties between parents and children. The individuality of each child and the unfolding of his talents and achievements became even more important. All the same, it was not until the end of the 19th century that it became the usual pattern in upper-class houses for children to have rooms of their own in which they could not only sleep but in which there was also sufficient space to play and do homework. The further extension of this aim, a separate room for each child, was, even in the upper classes, only realized at the turn of the century. Probably, moral considerations led originally to the decision in upper-class homes to give daughters separate rooms.

There seems to have been a close connection between the new structural changes in living areas and the interest of the upper classes in bringing sexual life under control. For instance, even in the 18th century, the bed was still a focal point of society in the salons of the houses of Rococo nobility. The bourgeois, however, found this decadent, and banished beds to secondary living areas. They made a point of keeping all professional and social encounters free of any affectual and drive-related behaviour. The whole sphere of sexual life was made private and was increasingly surrounded by a new type of psychological barrier connected with shame and fear of embarrassment, which eventually manifested itself in the form of actual walls for bedrooms. The taboo regarding parents' bedrooms, which has kept its hold from the 19th century until today, was supposed to delude children into thinking that their parents led a pure, sexless marital life.

There was considerable delay before the lower social strata took over these living patterns. Their living conditions were for a long time so unfavourable that they could not develop an independent family life in the patterns set by the upper classes. The housing of the lower classes usually consisted of one room with, at the most, a partition or tiny additional room. Cooking, living, sleeping, housework, and the work done at home for early capitalist enterpreneurs : all took place within these walls. These people could not allow themselves a distinct emotional life, gentle habits, and other new middle-class virtues, simply because the minimum of space needed for privacy was missing.

The first to try to follow the bourgeois pattern of living structure were the lower middle classes. The symbol of this effort was the parlor, usually a very small but well-furnished room. It was only used on Sundays and for special occasions but nevertheless gave the family the feeling of living like those in better circumstances. The rest of the dwelling included only one or two unheated bedrooms and a kitchen, in which most of the family's time was spent. This pattern is still typical today for a large proportion of the existing apartments in the Federal Republic of Germany. It is gradually being superseded by the modern type of rental apartment housing built after World War II.

The Child in the Family and Home Today

41 Influence of home environments on children

The portions of households with children under 15 years of age has gone down in the Federal Republic to about 30% of all private households. The average number of children per household has sunk from 1.7 in 1871 to 0.6 in 1975. The family with children no longer represents, therefore, the typical household. The most typical family household is the small, or nuclear, family, consisting of parents, or one parent, and children. The kind of family in which grandparents or other relations are included now numbers less than 3%. The household which also includes one or two servants, common at the beginning of the century, has now quite disappeared.

Most of the social and economic functions of family households in earlier times have now been taken over by social institutions. Functional changes are still under way. It has only become usual in recent times for such fundamental happenings as birth, death, or serious illness to be experienced outside the home. Even in rural areas, the habit of storage for economic reasons has diminished in the last generation. In addition, new household machines have reduced the amount of effort needed for housework. Thus the home has become a synonym in every respect for privacy and intimacy.

Socialization of domestic functions is accompanied by a withdrawal of other, bodily functions (which could have taken place in public in earlier times more or less without shyness) into privacy. This change not only applies to sexual life, but also to most other vital functions. That the separate bath and toilet are now common in the home is the result of this development.

The most important social function which the family has today is the primary socialization of the next generation, that is, bringing up and educating children. On evaluating the suitability of the rental apartments built after World War II for the socialization of children, it immediately becomes obvious that the modern apartments do not come up to the level already achieved by the upper classes at the turn of the century. In that these apartments have large living rooms, functional kitchens, baths and toilets, they have taken over typical upper-middle class structures. The parents' bedroom and the small children's rooms, however, cannot be called individual rooms in the bourgeois sense. Children's rooms, although now heated, tend to be just bedrooms, with insufficient space for play.

Research has shown that the smaller child needs both a

play area for his or her activities near to the caretaker (usually the mother), and an autonomous, less-controlled, individual area, as well as the possibility of moving freely from one area to the other. The apartments of the upper classes were spacious enough to allow for this, and there was, at least, the combined living room-kitchen or parlor-kitchen (Wohnküche) in the homes of those in poorer positions, where children could always play near their mothers. Children went into the street for games needing more space.

The living room-kitchen was narrowed down to a small functional kitchen in housing built after the war. Space thus won became part of the living room. Unfortunately, this is hardly acceptable as children's play space. The room itself usually lies somewhat apart from the working area of the mother, and is usually a forbidden area because of its expensive furnishings. In consequence, the play area near the mother no longer exists in either rented dwellings or in most of the privately-owned houses of today.

Simultaneously, playing possibilities on the street near the house have been greatly restricted due to increased motor traffic. And, last but not least, the high-rise blocks built today do not exactly make it easy for a child to move between indoor and outdoor play areas. All in all, spatial conditions for the development of small children have hardly improved in recent years. It may be reasonable to suppose that many children today are quite strongly "disciplined" in the home as a result of its construction and design, which means that they are hindered in learning to act autonomously. Another reason for disciplining children is a heightened sensitivity with regard to any disturbance of the private sphere, especially any kind of noise from neighbours. This constitutes the main source of arguments in rented dwellings. In consequence, the demand for soundproofing has risen to an extent which would have been unimaginable in the last century.

Further changes can be expected in the future. It is not improbable, for instance, that still visible remnants of purely societal functions in homes will gradually disappear completely. The dining room, indispensable until a few decades ago in upper-middle-class homes, is now either integrated into the living room or is part of a multipurpose area not far from the kitchen. With this multipurpose area, the old living room-kitchen celebrates its resurrection, in its new guise as a second living area. Parents and children are so fond of this area because there it is possible to live daily life without being under the restrictions presented by the living room, which still strongly maintains societal-presentational functions.

In actual fact, the much-respected living room suffered a severe blow with the rise of television culture. Once more, children were able to gain legitimate access to this room. This was made easier in that it was no longer necessary to adhere to formal etiquette in staging stiff, social evenings at regular intervals, as had once been so customary in the houses of the "better class". Seen objectively, it has now become paradoxical to retain the deeply-rooted practice of furnishing the living room as expensively as possible and keeping it fussily clean and tidy in consideration of some unexpected visitor. The question of how long this custom will be retained remains open. It does seem, though, as if a slow change is making itself felt, which would above all be of benefit with regard to the needs of children.

CROWDING AND THE DEVELOPMENT OF THE CHILD

These historical observations have shown that conceptions of the kind of space conditions positive for the development of children have changed much with time. Standards of education today, which put the development and protection of the ego-identity of the child first and foremost, would have been unrealizable in households in the Middle Ages. The fact that today, at a time when, at least in western Europe, the average living space per person is higher than ever before in history, so many families with several children feel that they are suffering from living "on top of one another", shows a serious change of outlook.

The Dwelling Situation of Young Families

The current legal standard in the Federal Republic of Germany is that each member of a household should have his or her own room. According to this criterion, young families with several children are indeed especially badly served. The standard is met, on the average, in 90% of all households. Apartments of standard or even larger than standard size are occupied by 99% of married couples without children. In contrast, only 86% of those nuclear families with two children reach the standard, as do 60% of those with three children, and of those with four children, just 29%, even though the kitchen is also counted as a room for these purposes. The situation for incomplete families is even worse. Summarizing, it can be said that almost half the children under 18 years of age today are living in conditions which do not correspond to standard. In low-income group families with four or more children, it is more than 90%.

There is, of course, a reason for this situation. It is precisely young families with small children in urban environments who constitute, by way of their socio-economic situation, a most critical problem group. Housewives with young children are especially immobile. They are not only more strongly dependent on the quality of the spatial environment than other groups, they are also less capable of compensating for shortcomings of the home by spatial mobility. Income per person is not yet generally very high in young families, especially when the wife no longer has paid employment or can only work part time after the birth of a child. Seldom do people have great savings in this phase of life. It is more usual to find debts due to investment in furnishing the home.

For this reason, the number of young families who have their own apartments is also very low. Certainly, the number of families with many children living in their own one-family houses in the Federal Republic of Germany is above average, but normally these people can only afford their own homes when their children have become so old that this form of living is no longer really necessary. When a young family has to move, either because of a change in place of work or owing to a new member of the family, the burden is excessive, due to moving costs and because, in their search for a new home, household members are limited to expensive, newly built apartments.

The Effects of Floor Plan Design on Family Life and the Socialization of Children

The variable, "crowding", is, no matter how sophisticated its definition, still only a very rough and inadequate measure for the influence of the architectural environment on the socialization of children. Insufficient attention is given to the fact that a number of different solutions to the problem of designing a particular number of rooms can be found, even when the available space is limited. Different ways that, for instance, rooms for one person, those for group activities, and those for specific purposes, as well as the ways in which passages that connect them, and indoor and outdoor areas of the home are related (that is, whether they are directly or indirectly connected to one another, or are entirely separate), set quite different limitations on the ways in which family members are able to organize their interactions with one another. The scope of various possible interactions is further dependent upon whether the means used to combine or separate rooms are rigid and unchangeable or whether they are such as can be manipulated by the inhabitants.

It seems, however, that information regarding the possibilities for influencing family life by means of the organization of the floor plan is better known to architects and tenants than to researchers. At least I know of no systematic, empirical investigation into the connection between floor plan design and familial interaction. Even descriptive investigations as to the actual utilization of given floor plans are still relatively rare. We only have a great many interview surveys of little informational value, questioning tenants as to their degree of satisfaction with their apartments.

This deficiency is also found in studies about children's living conditions. It is not usually borne in mind that basically all the rooms the family uses, not only the children's rooms, are, to a greater or lesser extent, also used by the children. Children are no isolated group; "living" or "playing" always means at the same time an interaction between the child and the rest of the family and their friends. Architects will have to orient themselves to the character of these interactions within the family.

Below, I shall try to sketch some important principles for spatial planning in the child's living area. They are based on a non-empirical study which had as its aim the translation of sociological findings into spatial criteria for floor plan design (Baumann and Zinn, 1973). It is typical for the situation in this country that a journalist, in consequence of her own experience and much intensive discussion with mothers, arrived at very similar conclusions and criteria; they are laid forth in her most remarkable and committed book (Dessai, 1976).

The relationship to the mother, who is usually the caretaker, is a determining factor in the primary socialization of small children in their first years. This relationship can be said to be successful when the child experiences security and protection, receives intensive emotional benefits, and learns to develop a personal identity, thus freeing himself or herself step by step from adult care in order to gain independence, competence, and autonomy in making decisions.

This process presupposes certain spatial necessities. The possibility for both child and caretaker to create and change both proximity and distance to each other in adjustment to their needs seems most important to me. "Proximity" and "distance" are key concepts in spatial socialization. These expressions are most ambivalent. Nearness to the mother usually means warmth, fondling, help and encouragement. This can, however, turn into unwelcome supervision and control leading to permanent interference and restriction of the child's activities. "Distance" can mean independence, privacy or freedom of action. But it can suddenly be felt by the child to be isolation, helplessness or despair. And in the adult caretaker, a loss of all hearing and visual contact can engender great uneasiness. The greatest benefits of both proximity and distance accrue only when both child and caretaker are able to keep control over the degree of mutual approach or reserve in every situation, adjusting proximity and distance as they wish, so that proximity does not necessarily mean interaction and distance does not enforce lack of interaction.

Whoever has watched children at play knows how short single play periods are and how often the place and the partners at play are changed. If the spatial environment facilitates this change of place, it helps, at the same time, the process of the gently growing autonomy of the child. In an appropriate setting, the child will start very early (at around one year of age) to remove himself or herself from the protective nearness of the mother in small experimental steps, in order to explore the environment. The spatial conditions are ideal when children can themselves decide the limits of their desire to pursue their own independence.

Deficiencies in Modern Housing

When evaluated according to the above principles, today's apartment buildings, especially, show many deficiencies. For instance, it is rare to find a play area that is large enough to allow mother and child to be close to each other without being cramped and to see and hear each other well. The kitchen is usually oriented towards the living room. But owing to its expensive furnishings and still existent presentational function, it is not possible for a small child to play there freely. Those toddlers who do so are constantly being cautioned to be careful, not to make the room dirty or untidy, not to spread their playthings around, and to remove them when they are in the way of adults.

Children's rooms are the smallest in modern rental apartments, offering, usually, only a minimum of space in which to play. In families with several children these rooms are turned into overcrowded bedrooms, which can hardly serve as individual areas of privacy, and still less can be used as a communal play area for several children.

Children's rooms are often isolated. A room at a distance provides needed privacy for older children and gives small children the chance to remove themselves consciously from parental control now and again. But the separate children's room remains, nevertheless, unsuitable as a daily play area for little ones. The distance to the mother is so great that casual communication, without interrupting either housework or play, is impossible. The consequence is that small children are usually to be found near the mother in the kitchen, where they get in her way. On the other hand, if the mother makes them stay in their rooms, they try to attract her attention loudly and incessantly. As a result, the mother constantly runs between kitchen and children, or else punishes the children so that they become resigned to their isolation. This situation is especially unfortunate in row houses, where the kitchen and the living room are on a different level from the children's rooms, and the way to the garden leads through the living room, the very area which is taboo for children.

In today's apartments, the parents' bedroom is seldom protected from children's noise. Conflicts become inevitable when a parent wishes to sleep during the day, which cannot be avoided when a parent works in shifts, or is ill and needs quiet. Further deficiencies result from the relationship between indoors and outdoors. The semi-private transitional zone outside the door, which for the child is a most interesting experiential area, is often only attainable with great difficulty. For instance, the child may have to use a dangerous or anonymous stairway, or a lift, or have to go onto a street full of traffic. In addition, it is often difficult to remain verbally or visually in contact with the home. In consequence, the child can only go out with the help of an adult. Once outside, he or she either feels isolated or, if accompanied by his or her mother, constantly under supervision; when the child wishes to return to the apartment, he or she is once more dependent on adult assistance. It is mainly for this reason, in my opinion, that high-rise blocks are unsuitable for young families with small children (Zinn, 1975).

Planning Requirements

The above considerations result in the following suggestions for apartment planning :

1. In the interests of smaller children, every dwelling should have a multi-purpose room related to the kitchen as the main working area of the mother. This should be at the disposal of the whole family as a daily living room for group games, housework and handiwork which do not disturb others, for mealtimes and for daily communication. It should, especially, give smaller children the advantage of being able to play in as varied and active a way as possible while still being near the mother. Attempts to reproduce a modern form of the old living room-kitchen can occasionally be found in newer dwellings in the form of a small dinette. It is important that this area be kept apart from the living room, with its remaining presentational function and associated standards of tidiness.

2. Attitudes in western Europe make the formal living room taboo for children. It is usually kept for quiet parental use and for receiving guests. It should therefore, be made smaller in favour of more space for the family room. In the dwelling, it should be placed so that guests can enter it easily without seeing the less formal family area.

3. Children should be able to retire into separate children's rooms whenever they feel the need. This need, however, varies according to age, so the spatial arrangements must be flexible. The individual rooms for smaller children should not be so small as to allow space only for sleeping, homework and games played alone, but should also make possible loud group games with brothers and sisters or friends, away from mother. This means that it is preferable, in smaller apartments, to give two smaller children one large room (at least $16m^2$) to share, which can later be divided into two single rooms, rather than to put them into small rooms with not enough space to play.

4. The requirements of preadolescents and adolescents differ somewhat from those of younger children. A part of their need to belong to a group is already satisfied outside

the home. Inside the home, such a child needs a room which may, of necessity, be small, but which should be an autonomous, individual area, respected as such by the parents and, for this reason, separate from the other rooms if possible. Ideally, it should have its own entrance. The differing requirements of younger and older children emphasize the usefulness of children's rooms which can be changed in size and be divided into two by moveable walls and doors.

5. Generally speaking, the rigid relating of a certain family type to a certain type of housing should not be assumed in planning dwelling units. It would be equally false to assume a rigid relationship between certain uses, functions and furnishing conceptions and certain rooms. The various rooms should rather be planned according to the principle of "multipurpose" rooms (interchangeability of the individual rooms for adults and children), so that the whole apartment can be used as flexibly as possible.

6. One of the most important demands included in planning today is for improved sound-proofing between various areas in the apartment itself, as well as to neighbouring apartments. This aim can be realized partly by skillful planning of passage areas in the apartment, and partly by increased technical effort, for instance by insulation against the sound of footsteps. Low-rise high-density buildings are preferable in this respect to multi-story buildings. Inside the home, areas for quiet, individual activities and loud group usage should be well isolated from one another, making sleep, work and active children's play compatible with one another.

An example, shown in Fig. 3.1 (a plan by the German architect Ferdinand Tjaden), meets all the above criteria.

All the recommendations for spatial planning which I have listed can be realized without great expenditure, since they involve simply more skillful use of available space. They can thus be of benefit to low-income groups.

May I note in conclusion that none of these ideas, of course, is really new. Good architects have always planned in this way. It is only that, today, there is greater uncertainty than ever before in recognizing good architecture and good apartment planning. For this reason, scientifically based criteria have become indispensable —even if, as a scientist, I repeatedly have the feeling of mainly uncovering wisdom which earlier generations have always intuitively known and used.

Fig. 3.1 : Alternative Floor Plan by Ferdinand Tjaden, Dortmund

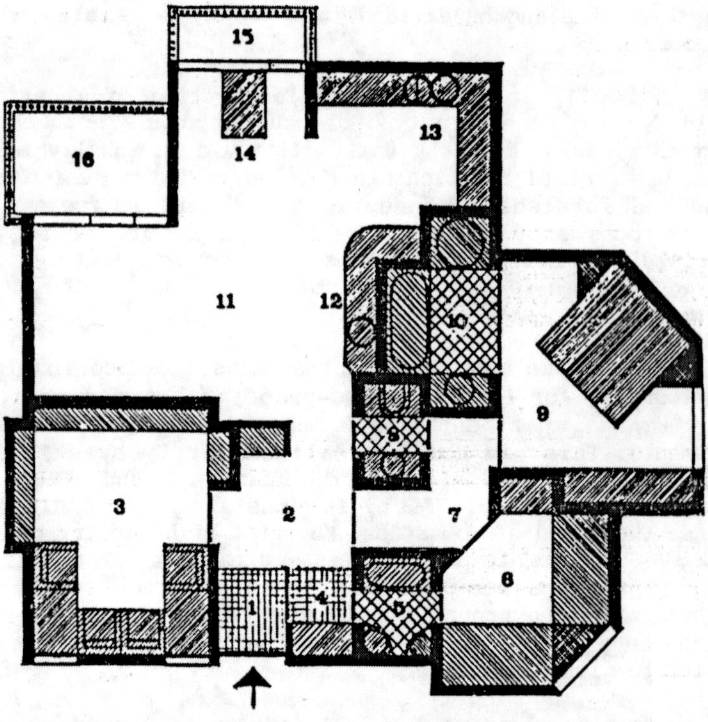

The size of the apartment is 95.35 sq.m. Children can go by way of a preliminary hall (1) into the children's cloakroom (4) and from there into their own bathroom (5)and children's bedroom (6) which is related to the parents' bedroom (9). The parents have a direct entrance to their bathroom (10) and to a separate WC (8), which is also available for guests, who can enter it from the hall. Playing children (11) do not disturb resting parents during the day but have direct verbal and visual contact to parents in the kitchen (13), dining area (14) and housework area (12). Guests can enter the formal living room (3) without noticing untidiness caused by children.

51 Influence of home environments on children

Source : Dessai (1976)

REFERENCES

Aries, P. **Geschichte der Kindheit**, Munchen, Wien, 1975.

Bahrdt, H.P. **Umwelterfahrung**, Munchen, 1974.

Baumann, R. and Zinn, H. **Kindergerechte Wohnungen fur Familien**, Bern, 1973.

Booth, A. **Urban Crowding and Its Consequences**, New York, 1976.

Chombart de Lauwe, M.J. Psychopathologie sociale de l' enfant inadapte, Paris, 1967.

DeMause, L. (ed.) **The History of Childhood**, London, 1976.

Dessai, E. Wohnen mit Kindern, in Dessai, E and Alt-Rosendahl, R. : **Wohnen und Spielen mit Kindern**, Dusseldorf, Wien, 1976.

Douglas, J.W.B. **The Home and the School**, London, 1966.

Elias, N. Uber den Prozess der Zivilisation, Bern, Stuttgart, 1969.

Gaunt, L. 158 smabarns bostadsanvandning, Stockholm, 1977.

Gehmacher, E., Kaufmann, A. and Strotzka, H. **Wohnen und psychische Gesundheit**, Wien, 1977.

Heckhausen, H. Entwurf einer Psychologie des Spielens, in **Psychologische Forschung** 27, 1964, 225-243.

Littmann, E. and Kasielke, E. Zur Diagnostik elterlichen Erziehungsverhaltens, in Probleme und Ergebnisse der Psychologie, **Beiheft** 2, 1970.

McCall, R.B. Exploratory Manipulation and Play in the Human Infant, in Monographs of the Society for Research in **Child Development** 39, 1974, No. 1550.

Michelson, W. The Physical Environment as a Mediating Factor in School Achievement, Paper presented at the annual meeting of the Canadian Sociological and Anthropological Association, Calgary, 1968.

Minturn, L. and Lambert, W.W. **Mothers of Six Cultures**, New York, 1964.

Murray, R. The Influence of Crowding on Children's Behavior, in Canter, D. and Lee, T. (eds.) : **Psychology and the Built Environment**, London, 1974.

Newson, J. and Newson, E. **Four Years Old in an Urban Community**, London, 1968.

Parke, R.D. Children's Home Environments, in Altman, I. and Wohlwill, J.F. (eds.) : **Children and the Environment**, New York, 1978.

Piaget, J. and Inhelder, B. Die Entwicklung des raumlichend Denkens beim Kinde, Stuttgart, 1971.

Roy, K. Parents' Attitudes Toward Their Children, in **Journal** of **Home Economics** 42 (1950), 652-653.

Wachs, T. The Measurement of Early Intellectual Functioning, in Meyers, C., Eyman, R. and Tarjan, G. (eds.) : **Socio-behavioral Studies in Mental Retardation**, Washington, 1973.

Wohlwill, J.F. and Heft, H. Environments Fit for the Developing Child, in McGurk, H. (ed.) : **Ecological Factors in Human Development**, Amsterdam, 1977.

Yarrow, L.J., Rubinstein, J.L. and Pedersen, F.A. **Infant and Environment : Early Cognitive and Motivational Development**, New York, 1975.

Zinn, H. Familie - Wohnbereich - Stadteplanung, in **Monatsschrift fur Kinderheikunde** 121, 1973, 427-431.

Zinn, H. Die gebaute Umwelt und ihr Einfluss auf den Menschen, das Beispiel Hochhaus, in Andritzky, M., Becker, P. and Selle, G. (eds.), **Labyrinth Stadt**. Koln, 1975.

Zinn, H. Entstehung und Wandel burgerlicher Wohngewohnheiten, in Niethammer, L. (ed.) : **Wohnen in Wandel**, Wuppertal, 1979.

FOUR

Roderick J. Lawrence

The Ideological Nature of Urban Dwellings in Geneva

INTRODUCTION

The prolific growth of interest in urban and housing history during the last two decades has meant that architectural, economic and social historians, urban geographers and others have published extensive descriptions of buildings and public spaces, and studied those policies and procedures which led to their construction (Daunton, 1983). Issues or themes such as public health and domestic sanitation, housing policies and building legislation have been the subject of many of these studies. There have been numerous analyses of dwellings built for different socio-economic classes in different societies, some examine specific towns or housing estates, whereas others are limited to a short period of time.

In the introduction to a recent monograph, Swenarton (1981) states that historians have dealt with politics, society and the economic cycles of the construction industry while over-looking the design of the built environment, whereas architectural and planning historians have ignored everything except the design of buildings. Nonetheless, Swenarton's own study considers the design of housing as a central issue of politics and government policy in Britain while failing to analyse the organization of the interior layout of dwellings, and the reasons for their design. Admittedly, his study does consider some issues that are related to site planning, but his analysis of the layout of residential areas is limited to the aesthetic composition of street-scapes. In essence, although we agree with Swenarton's diagnostic of much contemporary housing research, we cannot comply with his analysis of the ideological nature of house planning. This criticism is important and it now warrants more consideration.

The context in which houses are constructed, even those with significant government subsidies, cannot be reduced only to a political forum, as Swenarton implies. This reductionist stance is probably due to a misconception of the concepts of design and politics, which we have defined elsewhere :

"The term design can be used to denote :

(i) the ordering of the built environment; and
(ii) the scheme of action to achieve desired ends.

The term politics denotes

(i) government or government action ; or
(ii) it can also mean propoganda ; or
(iii) it can refer to the intentions and activities of eminent persons or groups of people."

(Lawrence, in press)

These definitions show that Swenarton adequately discusses the diverse meanings of politics but he underplays the first interpretation of the meaning of design. In this way, Swenarton does not present a balanced architectural and political analysis of the government housing campaign which he studied.

The shortcomings of Swenarton's contribution could have been overcome by a systemmatic analysis of the house plans that were proposed, coupled with the intentions of their architects and some housing reformers. This approach will be presented and illustrated in the following sections of this essay. Hence, it will be shown how and why certain ideas and values are attributed to house plans and the layout of residential quarters, rather than limiting the discussion to questions of housing policy devoid of spatial implications. Moreover, this approach suggests that attitudes and values about the planning of residential areas ought to be considered as part of a wider development in social policy and that these policies endow architectural designs with specific meanings that vary between different groups of people in the same society at a specific time. In sum, the intention of this essay is to develop an understanding of those kinds of factors which architects, building speculators, land owners and others have used with respect to the construction of urban housing since the mid-19th century. This discussion will be illustrated by refering to a long-term study of the design of rented dwelling units built in some towns in the French speaking Cantons of Switzerland (Lawrence, 1983). In this essay attention will focus on the town of Geneva. As a comprehensive analysis of building regulations, construction agencies and other factors has been presented elsewhere (Barbey, Brulhart et al., 1982) an account of how these parameters are implicated in house planning will not be repeated.

The period delimited for this study was chosen for the following reasons : 1860 corresponds with the beginning of industrialization in Switzerland, the opening of what became the densest railway network in the World, and the rapid development of popular housing for a rapidly increasing labour force in urban areas; it also indicates the decade when rented housing, including flats in multi-storey buildings, were constructed in large numbers.

In 1814, there were 1,900,000 inhabitants in Switzerland and Geneva was the largest town with 21,800 persons. By 1888 the population of the country had increased rapidly, so much so that Geneva had a population of approximately 52'000. With the proliferation of urban residents, a host of new functional building types - e.g. hotels, hospitals, prisons and schools - were constructed. Moreover, a new ordering of town layout and residential building design was engendered. Although a few utopian visions of communities had prefigured these innovative designs (Roseneau, 1959), it is instructive to examine how various actors - architects, landlords, planners, politicians and social reformers - answered the preeminent question of housing growing numbers of urban citizens. This is the intention of this chapter, which analyzes the design and management of shared, communal space and facilities in three types of urban dwellings built in Geneva from 1860. The collective space in buildings comprising several dwelling units not only provide access between the public realm of the street and the private realm of working-class residence but also include shared facilities (such as toilets and a laundry) and enabled interpersonal contact. This essay illustrates that the problem of accommodating as many tenants as possible in an orderly fashion was intimately linked to the design and intended use of these collective spaces.

METHODOLOGY

From the mid-19th century, there was a proliferation of interest and publications in Switzerland about housing for a growing urban population. These include public enquiries about sanitation, leading to the inspection of dwellings by health officers (Heller, 1979); the founding of benevolent societies that were concerned with housing issues, and the organization of architectural competitions to 'resolve' the shortage of houses. It is instructive to consult all of these sources, no matter how few they may be because, in tandem with an architectural analysis, such documents can enrich current understanding of the development of urban residential areas and housing types.

The method of study adopted includes both spatial and ethnographical analyses which employ an historical or temporal perspective. These analyses are founded upon :

(i) fieldwork studies of the layout and design of residential areas and specifically buildings which have been constructed between 1860 and 1960; and
(ii) analysis of diverse documentary sources including plans of extant and non-built housing schemes (such as projects for competitions) ; descriptions and articles by architects on housing; official publications including reports of government agencies, philanthropic societies, health and housing reformers; of building regulations and tenancy agreements; novels, autobiographies, brochures and newspaper articles.

This dual analysis suggests that as the amount of building construction increased after 1860, varied foreign and indigenous factors interacted in the development of urban dwellings (e.g. Gubler, 1975). This is ably illustrated in Geneva from 1851, the beginning of the gradual demolition of the fortifications around the mediaeval town. The ensuing urban expansion was influenced by foreign developments; for example, the monograph of house planning by Henry Roberts (1850) - an architect and housing reformer in London - was translated, published and debated; likewise, the National Exposition of 1896 in Geneva cannot be dissociated from the International Exposition in Paris of 1889. Consequently, it is too restrictive to analyse national or regional architecture of the 19th century in Switzerland only in terms of the totality of extant buildings. Therefore, in the following sections of this essay, the dual analysis presented here will be used to study three types of urban dwellings. The first type refers to tenements built for speculative purposes; one example (as illustrated in figure 4.1) shows that an artificially illuminated central circulation space of minimal dimensions provides access to each dwelling unit. In contrast, some model tenements (like those proposed in figure 4.2) provided a more liberal circulation space, with windows overlooking shared outdoor space. Finally, the example of the small semi-detached cottage or terrace house is considered. The latter were built by housing cooperatives and some factory owners. They exhalt independent household life, yet their generous volumes (as shown in figure 4.3) camouflage the strategies employed to direct and educate the lifestyle of the tenants. These strategies are expressed in the tenancy agreements. Following a comparison of these three types of houses, all intended for working-class families of similar socio-economic status, some theoretical and methodological issues will be formulated prior to the conclusion.

THE PROLIFERATION OF SPECULATIVE BUILDING

During the last half of the 19th century a new building type for residential use in Swiss towns evolved. The underlying concept which led to its design was that as many dwelling units as possible should be provided in the smallest space practicable over several floor levels. Today, after a century of continuous occupation, some of these buildings still retain their original spatial ordering. It is instructive to analyse these buildings, because they are generally considered to have presaged high-density flats that dominate the layout of many contemporary Swiss cities.

It is noteworthy that these massive buildings were not the product of a transformation of a type of agricultural building in an urban context. Rather, this kind of urban dwelling evokes a spatial organization like that of the monastry, the military barracks or the prison. In these kinds of disciplinary institutions the collective spaces are not residual zones that serve as circulation areas, but are intentionally designed to promote convergence, the disciplined interaction between people and favourize surveillance. If the hypothesis that some collective rented dwellings are descendants of these kinds of institutional buildings is valid, then it is necessary to show that those people responsible for housing the working-classes felt that it was necessary to accommodate as many people as possible while ensuring a harmonious and sanitary environment.

During the 19th century these kinds of buildings included at least three flats on each floor level. Each flat included two or three rooms, and was accessible from the communal staircase, landing and corridor at each floor level. Sanitary facilities were usually shared by the residents and were provided at each floor level; private bathrooms and laundries were rarely if ever provided in this kind of accommodation before the end of the century, whereas minimal cooking facilities were.

It is difficult to overlook the coercive nature of the access to each of the dwelling units. This characteristic became exacerbated towards the end of the century by an increasing tendency to dissociate the public realm of the street from the interior communal space of these kinds of buildings. Whereas there had been direct access from the footpath to the interior of the building, the distance between the two increased, with the adjunction of an outdoor space. Changes in the design of the interior collective space were engendered by restricting its size, eliminating decoration, and removing shared collective facilities. This transformation was accompanied by an increase in the surveillance of how tenants used these buildings, with the advent of caretakers, public health inspectors and street police.

An example of this kind of building in Geneva during the 19th century are the tenements aligning the Boulevard Carl-Vogt, built in 1897 by Jean Birmele, a building contractor. These tenements are one set of several buildings constructed by this person in diverse quarters of Geneva prior to 1900. In this example the plan layout, as illustrated in figure 4.1, is typical of the six main floor levels, which include five flats usually of two (sometimes three) habitable rooms; only the latter has a through floor plan. The communal lobby stair and corridor are of minimal dimensions; each tenement has its own toilet but no bathroom. The confined space of each flat is camouflaged by the carefully planned street elevations. Yet, the restricted space of the dwelling units is all the more noticeable given that the rooms of these dwellings are linked directly to one another, without a circulation space.

These buildings were commonly constructed by speculators including contractors, who invested their capital in land while accommodating some of their labourers. Therefore, it was not only important for them to include as many rentable units as possible, but also to minimize maintenance costs while retaining a clean, sanitary building. These ambitious intentions not only led to the design and the surveillance of these buildings, as noted above, but also prompted the regulation of how interior spaces were used by explicit codes of conduct that were contractually binding in tenancy agreements. These explicit codes of conduct were introduced by landlords and estate agents in Geneva from 1893.

Documentary evidence indicates that these regulations were intended to prohibit the occurrence of specific activities (for example, children's play, drying clothes and cleaning household wares) in the interior collective space. Given that these activities were intentionally prohibited in tenancy agreements suggests that they tended to occur against the wishes of landlords and estate agents. Analysis of the tenancy agreements which still exist today reveals the power and strategy of the providers of this kind of dwelling; they did not openly admit that these residential buildings were intended to accommodate a maximum number of tenants, thus yielding the highest economic returns, in an orderly fashion that ensured minimal maintenance costs.

Fig. 4.1 : Typical floor plan of tenement building constructed by Jean Birmele at the Boulevard Carl-Vogt in 1897

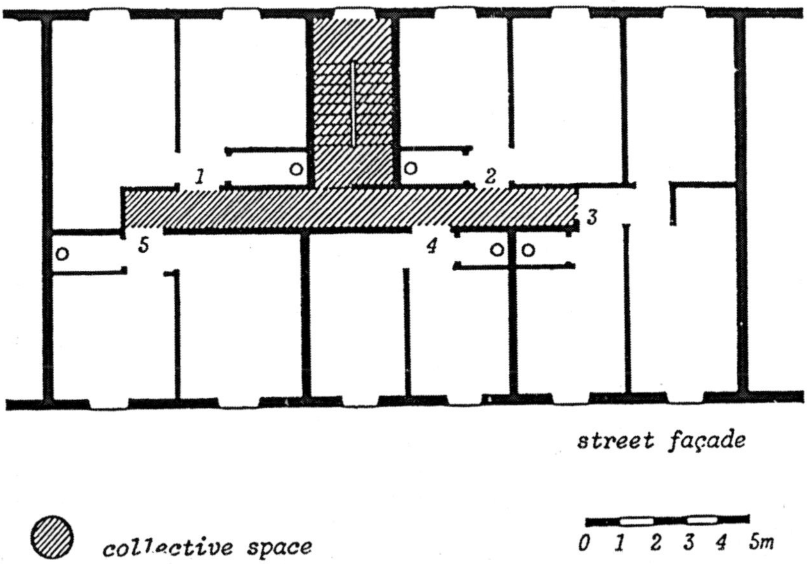

THE DEVELOPMENT OF MODEL DWELLINGS

In contrast to this kind of building with coercive communal space, there are examples of flats with more liberal shared areas built at the same time. On the one hand, various patrons of factories built apartments for their employers; these include the exemplary village at Niedertoss, Winterthur erected in 1852 by Heinrich Reiter : On the other hand, architectural competitions organized by benevolent societies or governments produced varied solutions to house urban populations; a notable example in Geneva, was the competition of the Municipal Government in 1877, which an architect won with a submission titled "une cité économique" (Lombard, 1877). Here is an explicit statement of certain criteria that were adopted for the design and management of urban dwellings.

Fig. 4.2 : Typical floor plan of flatted dwellings forming part of the winning design by Lombard for a competition in Geneva in 1877. (This design was never built).

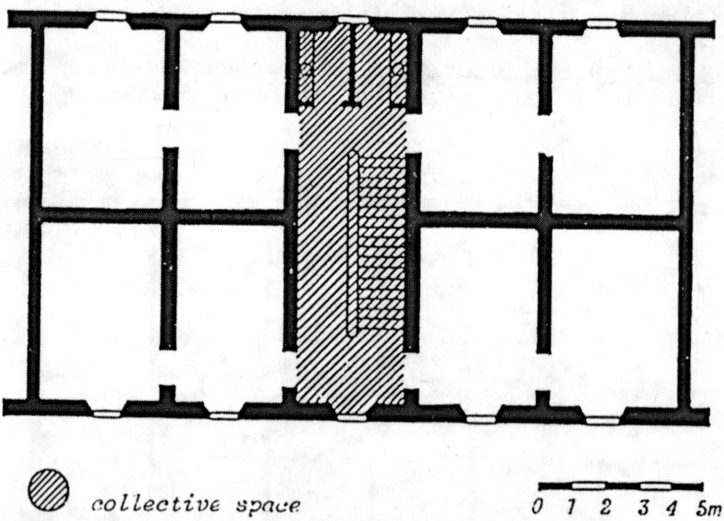

Analysis of the plans of this and other competitions shows the positive evaluation of shared communal facilities, which contradicts the devalorization noted in the preceding kind of tenement building. In his winning scheme Lombard designed a quadrangle 144 metres long and 140 metres wide surrounded by a series of 20 residential buildings, each 20 metres long and 12 metres deep. While some of these buildings had commercial arcades at ground level, the spatial arrangement of the upper floors was consistently like that shown in figure 4.2. This plan illustrates that four flats with two rooms were provided on each floor level. The tenements are small and are not self-contained, yet there are important differences between the way the collective interior space is treated in this and the previous example. Here the communal space is naturally illuminated by a window overlooking the public realm of the street. The surface area of this space assumes a larger proportion of the total floor area of the building compared with the example shown in figure 4.1. Here both the size and treatment of the interior, collective space enables (rather than discourages) it to be appropriated by the tenants.

Moreover, in the detailed report Lombard (1877) submitted with his plans for the competition he did not suggest how this space ought to be used, and there is no mention that it ought to be surveyed by a caretaker. In sum, the building design and the written intentions of the architect concur that the meaning of the interior communal space is quite different from the case of the tenement building discussed previously. In contrast to the notion of disciplined coresidence described earlier, the plan of Lombard can be interpreted as a derivative of the circulation schema of hotels and villas, in which a generous centralized collective space provides access to the private quarters of different members of the household. In this respect, Lombard's project illustrates an idealization of the kind of communal bonds that were expected to be nurtured by a specific kind of spatial arrangement of urban dwellings.

HOUSE AND GARDEN IDEOLOGY

The first Garden City was constructed in Letchworth, England in 1903. It was Parker's and Unwin's interpretation of Howard's (1898) vision, which projected a view of a total environment and a new urban society. Howard envisaged these cities in terms of social, economic and political factors, and linked these factors to the physical environment. In like manner, just prior to the First World War, garden cities or suburbs were constructed on the outskirts of some larger Swiss towns.

The "Cite-jardin d'Aire" is the result of a national competition organized by the automobile manufacturers Piccard and Pictet in 1919. Here there are similarities between Hoeschel's house plans and those designed by Tessenow in Germany (Tessenow, 1981); therefore, although one must examine links with the architecture of the Garden City Movement in England, it would be misleading to overlook influences from elsewhere. The realization at Aire, the largest of its kind in Geneva, now warrants further attention, not only with respect to its design, but also the values and ideas of those persons involved with its architecture and administration.

FIG. 4.3 : Floor plans of row houses built at the chemin de Sports, Aire according to the design of Hoeschel.

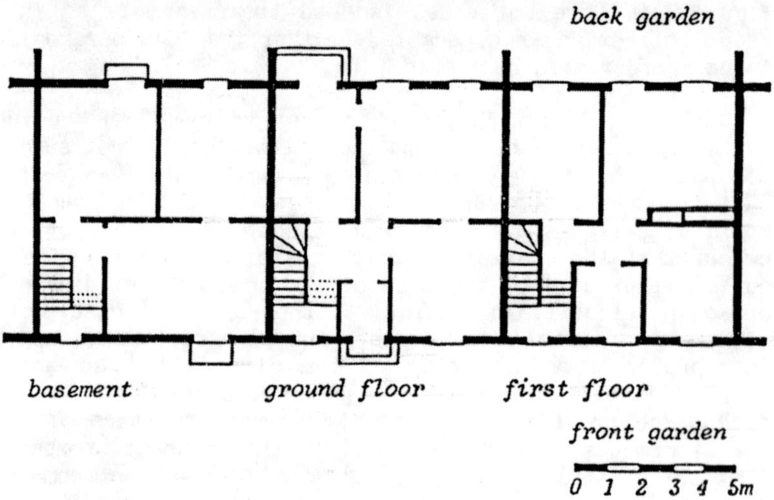

This garden suburb consists of semi-detached houses or rows of four or more dwellings aligned parallel to the principal roads. Each of these houses, with its own private garden, forms a self-contained household unit in a miniature social world, essentially romantic and individualistic in kind. These are various sizes of dwelling unit, but they are usually of two main floor levels with a basement and/or attic as shown in figure 4.3.

The house plan, as illustrated here, usually includes a kitchen and one or two other habitable rooms at ground level and three bedrooms, a bathroom and toilet upstairs. The basement includes a private laundry and storage rooms; the attic is intended solely for storage. As in Meyer's Freidorf (and elsewhere) instead of a dining-kitchen the architect provided a separate dining room, a parlour or living-room and a kitchen (not intended for family meals) on the ground floor. Moreover, a strong demarcation of the stair and circulation space from the habitable rooms enabled a range of diverse activities to be undertaken without hinderance from other activities including circulation. Clearly, privacy and order are paramount. These values are also reflected in the layout of the upper floor level which included three bedrooms that could enable the segregation of children of different ages and genders. By employing this spatial arrangement the principal concern of the architect Roberts (1850, p.10) was maintained, his contribution towards a better and healthier family life.

Clearly, the controlled liaison between rooms that was meant to accommodate specific activities, was intended to be the catalyst for the social reform of family life. Yet, architects went further than ascribing the layout of rooms and furniture therein; at Aire, like Freidorf near Basel, the architects supported the introduction of specific clauses in the tenancy agreement prescribing how space ought to be used by the residents. Moreover, there were specific requirements about what could be planted in the vegetable and flower gardens around each dwelling!

This example serves to illustrate that prescriptive behaviour patterns were evoked in houses of this kind, just as they had been introduced by landlords and estate agents in tenement buildings. Yet, too frequently urban studies have overlooked the presence of these conditions in realization of cottage building, while concentrating only on those that existed in flatted dwellings. This essay presents a more balanced account. It shows that the values and ideas of those who built tenements and those who designed cottages for the same sector of the population during the 19th century ought to be compared for several reasons. Firstly, both these sets of actors shared fundamental ideas about the need to prescribe the behaviour of the residents; thus by itself architecture was not the sole vehicle for assuring a sane domestic environment. Secondly, these two kinds of house form express different ideas and values about the nature of dwellings for the urban population; tenement construction was intentionally coercive primarily linked to financial investment and profit motives, whereas the idealism invested in the Garden City or suburb was not ranked below return on capital investment, and engendered the design of a spatially generous yet prescriptive domestic environment.

SYNTHESIS

The preceding sections of this essay have examined the

spatial order of, and those ideas and intentions endowed in, three pre-dominant kinds of urban dwelling constructed in Geneva as early as 1860. Specific attention has been given to those house forms built at the end of the 19th century; therefore, certain qualifications are necessary.

Firstly, although the kinds of urban dwellings described here are representative of those built in diverse towns of Switzerland, it is crucial to note that examples of the Garden City were no longer built after the 1940's, whilst flats in multi-storey buildings proliferated; secondly, the numbers of these kinds of dwellings constructed in the 19th century varied between the towns; for example, there is no evidence of a Garden City or suburb being built in some towns. In sum, there is no general, chronological sequence of constructed examples.

During the period of this study the interior layout of flatted dwelling units has undergone only minor changes including an increase in size, which can be attributed to the inclusion of a bathroom, additional storage space in the kitchen and elsewhere, and (sometimes) an additional room.

In sharp contrast, however, this study shows that the collective, interior spaces (i.e. the lobby at ground level, the stair and its landings at the upper levels) have undergone significant spatial transformation, including the suppression of natural daylight, subtle changes of floor level, and a reduction in size and decoration. This trend has been observed in all of the towns from the earliest decades of this century. The catalysts for this change were manifold : On the one hand, they included technical innovations such as the inclusion of the lift as a vertical means of transport; on the other hand, a fundamental idea shared by many housing reformers of the late 19th century was that different spatial relationships in urban dwellings engender different kinds of human contact. This principle generated a concept of domestic culture which the reformers applied to the design of popular urban dwellings by :

(i) reducing the size of shared communal space and eliminating shared facilities (notably sanitary services) to minimize contact between residents;
(ii) providing private facilities in each dwelling;
(iii) designating an independent access for each room in the dwelling by including a demarcated circulation space; and
(iv) prescribing how both interior spaces and 'private'

gardens ought to be used by tenants, including these prescriptions in tenancy agreements, and employing caretakers to regulate behaviour.

Moreover, during the period of this study rented dwelling units have become more strongly demarcated from the public realm of the street. Fieldwork has shown that since the First World War it has been increasingly common for tenement buildings to be setback from rather than aligned along, streets and courts as had been customary during the 19th century. This transformation has meant that the collective interior space is no longer directly linked to the public realm; now an external space separates these two domains. It has been observed in many towns that this external space was often a small garden between the building and footpath, but since the Second World War it has become a vast landscaped area encircling tenement blocks.

The morphogenesis of urban dwellings analyzed here expresses specific architectural, economic and socio-political factors that ought to be considered with the production of other kinds of buildings, such as the proliferation of administrative offices for private corporations, or the replacement of the local grocery shop by the multi-chain store in a shopping centre. Thus, at a more general level, this study illustrates the increasing specialization of buildings in terms of social purposes as opposed to the growing anonimity of external spaces around buildings. It also shows how the regulation of the design and use of the built environment has become more explicit during this century. Moreover, it suggests that architects and planners have assumed a collaborative role with public and private developers to design buildings, as components of a total, model environment.

The analysis presented in this essay could be extended to examine the ideological nature of the interior layout of dwelling units in different types of buildings. Moreover, the comparisons could be enlarged to contrast those dwellings built in 1860 with those constructed a century later. Although there is insufficient space to present this research here, it is appropriate to illustrate a conceptual model which can be applied to extend the interpretation presented here in the future.

The conceptual model presented here for the analysis of the ideological nature of dwelling design implies that houses ought to be studied in terms of holistic and dynamic processes, which are represented in figure 4.4. The left side of the diagram shows that those actors involved in the design and management of houses are motivated by rational parameters (P1) such as economic return on the invested capital, and prescriptive ideals (P2) such as disciplinary notions concerning the way tenant ought to use domestic space and facilities. The influence of these two sets of factors has been ably illustrated earlier in this essay. Furthermore, the examples presented earlier also indicate that the tenants did not necessarily conform to the intentions or prescriptions of the landlords and estate agents. The ways in which tenants appropriate space are accounted for on the right side of figure 4.4, by those factors of independent action (R1). Nonetheless, the fact that some tenants undoubtably conform to prescriptions in tenancy agreements for fear of eviction cannot be denied, and is represented by auto-coercive factors (R2) in the figure.

Fig. 4.4 : Graphic representation of the processes implicated in the planning and use of rented dwelling units

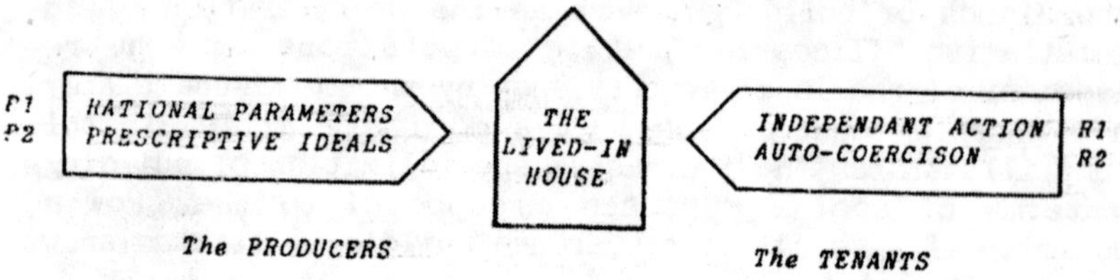

In sum, dwellings are not merely bricks and mortar, but they express diverse intentions and house a range of daily activities. This essay has shown that there is no direct correspondence between those activities of the tenants and the intentions of the producers of houses.

CONCLUSION

In recent years there has been a growing interest in urban environments including house planning, the layout of residential quarters and the daily life therein. There have been many studies of urban residences either solely in terms of building design or only in terms of political intent. Both these recurrent interpretations of urban environments are incomplete, for reasons which this essay has discussed and illustrated.

This study illustrates that different groups of people partake of different ideas about the design and use of domestic buildings; just as the landlords and tenants of 19th century tenement buildings in Switzerland had divergent views about the design and use of space, so this divergence is still evident today with the respect to the definition and regulation of public and private domains in rented dwelling units. In like manner, there was a divergence within professional groups; for example, between those architects who designed rented dwelling units for building contractors and those, like Lombard, who sought social reform in an efficient manner by the design of model apartments.

In sum, it is illusory to ignore those ideas and values that presaged the construction of certain types of urban dwelling units from 1860 and which became endowed in these buildings. Nonetheless, the ideological nature of building layout and house plans has largely been overlooked by recent analyses of urban environments. This study has indicated however, that ideas and values become operative through the vehicle of building design; moreover, it has illustrated how certain plan layouts were employed to install certain kinds of behaviours and that these layouts were not the sole responsibility of architects but a range of actors involved with the morpho-genesis of urban dwellings. Thus current and future concern with the urban housing cannot be stifled by an interpretation that treats buildings as if they were autonomous objects. The buildings in Swiss towns, and elsewhere, we experience today are complex artefacts which are endowed with meanings, and these meanings express specific socio-economic, cultural and political factors.

REFERENCES

Barbey, G., Brulhart, A., Germann, G., and Gubler, J., "Geneve". **Inventaire Suisse d' Architecture : 1850-1920.** Volume 4. (Societe d' Histoire de l' Art en Suisse, Berne, 1982, pp.249-404).

Daunton, M., Experts and the environment : approaches to planning history". Journal of Urban History 9 (2) 1983, pp. 233-250.

Gubler, J., **Nationalisme et internationalisme dans l'architecture moderne de la Suisse.** (Editions L' Age d' Homme, Lausanne) 1975.

Heller, G., **Propre en ordre : habitation et vie domestique 1850-1930** : l' exemple vaudois. (Editions d' En-Bas,

Lausanne) 1979.

Howard, E., **Tomorrow : A peaceful path to real reform** (Swan Sonnenschein, London) 1898.

Lawrence, R., Espace prive-espace collectif-espace public : l'exemple du logement populaire en Suisse romande, 1860-1960. Doctoral dissertation at E.P.F.L. 1983.

Lawrence, R., (in press). "Urban history, housing and politics in Britain : A review essay" Social Science Information.

Lomabard, B., "Projet d'une cite economique a Geneve". Memoires couronnes a la suite du concours institue par la Ville de Geneve sur la question des petits logements. (Imprimeries J. Carey, Geneve) 1877,.

Roberts, H., The dwellings of the labouring classes. (Society for Improving the conditions of the Labouring classes, London) 1850.

Roseneau, J., The Ideal City (Studio Vista, London) 1959,.

Swenarton, M., Homes fit for heroes (Heinemann, London)1981,.

Tessenow, H., La cite et l'artisan. (Archives d' Architecture Moderne Bruxelles). (1st German edition, Berlin, 1916) 1981,.

FIVE

Gary Sands

Housing Conservation in Detroit's Harmony Village[1]

INTRODUCTION

In the United States, individual preferences have traditionally favoured new development over conservation. This attitude has been fostered by the abundance of land available for development and a generally high level of affluence. Public policies have further reinforced the preference for new housing. A number of government programs and policies encourage new housing construction while substantially less assistance has been provided for the maintenance of the existing housing stock.

The emphasis on production of new housing has also indirectly contributed to the deterioration of the housing stock. America's housing policy has traditionally relied on filtering strategies the deliberate creation of a surplus of higher quality housing in order to create housing bargains which are accessible to lower income households.[2] Unfortunately the persistence of surplus housing may cause a decline in housing quality as well as price. If a balance is not maintained between supply and demand (by the removal of the poorest quality existing dwellings), not only will blight and deterioration spread, but the cost of encouraging additional new production will increase.[3]

An example of some of the adverse consequences of production oriented housing strategies is provided by the Detroit metropolitan housing market. Between 1970 and 1980, there was a net increase of about 160,000 units in the housing stock in the three county area.[4] During the same period, the population of this area fell by almost 170,000. Although average household size declined, the number of surplus housing units increased sharply.

Much of this housing surplus came to be concentrated in the City of Detroit. Despite a net loss of some 60,000 dwelling units, excess housing increased as the City's population declined by about 300,000. Units which remained vacant for long periods frequently became vandalized, increasing the blighting effect on nearby properties. (This problem was exacerbated by the lengthy time required to complete legal proceedings against tax or mortgage delinquent properties.) Many neighborhoods were caught in a self-perpetuating spiral of decline.

The Harmony Village program was initiated in an attempt to preserve one Detroit neighbourhood which contained substantial amounts of better quality housing. The program was established as a joint effort of the City of Detroit, the State of Michigan (through the Michigan State Housing Development Authority), the Federal government (through the Department of Housing and Urban Development) and residents of the community. The program committed all four participants to a concentrated effort to restore the housing in the area to productive use. This was to be done through public improvement programs, the upgrading of the commercial areas, and the provision of loans for home improvements and housing rehabilitation. Funding for these activities was provided primarily by the City of Detroit through its Community Development Block Grant allocation.

In addition to these efforts to maintain and upgrade currently occupied housing units, the Harmony Village program also addressed the large number of vacant homes in the neighbourhood. The reduction of the number of vacant and abandoned structures was seen as a means not only of conserving these units but also of protecting the other housing units in the neighbourhood.

HARMONY VILLAGE

Harmony Village is a 900 hectare area located about 15 kilometres northwest of the Detroit central business district. In 1970, the area contained about 14,800 dwelling units. About two-thirds of these were in single family structures. An additional 30 per cent of the dwellings were in structures with 2-4 units and only four per cent were in structures containing five or more units. Almost all of the single family units and many of the small multifamily units were owner occupied. Seven out of every ten dwellings were owner occupied, a slightly higher percentage than for the City as a whole. The median value of owner occupied units was $15,900, comparable to the city-wide median of $15,600.

Almost 49,000 people lived in Harmony Village in 1970. The average household size was 3.4 persons, somewhat above the city-wide average size of 3.0. Four out of five households were families (i.e., consisted of related individuals). Just over 70 per cent of the population was black.

The occupational characteristics of Harmony Village residents closely paralleled those of the City as a whole. About one-third of employed area residents held jobs in manufacturing, primarily in automotive related industries. Substantial numbers of persons were employed in retail trade, government and health services. Unemployment was about seven per cent in both Harmony Village and the City as a whole. The median income in the area was approximately $9,000, about $1,000 less than the median for all Detroit households.

Harmony Village experienced significant changes during the early 1970's.[5] The population of Harmony Village declined by almost one-sixth, to 41,000. The white population of the area fell from 13,700 to 3,200. Although the occupational profile of the area did not change significantly, median income rose by almost 50 per cent, to $13,300. This compares with an increase in the city-wide median of only 14 per cent. (Table 5.1)

The area also experienced dramatic changes in its housing stock. Between 1970 and 1975, about 850 dwelling units were demolished. Despite these removals, the vacancy rate tripled. In 1975, over 1,500 units were vacant, 400 of which were vacant and boarded. The federal government had acquired through foreclosure almost 1,000 units, most of which were vacant.[6] The number of owner occupied units in the area declined by about 900. Home values in the area remained virtually unchanged throughout the period.

THE CONSERVATION PROGRAM

Initial efforts to conserve the housing stock in Harmony Village focussed on those units owned by the Federal Department of Housing and Urban Development (HUD). Vacant units from HUD's inventory were offered to the Michigan State

Housing Development Authority (MSHDA). The state agency determined what repairs and improvements were required to place the units in sound marketable condition. If the estimated cost of rehabilitation was equal to or less than the mortgage commitment which HUD was willing to offer, MSHDA would acquire the properties at nominal cost.[7] When repairs had been completed (by a licensed contractor), the unit was sold to a moderate income purchaser subject to a HUD insured, MSHDA financed mortgage. Units carried a one-year warranty on major systems, including heating, plumbing and electrical. The sales of rehabilitated units began late in 1975. Through 1979, some 450 units were sold through the program, with peak sales occurring in 1977 when 145 units were sold.

TABLE 5.1

Harmony Village
Housing and Population Characteristics

	1970	1975
Number of Housing Units	14,855	14,202
Tenure		
Owner Occupied	73.1%	69.8%
Renter Occupied	23.3%	18.6%
Vacant	3.6%	11.6%
Median Value		
Owner Occupied	$15,866	$16,671
Number of persons	48,753	41,081
Number of Households	14,315	12,555
Median Income	$9,000	$13,300
Per cent Black	71.0%	92.1%

Sources : 1970 U.S. Census Population and Housing: 1975 City of Detroit Citizen Survey

Unit Characteristics. The typical home purchased through this program was a six room, three bedroom unit either partially or wholly of brick construction. About one-quarter had four or more bedrooms. Only two of ten had more than a single bath. In terms of square feet of living area, the average home contained about 100 square metres. Sales activity was highly concentrated. About two-thirds of all sales were in a 250 hectare area in the southwest corner of the project. This subarea contains some of the best quality housing in all of Harmony Village. About seven and a half per cent of all of the homes in this subarea were rehabilitated and sold through the Harmony Village program in a three-year period.

The average sales price of a rehabilitated home was $17,600 (median $17,850). The price of most of the units fell within a fairly narrow range 86 per cent of the units cost between $15,000 and $20,000. Monthly housing payments (including interest and principle) averaged just over $200. For 85 per cent of the mortgagors, the mortgage payment represented less than one-fifth of their monthly income.

Over the years during which the Harmony Village program has been in operation there has been a steady increase in the price of homes sold. In 1976, the average price of the rehabilitated homes was just over $17,000. Subsequently, the average rose to $17,600 in 1977 and $18,250 in 1978. These prices are comparable to the average sales price of other homes in the area. The Detroit Board of Assessor's reported that the average sales price of homes in Harmony Village, excluding those sold through the program, was $18,000 in 1977 and $18,550 in 1978.

Household characteristics. In several respects the program has not changed the type of household moving into the area. All of the purchasers are black. Almost 45 per cent of the mortgagors were females, a figure identical to the proportion of female headed households in the area in 1975. The average household size was 3.2; again, about the same as the 1975 average for all households in the area.

TABLE 5.2

Characteristics of Housing Units sold through Harmony Village Program, 1976-78

Average Number of Rooms	6.2
Average Number of Bedrooms	3.2
Average Size In Square Feet	998
Construction Type:	
Brick.	84.9%
Aluminum	6.9%
Wood	8.2%
Sales Price	
- Average	$17,600
- Median	$17,850
Average Mortgage Payment	$205

The median age of Harmony Village purchasers was 29, with nearly one-quarter of the program participants under the age of 25. Less than half of the Harmony Village mortgagors were married couples. This low proportion of married couples is related to the high proportion of female mortgagors.

More than three-quarters of the program participants were households with minor children. Although a large proportion of the married couples had no children, about three-eighths of all mortgagors were single parents with minor children. The single parents were predominantly (94 per cent) females.

The mortgagors previously resided in all areas of Detroit, as well as in a number of suburban communities. There was, however, a heavy concentration of previous addresses in the immediate vicinity of the project. Less than five per cent of the purchasers were previously homeowners. In fact, about one of every eight of the mortgagors had not been maintaining their own household prior to their move to Harmony Village (e.g., had been living with parents or other relatives).

The mortgagors were comparable to other area residents in respect to their employment characteristics. The largest proportion of mortgagors were employed as operatives (machine operators, assemblers, etc.), mainly in the automotive industry. About 22 per cent of all purchasers (45 per cent of couples) were families with two wage earners. The median length of employment for all mortgagors was just over four years. Almost one-fifth of the mortgagors and an even larger proportion of the co-mortgagors had held their current job for less than one year.

Financial Characteristics. The median income of mortgagors was $14,900. About nine per cent had incomes of more than $25,000 a year, while six per cent earned less than $10,000. Data from the 1974 Annual Housing Survey of Detroit indicate that Harmony Village Program participants had slightly higher incomes than other Detroit home purchasers.[8]

Most mortgagors had only limited financial assets. The median value of cash accounts for all mortgagors was just under $400. About one-third lacked cash reserves equal to one month's mortgage payment, while one out of five had ready cash of less than $100. Although the median value of the mortgagor's noncash assets was about $4,000, most of these assets consisted of household furnishings, which are generally not readily convertible to cash.

TABLE 5.3

Characteristics of Harmony Village Mortgagors

Median Age	29 Years
Per cent Male	55%
Household Composition	
Single, Individual	13.6%
Couple, No Children	8.2%
Couple, With Children	40.6%
Single, With Children	37.6%
Average Family Size	3.2 Persons
Previous Tenure	
Own	4.8%
Rent	81.9%
Board	13.3%

DELINQUENCIES AND DEFAULTS

Although the program has been successful in restoring and marketing more than 400 units, it has encountered some problems in terms of delinquencies and defaults. As of August, 1979 about one of every five mortgages in the program was 30 days or more delinquent. About five per cent of the mortgages had been foreclosed and foreclosure proceedings were in progress for an additional five per cent of the mortgages.[9]

This rate of mortgage default is high by most standards. While an above average default rate might be expected for a program serving low and moderate income households, it is counterproductive to a program the primary objective of which is to restore housing units to productive use. A unit which has been foreclosed is likely to become vacant, possibly vandalized and a potential blighting influence on the neighbourhood. Thus it seems to be worthwhile to consider whether defaults and foreclosures could have been minimized.

A review of the Harmony Village mortgage records identified several factors which appeared to be associated with mortgage default. Among these were low income, low cash assets, large housing cost increase and an absence of installment debt. (This last factor probably serves as a proxy to identify borrowers not found credit worthy by other lenders.) Factors which were found to be poor predictors of default included marital status, sex of borrower, age of borrower and previous tenure.

Any of the variables which were found to be good predictors (income, cash assets, change in housing costs, installment debt) could be incorporated into an underwriting criterion which would have produced a lower default rate. For example, granting mortgages only to borrowers with incomes in excess of $15,000 a year would have eliminated approximately half of the mortgages which had gone into foreclosure. The proportion of mortgages foreclosed, however, would only have been reduced from 4.9 per cent to 4.7 per cent. Imposing this limit would have denied mortgages to 194 borrowers, 184 of whom were not in default.

A much more effective criterion for identifying potential problem mortgages would seem to be the amount of cash assets held by the mortgage applicant. Simply by requiring that applicants have cash accounts (over and above funds required for downpayment and closing costs) equivalent to one month's mortgage payment (generally about $200), seven-tenths of the foreclosures could have been avoided. Even if the standard is lowered to a minimum of $100 in ready cash, the overall foreclosure rate would have been cut in half, to 2.4 per cent. Under this latter standard, 83 borrowers would have been denied mortgages, 70 of whom had not been foreclosed.

CONCLUSIONS

It would appear that, overall, the Harmony Village program has been successful in achieving many of its objectives. The program has marketed and returned to occupancy a substantial number of housing units. Where prior to the program housing in Harmony Village was being abandoned because no purchasers could be found, by 1979, there was a reasonably strong market for both rehabilitated and non-rehabilitated units. There were significant increases in both home sales prices and residential assessed valuations between 1974 and 1979 indicating a strengthening of the market.

The Harmony Village program has not been an unqualified success. The program has had its greatest impact in the southwest part of the area with other parts of the neighbourhood apparently receiving few spill-over benefits. The program has also experienced some relatively high rates of mortgage foreclosure. These defaults are perhaps more appropriately viewed as failures to return properties to continued occupancy, rather than primarily as financial losses. In order to minimize the adverse neighbourhood effects of new defaults, it would seem advisable to introduce new mortgage underwriting criteria. While this would not change the probability of default or foreclosure for mortgages which have already been made, the risk of default could be minimized for new mortgages. The single criterion which would seem to be most effective in reducing the risk of foreclosure would be to require that mortgagors have a reasonable minimum amount of cash assets.

Finally, a brief comment about the cost of the program to the various participants is appropriate. Neither the City of Detroit nor the Michigan State Housing Development Authority bear any extraordinary costs for this program, although the City does concentrate its public improvement activity in the project area. MSHDA's policy has been to recover all of its cost of acquisition and rehabilitation in the sales price of the properties sold. (Some of the State's overhead costs for the program may not be recovered.)

The largest financial contribution to the program is provided by HUD in making available to MSHDA the vacant units for rehabilitation. The loss to HUD's insurance fund on these transfers may amount to $10,000 to $15,000 or more per unit. The nominal payment for the units by MSHDA is less than what HUD might be able to realize through sales to private individuals. The Federal agency does, however, benefit by being able to reduce its inventory, ensuring that necessary repairs are made competently and expeditiously and improving the marketability of other federally insured properties in the neighbourhood. Although these factors may not offset all of the losses to the insurance fund in a strict cost-benefit calculus, it would appear that this type of program nevertheless provides an attractive alternative for HUD in areas where the private market is extremely weak.

NOTES

1 The cooperation and financial support of the Michigan State Housing Development Authority for this study is gratefully acknowledged. The interpretations and conclusions expressed herein are those of the author and do not reflect the position of the Michigan State Housing Development Authority.

2 Henry Aaron, **Shelter and Subsidies**, D.C. : The Brookings Institution, Washington, D.C., 1972.

3 Richard U. Ratcliff, **Urban Land Economics** McGraw Hill Book Company, New York, 1949.

4 U. S. Bureau of the Census, **Census of Population and Housing**, 1970 and 1980, Detroit, Michigan SMSA. The 1970 metropolitan area definition of Wayne, Oakland and Macomb counties is used throughout this paper.

5 Estimates of change from 1970 to 1975 based on unpublished data from the City of Detroit Planning Department, **Detroit Citizen Survey**, Rounds 1 and 2.

6 The reasons for the high rate of foreclosures are complex, but generally seem to be a result of the desire to achieve high levels of production in a short time and, in some cases, the dishonest practices of some government officials. See Brian Boyer, **Cities Destroyed for Cash** Follett, Chicago, 1973).

7 For purposes of determining rehabilitation feasibility, both the costs of repairs and the amount of the mortgage commitment were pooled for several properties. As a result, the "profit" from a unit requiring only modest improvements could be transferred to other properties where the extent of repairs needed might exceed that property's market value.

8 U.S. Bureau of the Census, **Annual Housing Survey Detroit 1974**, Part D Characteristics of Recent Movers (Washington, D.C. : GPO, n.d.).

9 Unpublished data, Michigan State Housing Development Authority.

SIX

Zbigniew Pucek and Kazimierz Z. Sowa

Changes in the Living Habits in Modern Dwelling-Houses in Iraq

INTRODUCTION

Improvement of the living conditions belongs actually to the most important problems which face developing countries. In order to achieve the improvement some of the countries accept indiscriminately living patterns and related technologies from advanced industrial countries. These imported patterns and technologies are usually deeply rooted in specific, most often European cultural tradition and circumstances. Their successful implementation depends upon determined social, cultural and economic as well as physical and climatic conditions which are not always obtainable in particular developing countries. One can notice it in connection with the modernizing tendency shown by housing programs launched in some of the Third World countries. Such a program was started in seventies also in Iraq. This paper deals with distinctive features of the adaptation process of Iraqi population to a new and rather alien housing conditions.

Iraqi are strongly attached to a traditional living habits which are still commonly practiced. These are based not only on local needs but also on general Muslim rules. Most important of them are : isolation of the family private life from outsiders, continuation of the large family structure, keeping on close relationships with relatives or even with tribe members. There are also some demands resulting from climatic conditions, namely effective cooling and heating facilities. Traditional Iraqi types of house meet all these task very well, however in the way which cannot be evaluated as modern. What is more they are in accordance with daily and seasonal changes in the occupants' course of life and fit to the dominant traditional type of living equipment and furniture. On the other side, modern houses are sometimes unpropitious to the rules, which simply cannot be abide or observed in the conditions offered by living structure taken from a different culture. In this situation some adaptative changes begin

The following analysis results from research program carried out late in the seventies in three biggest towns of Iraq, i.e., Baghdad, Mosul and Basra. The research program was a part of the comprehensive Governmental housing program for Iraq charged to Polish contractor with a commission. It is based on scores of detailed problem inquiries held with families which occupy flats in modern multifamily buildings. In addition to the inquiry with lodgers, some interviews were also carried out with social experts—owners of apartment houses, building contractors—and this led to more comprehensive discussion on a number of problems.

TYPES OF MODERN HOUSES UNDER ANALYSIS

The lodging quarters occupied by the families under investigation may be divided into two groups. The first group includes typical multifamily buildings which form districts (the so-called blocks) and are found in various parts of Iraq. They follow the same building design. The second group includes a few multifamily buildings spread all over the towns which have been built after individual designs. Survey in Baghdad and in Mosul involved mainly the families living in the first type of houses, while the survey in Basra, where the multifamily block building system is absent included people residing in the second type of buildings.

In Baghdad, the Palestine Str. (Wazirija district) housing estate was investigated, which had been built for the Electro-technical Equipment National Works. It is a typical industrial next-to-plant-housing estate which is occupied by the families of the plant employees and is located in a very short distance of half a kilometer from the Works. It is still being expanded : at present four blocks of 36 flats each have been occupied. All the flats have the same floor space and room composition. All the blocks of flats have three storeys and three stairways each equipped with open landings. At each landing there are entrance doors to four flats. Entrance doors are located in couples on the right and on the left landing, opposite to each other. The other two sides of the landing are open and secured only with railing. The approximate landing surface varies from 30 to 40 square metres. Because of its open structure it is called "bower" by the tenants. The building is topped with a vast terrace provided with water, sewage and electric installation. The estate area is not kept in order and absolutely not managed. Shops and all kinds of services are missing.

The Mosul housing estate is located in Mansui district. This is also an industrial next-to-plant settlement belonging to National Textile Works. It includes four blocks of 36 flats each built after the same design as the Baghdad housing estates described yet. The block of flats is a spatially separated component of a larger district consisting mainly of detached small houses. It has not yet been completed. The inhibited part is kept relatively in order, the estate is provided with certain social objects/school and ambulatory/and market centre, so called suq.

A flat located in block housing in either of the districts i.e., in Baghdad and Mosul, consists of a hall, two dwelling rooms and a kitchen, a bath-room with shower, WC of eastern type, and a balcony. The entrance door opens directly to the hall, wherefrom an open passage leads to the two dwelling rooms, as well as to the bath-room and WC. The entrance to the kitchen is from the hall directly. In the flats on the first floor there is an additional exit from the passage to the small yard where an illuminatory shaft is situated. The shaft opens from the top only. The yard is a common place to all four flats. The total of the functional floor space of the flat is about 70 square metres.

The flats in Baghdad housing estate were populated in 1974-1976, whilst the Mosul flats in 1975-1976.

In Basra inquiries covered the families who lived in various types of non-typical buildings scattered all over the town. A half of the accommodation is rented from private housing estate owners, the other half is a property of the Wakf Ministry, i.e. Social Welfare Department. The flats in this type of buildings have one, two or three rooms, a hall, a bath-room and WC. They have got electric installation. The age of the buildings ranges from seven to more than ten years.

A certain number of flats in the non-typical multifamily buildings were also investigated in Baghdad. The majority of such buildings turned out to have shops and other utilities situated on the first floor. The non-typical buildings involved in the studies were located in the central parts of the city, while the housing estates were found on the outskirts.

TYPE OF FAMILIES UNDER INVESTIGATION

With respect to their social and professional features, the families under investigation form a considerably homogeneous category. Most of the interviewed heads of families were low-salaried workers and clerks. However, from the viewpoint of income level, the families living in non-typical multifamily buildings differ much from the ones living in the industrial next-to-plant housing estates. In the latter group, an average monthly income per one household ranged from 100 to 150 ID, while in the former from 40 to 50 ID. The percentage of rent-charge in the monthly budget is different in both groups. The rent for the plant housing calculated by the employers reached 7 per cent of an employee's monthly salary, while in non-typical buildings it is generally much higher and ranges from more than ten per cent of much higher multiples of the monthly income of the families under investigation.

A standard level of education of the heads of households is not more than four to five elementary school courses. In Basra families the average education level was relatively higher (a few grades of a secondary school), while in Mosul most of the heads of households were illiterates. The young generation of the interviewed families (grown or growing up children) showed moderate educational aspirations and did not promise a considerable advance in this respect in comparison with their parents. However, in a number of cases, especially in Baghdad, parents showed higher and more concrete purposes concerning education of their children.

As far as the territorial topography is concerned, three categories of families could be distinguished. The first category includes families which were born in the town they live in ("native" group). The second category are families whose parents were born outside their living place, but whose flats they occupied was not their first lodging in this locality ("adapted" immigrant group). As a rule, these families had been living in the town for more than ten years. The third category are families who had just moved in to their houses and came to them directly from the outside, mainly from villages and small towns ("non-adapted" immigrant group).

83 Changes in living habits in modern dwelling-houses

The immigration mechanism which has shown up in our studies deserves some attention. It originates from family relationships. In general, immigrants arrive to a town being encouraged and supported by some members of their families who had settled there before. The houses of those relatives were the first immigrants shelter - sometimes even for a long time. The same mechanism may be observed also in the industrial next-to-plant housing estates under investigation. It causes, of course, relative deterioration of living conditions. A trend is also noticed of family in one building grouping, which is, however, restricted by the lodging possibility. Immigrant families living in Baghdad, arrived to the town from the South of the country (vicinities of Kut, Amara, Divanili). In Mosul the immigrant families arrived from nearby towns (Bashika, Sanjar).

Before moving into their present flats, most families occupied a small conventional Arab low-standard house or a part of it. In case of the immigrants from villages the house was a "sarif" built of clay or less frequently of stone. Generally, the former living conditions are worse both in respect of their standard and floor space. Usually the houses were not owned by interviewed lodgers but only rented jointly with other families, frequently with relatives. Nevertheless the rent-charges were much higher than the ones paid for accommodation in the block of flats. In spite of their low standard, those houses had some advantages much appreciated by lodgers, namely : sleeping terraces and gardens.

A typical family living in a flat in a multifamily building consists of two generations, and is frequently enlarged by cousins which associates with the aforementioned migration mechanism. As a rule, it is also a multi-children family. The most typical is a family with four, five or six children. A smaller number of children is more specific of a young married couples. A special, subjective indicator of the large number of children the interviewed families had is the parents lack of knowledge often of the exact number of their progeny. When asked about the number of children they answered for instance : "About seven or eight".

A typical family shows a permanent survival of the Muslim rule of the family endogamy and tribe endogamy in the North of the country. The surveyed married couples in Baghdad and in Basra are usually relatives to themselves of the second order, e.g., the wife is a daughter of the husband's uncle etc. Due to this, the family bonds are substantially petrified, which is reflected in the intensity of social family life in the flat. Of course, few Christian families are excluded from this rule.

LIFE ORGANIZATION IN THE FLAT

Flat equipment

All surveyed flats follow West European organization patterns of life in the flat. The flat structure is based on the separated rooms to which particular life functions of the family have been attributed somewhat in advance. Thus a typical flat consists of markedly isolated sleeping rooms, a room designed for social family life (either a hall or a sitting room), a kitchen, sanitary accommodations and a balcony. Because the surveyed families belong to a specific culture tradition which differs from the European one, the European flat philosophy give rise to a number of adaptation problems. When analysing these problems, we shall focus our attention on the housing estate conditions because of the probably wide prospects of such a building type in Iraq.

The flat equipment may be divided into portable and non-portable. A typical flat is furnished mainly with the former kind of equipment. It includes : bed-spreads, coverlets, blankets, pillows, mattresses usually gathered at day-time in one room in a high stack. At night and during the afternoon siesta they are spread in various rooms according to actual needs. This group includes also camping and garden chairs which being portable by nature are actually all the time moved from place to place in the flat. Also portable are commonly used small tables (so called "coctail tables"), movable stools for beverages and ash trays. Also portable radio sets and fans are frequently met. This group of equipment involves also various heaters and little stoves used in winter. Great freedom with which the lodgers organize ad hoc the floor space and distribute the portable furniture is a striking feature of how they utilize the flat.

The non-portable equipment includes first of all benches which is a typical hall furniture. There are beds in a majority of flats, particularly in Baghdad but their number is never sufficient to meet all family members' needs. Only some members of family have beds to sleep in. A similar number of flats is furnished with one or less frequently with two wardrobes; however, the wardrobes are usually too small to contain clothing and linen so part of clothing is hung on nails or on freestanding coat-stands. In some flats there are glassed cupboards and cabinets which are used to store the table ware. Beds, wardrobes and cupboards are distributed in the rooms which have been designed for sleeping. Other non-portable equipment are refrigerators and television sets. In general, they are the commonest parts of flat equipment. Television sets are put in hall, as a rule, while the refrigerators in one of the sleeping rooms or sometimes in the hall. Actually, the refrigerators are never located in the kitchens.

The standard kitchen equipment is a drainboard sink and (in Mosul) also a water heating gas boiler. The equipment installed by the lodgers themselves is the following : a gas-stove for cooking (sometimes portable gas burner or primus, more frequently, however, non-portable stove with several burners and baking oven), less frequently a table and an auxiliary cabinet.

The bathroom appliances include a wash-hand basin and a shower without a spraying head or with one made by the lodger themselves from an adapted plastic bottle. The WC is equipped with an East-type lavatory pan and a tap with running water (in Baghdad) and also, but less frequently, with a water-closet (Mosul).

In a majority of flats there are ceiling fans installed by the lodgers themselves, however, usually in the hall only. Moreover, some flats in Baghdad are furnished with air coolers also on lodgers' own initiative.

Baghdad and Mosul housing estates are different in individual furnishing of the flats. The difference is noticeable in flat furnishing with portable and non-portable equipment. Unlikely the Baghdad housing estate where there is some equilibrium between both types of equipment, the Mosul flats have only a typical portable equipment.

Flat utilization

A striking feature of the flats utilization is that they are occupied by the lodgers permanently all day long. Such continuous stay of the whole family or some of its members in the flat is accompanied by its "opening" on the adjacent areas of the building (landing, staircase and neighbours' flats). This means that the family members,and particularly women and children, are leaving the flat and returning there unceasingly. Since other lodgers of the block of flats take part in this process too, outsiders pass the family flat, or rather its permissive part, continuously. Usually only late in the evening the family life is almost totally confined within the flat.

In spite of such lodgers' activity and permanent "outflow" of the family life outside the flat, the flat is the place where most of the family needs are met. The needs may be set into four groups : biological, household, culture and social needs. In the terms used by the architects, the flat capacity to satisfy these needs is called its function. The functions in turn are specified and closely relate to each room of the flat. Taking into account the culture features and especially living habits of the community under investigation, such a close linked to the Western tradition defining formulation seems difficult to accept.

Biological needs include primarily sleep and food. Contrary to conditions in a conventional Arab house, where seasonal use of the terrace to sleep at night is typical, flats in a housing estate bring about a necessity of night rest inside them. Our studies have shown that the family members do not invariably sleep in a particular room of the flat or even in a particular bed; this holds true especially about children. The family night rest is not restricted to sleeping rooms. Very often people sleep in the hall, on the balcony and even in the corridor. It happens that a sleeping place could be arranged outside the sleeping room altogether.

Three basic patterns can be observed in the room utilisation during the night rest. One refers to distributing of people in each room according to a generation principle, i.e., parents sleep in a separate room, while children (except babies) sleep in another room or rooms, often in neither of the sleeping rooms but just in the hall. The second pattern is based on the distribution of sleepers according to their sex. Mother and daughters sleep together in one room while father and sons in another. The third pattern is of eclectic nature and is based on a random distribution of the sleepers in the rooms. In three-generation families and in enlarged families there is a trend to assign separate sleeping rooms for relatives. In summer children sleep often on balconies in flats on higher floors.

In general, it is only the kitchen and the sanitary accommodations which are not utilised for the night rest. For daytime rest and sleep the hall is used usually, or in the case of very large families also the sleeping room. Beds, both for daytime and for night rest, are mostly portable ones and are made directly on the floor and on the benches.

Foodtaking is difficult to formulate in clearly defined patterns. As a rule, food is taken in the hall, less frequently in the kitchen. Food is taken in a conventional way, on the floor, without any equipment except a few vessels. Only rarely are the meals taken at table, which is practiced sometimes in the families the members of which have visited European countries. Besides, a table is quite unusual as a part of furniture in the flats.

It has been found that only rarely the meals is taken by the whole family together. This is only due to lack of tradition, and due to multi-shift system of work of the family members.

The so called physiological and sanitary functions are performed in the accommodations provided for these purposes. In some flats the doors to the bathroom and to the WC have been removed and replaced by linen curtains.

Household needs include meal preparation, washing and drying as well as storage of household objects and equipment. In principle, these needs are met in rather close relations to the accommodations provided for this purpose. In general meals are prepared in the kitchen with gas stoves and much less frequently with a primus. Bread baking, in which nearly a half of the family participate, is an exception. The bread is baked in so called "tenures" which are bread ovens built of clay or of stone. These are most frequently common "cooperative" installations, i.e., they are erected near the blocks of flats and used by several or even more than ten families.

In all flats under consideration, people wash the clothes in the bathroom; for drying them, besides the balcony the landing, the roof terrace, the space in front of the block and the yard are as well used. The terrace and the yard are utilised mainly by families living respectively on the highest and on the first floor. At times, the hall also is used for this purpose.

Besides the typical storage forms (e.g., kitchen cupboard for vessels), there are no clearly defined storage rooms in the flats. Neither have they been designed by the architect, except the aforementioned storing forms for beds and clothes. It is noteworthy, that frequently a balcony is used as a storage place for bread-oven fuel (mainly old cardboard and papers) and for various odds and ends, rags and worn out household equipment. In some flats domestic animals like rabbits, sheep and hen, were found moving all around.

Culture needs which are met within the flat are : television watching, listening to the radio and much less frequently newspaper and book reading. This social behaviour includes also self-teaching within a family. From the aforementioned forms, television watching is of particular importance because it is a very widespread time pass. Its external symptom are television sets of the commonest design in the whole interviewed population except the poorest families in Mosul. As a rule, the sets are permanently fixed in the hall at the most exposed place. This indicates that, apart from its proper function, they are a symbol of social position in the environment. One well-to-do family in Basra had as many as three television sets, purchasing better and better models up to the coloured one. In general, television is watched for the better part of the day with the viewers partially changing and including some people from outside the family circle (neighbours and their children). The inquiries show that in the evening the whole family is centred at the television set. However, the social life within the family is so intense at day, that isolation of special time of dense family communication and assigning it certain separate rooms seems neither reasonable nor justified. Because of great importance of television, radio is a minor and less attractive source of amusement in the flat.

Only in a few houses were newspapers and books found. The marginal role of reading in the cultural life of this circle is one of its characteristic features.

It is noteworthy that there were no separate places for children to study within the flats. They try to find an empty place and study there. Studying is a function frequently performed outside the flat on landings, staircases, terraces, in public gardens and even in cementerie. Certainly it is partially due to the lack of the tradition in this respect.

Social needs include various forms of communication with more distant relatives and with neighbours. All families under consideration were in close communication with their numerous relatives living in the same locality or outside it. The importance of family relationships originates in the tribe tradition which has survived up till today and had been reinforced by aforementioned principle of the family endogamy. The family intercommunication function affects the patterns of flat utilization. It is reflected in a visiting habit. Which runs for several days or even for several weeks at a stretch. These visit are paid to relatives occupying the flats under consideration. One of the rooms in the flat, usually the hall, is then given to the visitors for their night rest. The host suffer the lack of a spare room for visitors. Fairly regular and prolonged visits of either the wife's or the husband's parents occur frequently and seem typical.

Neighbourly relationships are an important and much developed component of social life in all families. Almost all day long neighbours_ especially women and children_ frequents move place to place at the flat hall. Neighbours one at liberty to go into the hall & the kitchen, than the other rooms. Therefore, complete Neighborly isolation, that in witnessed in European towns is not seen here.

LIFE ORGANIZATION IN THE BUILDING

A typical block of flats consist of three identical segments, each one having its own isolated staircase from which one enters into twelve flats located on three floors. A segment like this is a structural framework of lodgers' social life within the building. The families occupying flats within the same segment may then be considered a primary neighbours' community. It does not mean, however, that there is no neighbourly communication among the families who live in different sections of a block of flats or in different buildings even. However, there is a particular intensity of social and neighbourly relationships within a segment as a clearly defined natural entity. Within this unit the landing onto which four doors are open is a basic link of the social and neighbourly life. The doors remain mostly open during the day.

It is on the landing where the lodgers are most socially active. The landing is used especially by children who use to play there, as well as by women who do their like sewing, mending the clothes and preparing the meals. It is also a place to both men & women for meeting, chatting idling (just sitting without doing anything) and even for slumbering. Hence, the landing is considered by the lodgers to be a sort of extention of the Hat. Contrary to European blocks of flats where the landing and the staircase are meant rather to separate flats from one another, in the buildings under examination both elements are a strongly integrating factor erasing the spatial and social flat limits. In such a situation social neighbourly life easily penetrates inside each flat.

A landing place being a part of the building communication system, allows for expansion of social life (meetings, conversations, plays) unlikely to the household functions on other landings with in the same segment. The landings are not only a place of neighbours' contacts, but also a place to exchange goods and values among the families. All persons interviewed stated that their neighbourly relationships involve mutual help, i.e., borrowing household equipment, money and even food. A typical answer to the question of evaluation of the neighbourly relationships was a statement that all lodgers of the segment are "one large family". It shall be pointed out that neighbourly life in non-typical multifamily buildings which have been examined is of similar importance. It is characteristic that this actual abundance of social life is in contrast with a frequently declared wish to live in a relative isolation from neighbours (a wish to have a house of their own, motivated by a chance of isolation given). This interesting antinomy between the active acceptance of spontaneous social and neighbourly life in the block of flats and a declared preference to traditional isolation may be explained by a specific lodgers' attitude towards this housing form, where they live, i.e., the block of flats. In the traditionally framed consciousness of the interviewed people most of whom had lived previously in Arabian houses, a block of flats or one of the segments identifies with one common house for all lodgers. Flats are not considered to be isolated closed entities but parts of a main unit which is the house, a common residence of all families occupying it. That consciousness is well reflected in the aforementioned statement : "We all here are one large family". It is probably a crucial element in the mechanism of both flat and building utilization pattern.

The closeness of social and neighbourly bonds, however, is somehow restricted because of the actual strangeness among the families. Among other things, the restrictions show up in various intimate functions of family life confined within the flats as we have mentioned yet. One of these restricting functions is night sleep. Although the blocks of flats were provided with terraces, the lodgers were reluctant to use them in respective seasons to sleep despite their also generally declared need to have terraces available for sleeping. Only in a few cases has the terrace been found to be used for this purpose by the families living on the top floor. This reluctance is due to the lack of isolation from the other terrace users.

LIFE ORGANIZATION IN THE HOUSING ESTATE

Unlikely the building, the nousing quarters under investigation do not create proper conditions for social life and housing bonds within them. Especially in Baghdad the housing estate is simply reduced to a group of free-standing blocks of flats and has no facilities at all. The Mosul housing estate is kept in better order and has a suq and a school as well, but also there are neither green grass, trees, shaded places, playing-squares for children, benches nor small architecture. Because of the climatic conditions, life is centred mainly within the building and directly nearby its walls on the shadowed area. Because the housing estate does not meet the lodgers needs, the tenants themselves make characteristic attempts at self-management. First of all, we should mention mini gardens which the first floor lodgers form directly in front of their flats. The gardens are not only a source of recreation, but also used for vegetable cultivation attempts. The gardens are usually fenced and used mainly by the "owner's" family. Nevertheless, it was often observed that neighbours were welcome. Another form of the housing estate self-management are the aforesaid bread-ovens. The third form are the mobile and fixed little stalls used for marketing some food articles. Usually, such stalls consist of goods simply exhibited on a piece of paper in a shaded place. Additional problems of the Baghdad housing estate are total disorder and negligence of the housing area. All over the place adjacent to the blocks flow sewage and faeces. They stream out in many places from malfunctioning sewage system. The odour penetrates into the flats on the lower floors. Also mains failures occur frequently which is due to extremely primitive electric installation. These technical problems result from a low manufacturing standard in mass building.

LODGERS' OPINIONS AND DESIRES

Opinions Concerning the Flats

The lodgers, attitude towards the flats they live in ranges from full acceptance to extremely critical opinions. In general, positive opinions prevail; however, very often they are based on an unreflective attitude towards lodging needs and the degree of their satisfaction. Because of this, those positive opinions cannot be considered as indicators of real adaptation to the type of flat which is met in the building under discussion. Rather they result from ignorance of the utilization pattern for which the flats were designed. Usually, the opinion express satisfaction because for lodgers to have a flat means to eliminate previous lodging and living difficulties. A very low rent-charge is not to be disregarded either. Despite the higher technical standard of the Mosul flats and of their better construction these flats have been more critically evaluated than the ones in Baghdad. This criticism is due to the more recent experience of the traditional living habits and housing conditions. The Mosul housing estate is occupied mainly by Kurds people who moved in there rather recently and came directly from old villages and small towns.

The occupants' critical comments refer first of all to flat equipment and especially lack of cooling installation. This is a wide spread disadvantage. Some flat users installed air coolers on their own expense. It is noteworthy that air coolers belong to the standard flat equipment. However, this has never been actually achieved. Because of a high price of air coolers, the cooling problem in most flats has remained unsolved yet. It should be stressed, however, that the modern concrete based building technology does not fit well to climatic conditions of Iraq as compared with the traditional clay, baked brick or even stone technologies. One can doubt if this is really "appropriate technology" for Iraq. But living in a concrete just not possible without expensive and sophisticated modern cooling as well as heating equipment.

The tenants of the Baghdad quarters suffer also without gas boilers to heat water. Also the room distribution in a housing estate flat is commented critically. We listened to repeated complaints about the bad kitchen location in the flat. The kitchen is entered directly from the hall, which is both awkward for visitors and inconvenient for lodgers because kitchen odours all over the flat. They are a great nuisance especially in the hall where the lodgers stay most frequently. Also the WC and bath-room entrances being located very close to the hall these were critically evaluated, too. In cases where the balconies are turned out to be too small the number of rooms has been evaluated critically. The lodgers were particularly critical about not having a separate room which could be used to store the household equipment and objects.

Generally, lodgers are satisfied with their flat surface area, though some believed it to be too small as compared to their size of the family. Actually own lodgers' subjective opinions on their flats were not influenced by the factor of the number of family members. Although the floor space of each flat is the same, very often large families believe it sufficient, while the smaller ones complain that they are too confined in the flat. A very specific feature of an absolutely erroneous estimation of the floor space is doubling its dimensions or even enlarging it three times. A flat, the floor surface of which in our opinion equals about 70 square metres, is estimated by its users to be about 150-200 square metres.

Opinions Concerning the Building

The first matter to mention because of its being partially involved in the flat problems, is the question of terrace as a possible place of a seasonal night rest. The several segments of a block of flats have their own individual terraces. However, in spite of deeply rooted traditional Iraqi habits as well as climatic conditions they are almost never used by the lodgers as a sleeping place. The critically accepted reason for this is the lack of possibility of isolation from other possible terrace users. At the same time, all persons interviewed stated they suffered from not being able to sleep outdoors and that they would gladly use the terrace provided its structure allowed each family sleeping intimacy according to the Muslim decencies (a proposal to divide the terrace into a given number of boxes).

Also the size of the building as a housing unit was evaluated by the lodgers. Most of them had no complaints in this respect. A few people only announced the lodging quarters to be too large (too many flats in one building). A more frequently commented aspect of flat utilization was the number of floors and their convenience from the point of view of flat location. The families living on the third floor frequently complained they had to climb too many stairs which was tiresome. It is reasonable that the first floor flats were appreciated most. A common opinion was that they were most convenient for families with children. Though the number of floors was not great most lodgers believed lifts were necessary in such buildings. In the Baghdad housing estate the sewerage system and the electric installation were the objects to complain about. A new but constant problem in Basra was a constant water supply to higher flats. The floors above the second floor got water only at nights.

Opinions Concerning the Housing Estate

According to the lodgers' opinions an essential drawback of the housing estate was insufficient management. People suffered particularly from the lack of shopping possibilities and utilities. It should be pointed out here that a majority of lodgers wanted to have a commercial and service centre within the housing estate which would be a sort of traditional suq, i.e., oriental bazaar. The idea of installing shops and service centres on first floors of the blocks of flats was not popular, because of three reasons : difficulty in buying various things in shops spread all over the district, troubles in keeping a block of flats in order and in proper sanitary conditions in case such services were located in it, and finally, the lodgers' peace.

The next proposal was to arrange green gardens and recreation areas within the housing estate. Playing yards for children properly located and prepared were badly needed. The interviewed families pointed out that blocks of flats located in a row and separated only by a narrow space allowed for needless observation of the flats and of the life inside them (peeping through each other's windows). It is, of course, against traditional sense of privacy. The last problem discussed by the lodgers was the location of the housing estate in relation to the larger city units. Though lodgers were glad because of the vicinity of their working place, they were critical about living on the outskirts. This was of vital importance in Baghdad because of the aforementioned poor management of the quarter in the commercial, service and recreation respect.

CONCLUSION

Due to a number of reasons among which equally important were the objective social and demographic phenomena as well as considerations of social politics, the multifamily buildings may be expected to become a principal housing form for Iraq population. In connection with this the question of how the population adapts to new forms of housing buildings is of great importance. Our study has stated essential forms and direction of the adaptation.

The spontaneous process of two-sided adaptation takes

place in the interviewed population. The lodgers adapt themselves to new life situations in the block of flats and adapt both the block and the flats to the users' traditional needs, living habits and patterns. In such a spontaneous two-sided adaptation, new specific forms arise of utilizing this new element of material culture, which is the European form of multifamily building. The formation of a new housing system which exceeds the flat limits and simultaneously integrates them both spatially and socially in some new entity is a striking and a very specific feature of this adaptation. The new housing entity is made up of flats which give to the same landing. The system is therefore formed of the landing and halls of the adjacent flats. It spatially determines a basic zone of common social and public life of group of families, outside which all other sections of the flat form a spatial zone of social and private family life. This new double-zone spatial and social structure of a housing unit somehow replaces the traditional division of Arabian house into social, family and intimate life zones. This structure is a spontaneously formulated solution of the problems arising from living of a number of families strange to each other in one building, which is something outside the local cultural tradition. The solution consist in treating other inmates of the house or at least of a part of it in the same way as if they were the inmates of a traditional Arabian house and according to all rules applicable there.

The organization of social, private and intimate family life is confined within the material framework of the flat. We have stated yet a specific structural feature of this organization, which was the fact of no precise and fixed assignment of a function to a particular room. This "functional mobility" which takes form of some kind of indoor nomadism within the stable flat structure, on the one hand results from the adaptation difficulties within a typical house in a block of flats and on the other hand it associates with the flat congestion. The first reason may be thought to have arisen from the traditional living habits of the first generation to live in such buildings. The flat congestion, however, is a function of the number of family members only because all flats in the housing estate have the same uniform floor space.

In our opinion neither the tradition nor the flat congestion favour the concept of a flat as a stable and non-adaptable structure. Surely a better-suited to the mass users' actual lodging habits and needs will be a flat that is partially flexible structure somehow allowing for reshaping by the lodgers.

As far as the housing quarter organization is concerned, its problems are in general the same to the well-known problems in other countries, also in Europe - they involve the lack or severe shortage of the shopping and service system, recreation areas and playing yards for children. However, this makes the lodgers' tendency to adapt public but unorganized space to the functions grounded in their traditional needs even more strong. It results in such activities as mentioned private bread baking in the "ad hoc" arranged bread-ovens which are erected all over the housing estates and founding private gardens against local regulations.

Finally, it seems clear that estate projects and proper preparation of lodging should be accompanied by right educational policy both on macro and micro scale. It is noteworthy that adaptation problems are reflected not only in the organization of life within flat or a block of flats or in how to live in new housing conditions, but they refer to more primitive aspects of how to use the modern technical facilities a present-day multifamily building is equipped with.

SEVEN

John C. Weaver

Capitalism, Land Development and Housing in a New Society

The Case of Urban Canada, 1800-1980

In Contrast to the United States, Canada has had a mild reputation for a mixed political economy expressed in major public-owned corporations in transportation (Air Canada, Canadian National Railways), communications (Canadian Broadcasting Corporation, National Film Board), and recently in petroleum (Petro Canada). The provinces also have embarked on state ownership, mostly in electric power development and distribution, and in investment in energy corporation. As well, a universal health-care insurance plan has been taken to demonstrate the possibility of a some-what distinctive national character. Many Canadian observers have chosen a sweeping interpretation for these supposedly unique Canadian ventures and have proposed a Tory or British paternalistic quality in Canadian historical development that has contrasted with the more completely liberal or laissez-faire traditions formulated in the United States. The American Revolution, it is alleged, split the continent along ideological lines. The inadequacy of this interpretation is evident in the historical evolution of land use and housing in the northern society's urban centres.

According to the categories of housing policy established by D.V. Donnison, a British housing authority who undertook a study of European housing policies for the United Nations in the 1960s, Canada's assisted free market approach pre-dominated in nations in the early stages of industrialization, ruled by repressive regimes such as Greece, Spain, Turkey and Portugal. From 1949 to 1963, only 11,000 units of public housing were produced or 0.7 per cent of all new residential construction in this era. A revised National Housing Act (1964) altered the pace of public housing construction so that from 1964 to 1972, 98,000 units of public housing were constructed, roughly 9% of new units built during that period. Nevertheless, the official position emphasized that public housing was merely an aid to families extended to them until they would be able to avail themselves of private sector accommodation.

The argument that proposes Canada as a Tory fragment explains very little. State ownership has been adopted as an aid to national survival, countering American continentalism, or, in the case of the CNR, as an expedient to salvage bankrupt private enterprises. Canadian social policies arose from the pressures of the political left and not from a conservative philosophy of paternalism. It is necessary to explain this background in order to clear the way for a discussion of housing that argues that Canada is a relatively unexceptional capitalist society where private land assembly, construction industry interests, and financial institutions have asserted themselves to develop and protect a societal commitment to private property. Similar to other western capitalist societies, pressure from the left and from organized labour has forced some concessions; but the measures came late and the emphasis has remained on assisted home ownership. In part, this want of a significant public housing tradition reflects the relatively successful operations of the private housing sector. Until very recently, barring a few exceptional crises, private entrepreneurship supplied adequate rental accommodations and held out the prospect of home-ownership for the majority of Canadian households (Table 7.1).

TABLE 7.1

Percentage Dwellings with Owner Occupants in Urban Canada and Selected Cities 1921-1981

	1921	1931	1941	1951	1961	1971	1981
Urban Canada	46%	43	41	56	59	54	55
Montreal	15	14	12	18	20	19	22
Toronto	47	42	42	62	56	42	41
Winnipeg	43	43	44	53	57	47	42
Vancouver	35	46	50	63	61	47	55

Source: Census of Canada

Note : The declines in home ownership in some Canadian cities in the 1960s appear to be due to the arrival of the "baby boom" generation on the shelter market and the corresponding construction of rental accommodations for young families.

In sum, it will be argued in this discussion that the history of housing locates Canada squarely in the mainstream of advanced capitalism. Moreover, by retaining a sense of how abundant resources for housing construction and how certain technological and financing innovations have assisted the performance of the private sector it is possible to explain why the provision of shelter in Canada has differed from many western societies in its limited recourse to government land banking or public ownership of housing. In the broadest sense, Canada's experience is typical of a capitalist political economy : in a more particular way, the environment, settlement history, and other local factors like abundant resources point toward an especially strong role for the private institutions banks, insurance companies, land development companies, construction firms, and small scale contractors. Shelter has not presented an enduring problem for the great majority of Canadians (Table 7.2), although the current economic slump may be of such a magnitude as to force new policies and a shedding of the expectation of wide-spread home ownership.

TABLE 7.2

Average Number of Persons per Room in Canadian Dwellings, 1881-1981

Year	Average Number
(1881)	(1.0)*
1891	n.a
1901	0.86
1911	0.83
1921	0.80
1931	0.79
1941	0.78
1951	0.70
1961	0.73
1971	0.63
1981	n.a

Source : Census of Canada: Dominion Bureau of Statistics, Housing In Canada (1931) (Ottawa, 1941).

* An estimate based on the census figure of 6 persons per dwelling and the observation that a 6 room dwelling was the average at the turn-of-the-century.

To clarify the history and historical geography of housing in urban Canada, the following discussion considers these themes : the patterns of land tenure and property development; construction practices in the shelter industry;

home ownership and tenancy; the social patterns of residential space.[1]

THE PATTERNS OF LAND TENURE AND PROPERTY DEVELOPMENT

As late as the Napoleonic wars, British North America encompassed an assortment of quite different colonies with distinctive land tenure laws and singular land-use characteristics. In the Atlantic fishery colony of Newfoundland, ownership of land by settlers had been discouraged by the British government from the early 1600s to the early 1800s to guard against the establishment of a colonial rival to the English fishing fleet. In the relatively small urban community of St. John's, Newfoundland, much of the property was held by absentee landlords who were to oppose municipal improvement as late as the 1880s in order to hold down the tax rate. Leasehold tenure has remained a complication in the city's affairs to the present.[2]

In Prince Edward Island, captured from the French in 1758, the British disposed of the colonial land by a 1767 lottery in which 67 estates were granted to absentee owners. Often their interest in the property was impersonal and fully one fourth of the townships changed hands in ten years. Absentee landlords were the rule until the mid-nineteenth century. In Quebec, a much modified feudal land tenure arrangement - the seigneural system - was retained by the British conquerors from 1759 to the 1850s when a series of acts sped its liquidation. In the cities of Montreal and Quebec, especially the former, estates granted to religious orders and to individuals in the seventeenth century continued to provide leasehold tenure revenues well into the nineteenth century.[3] Land speculation, the quick sale of parcels of land for large gains or would-be large gains, was not unknown, but the legal and institutional developments necessary for widespread speculation were not in place nor was immigration substantial enough to precipitate speculative activity in land and in construction.

The first significant break from traditional modes of land tenure with their accent on rental or leasehold revenues came with the creation of a new colony in 1791. Upper Canada, most of the eastern and southern portions of present-day Ontario, was a virgin landscape onto which the colonial authorities affixed a grid survey of land thereby establishing uniform parcels of land and onto which they extended freehold tenure. As well, in 1795, an Act established a system for the registration of property instruments. For the next half century, the agricultural and commercial expansion of this new society and the arrival of 900,000 United Kingdom immigrants between 1815 and 1850 excited a land market[4]. Dealing in land became a notable enterprise. To help guarantee that purchasers received a strong title, Canada adopted mandatory land registration in 1849. All transactions involving a parcel had to be registered at a county land office. The 1795 Act only had established mechanisms for voluntary registration. The notion of the Crown's stewardship over land, an impulse behind the French seigneurial estates, had been replaced two centuries later by the concept of the Crown as regulator of a bourse or exchange. Crudely stated, a feudal notion of land tenure had been replaced by a bourgeois conception of property complete with a government sponsored exchange. Additionally, the merchants and agriculturalists of Ontario articulated an expansionist vision of their society and coveted the lands held by the Hudson Bay Company since 1670. The purchase of the company's domains in the North American interior by the newly established Dominion of Canada in 1869 represented a further advance of Ontario's new social vision - a nation of small proprietors. From 1870 to 1890 and again from 1900 to 1914, settlers from the east precipitated western real estate speculation; the initial wave extirpated the small but viable hunting cultures of Amerindian and Metis (mixed blood) peoples. Private property not collective concepts of land occupation had triumphed from sea to sea by the late nineteenth century.

In terms of urban form and property development, colonial governments and official designs had a role in townsite selection and some features of land use from the mid-seventeenth century until the early nineteenth century. However, neither the French nor the British empires demonstrated as much interest in urban planning as did the Spanish well to the south. The French Crown granted the island of Montreal to a missionary enterprise in 1642; the planned military base of Louisbourg was erected in the early eighteenth century by the French to safeguard their North American empire. The British countered by founding Halifax in 1749, Toronto, originally named York, was created according to government plans to serve as a colonial capital with grand park lots for a wilderness aristocracy. In the interior of the continent, the Hudson Bay Company had established its trading posts. Upper Fort Garry and Lower Fort Garry drew settlements in the early 1800s that would evolve into the city of Winnipeg; Fort Edmonton became the city of

Edmonton. The general point is that urban sites had been engendered by distant imperial authorities acting on behalf of religious, military, and commercial concerns. Colonists were not selecting and developing settlements; they were not engaged in the private enterprise of surveying town lots and selling them to new arrivals for speculative investment or construction purposes.

In 1816, George Hamilton, a colonial merchant, established a townsite in Upper Canada as a speculative venture. The founder surveyed his townsite of Hamilton on a grid layout that mirrored the general pattern of rural land surveying found throughout the colony. Lots were numbered and sold to assorted investors. Hamilton was the first significant Canadian community created as a private enterprise.[5] In 1826, to raise revenue, the government of Upper Canada sold tracts of government or Crown land to British investors who constituted a chartered land sales company. In the late 1820s, the Canada Company laid out two townsites, Guelph and Goderich, with more imaginative layouts than the grid survey. In Goderich, the streets radiated outward from a central hub like the spokes of a cart wheel.[6] The company's creation and its role in establishing towns confirmed the paramountcy of private enterprise in urban growth. In subsequent decades, especially the years from 1870 to 1914, the Upper Canadian or Ontario model of having private individuals or companies engaged in urban layout and promotion would apply to the new settlement areas of the Canadian west. Land had become a major commodity to be traded among the bourgoisie and, along with the government regulation of the exchange through land registry offices, the market had stimulated a host of suppliers and service specialists : subdivision land surveyors, large scale investors, small speculators, real estate agents, mortgage brokers, and many others. Even before 1900, two companies well endowed with western Canadian land—the Hudson's Bay Company and the Canadian Pacific Railway—had considerable experience with townsite preparation and promotional activity.[7] Some western Canadian cities in their era of boom growth just before 1914 were reputed to have more real estate agents than grocery stores. The point is that Canada came to harbour an especially vigorous and sophisticated economic sector specializing in land sales.

Once established, the real estate industry encountered problems and evolved in ways that were meant to overcome land use uncertainties and market crises. There was always the risk of over supply in a sparsley populated society with small cities and with a dependency upon growth by immigration and imported capital. Then, too, there remained the challenge of calculating how best to develop the land : many small lots for labourers' cottages or a few larger plots of land for middle-class or elite areas? Non-conforming land uses like industries or railways complicated the calculation by introducing, in the era before urban planning, an element of chance that could upset land values. The usual land sale practices on the urban fringe during the nineteenth century were aimed at making quick sales; auctions, lottery disposals, and newspaper promotions were typical devices that left the land developer with little influence on the shape of that portion of the city in which he operated.[8] However, like other major sectors of capitalist economic activity, the unregulated market in land brought risks that consolidation could reduce. Unconditional sales by a number of independent land developers meant that purchasers could erect shacks or an obnoxious business within a survey or on an adjacent plot of land. These actions resulted in depreciating the value of adjacent property or driving potential purchasers toward another area of city. Consequently, land developers progressed toward accepting a degree of urban planning, toward corporate integration, and toward oligopoly in urban land markets.

Initial controls included informal agreements between land developers and purchasers (building contractors or investors in rental housing) to conform to certain building standards. Land developers tried to sell a row of lots to a single contractor knowing that he would erect a uniform streetscape. Provincial and local governments aided this process of modest land use regulation in the late nineteenth century by establishing fire and health codes. By the early 1900s, a few subdivisions were governed by covenants attached to deeds that outlined the minimum value of houses to be constructed and that sometimes included racial clauses. Racial covenants were struck down by the Canadian courts in the early 1950s. Meanwhile, property development companies had evolved which dealt with hundreds or even thousands of city lots and employed urban planners.[9]

In Hamilton a local syndicate of powerful businessmen assembled a 1700 lot community complete with shopping area by 1919. Unlike earlier developers who might have surveyed 100 or 200 lots and hoped for a rapid turnover of inventory, the development syndicate could holdout for a long term return. In some instances, major foreign enterprises invested in the Canadian property industry. For example, the

Guinness interests from the United Kingdom developed the prestigious area of British Properties in North Vancouver beginning in the 1930s. Indicative of the growing capital investment, the company constructed the Lions Gage suspension bridge to link its tract with central Vancouver. In the early 1950s, the ultimate steps in consolidation was taken with the development of the Toronto suburb of Don Mills. Planning, surveying, construction of streets and erection of homes came under the control of single corporation. The fusion of the construction industry with land development increased, conceivably making it more difficult for small building contractors to find lots.[10] This alleged problem has figured in an unresolved and probably unresolvable dispute in urban literature as to whether or not land developers function in an oligolpolistic market place.[11]

CONSTRUCTION PRACTICES, HOMEOWNERSHIP AND TENANCY

Homeownership among households in Canadian cities has varied from centre to centre. For example, homeownership in Montreal historically has been lower than that in Toronto. The labour composition of each city and the corresponding wages and numbers of weeks work annually have differed presenting an important variable in any discussion of residential quality of ownership.[12] Regional variations not withstanding, the trend from the mid-nineteenth century to the present has been one of increasing ownership (Tables 7.1 and 7.3). Many complications have to be borne in mind when discussing ownership. The essential components, however, have included the extraordinary material resources in Canadian urban hinterlands and the ingenuity of evolving capitalist institutions in furthering technological and financial innovations in the service of potential home buyers.

In the early nineteenth century, the British North American colonies exploited timber resources for export to the United Kingdom and the United States. There was no shortage of building material, but the colonies lacked a pool of skilled labour so that from the 1830s forward it is certain that housing construction practices evaded craftsmanship and brought together inexpensive material, simple plans, and casual labour. Skilled carpenters endeavoured but failed to control the building industry through craft unions in the 1830s; investors in housing and commercial property could find adequate labour without having to have recourse to the crafts.[13] In special circumstances, such as the construction of churches or mansions, stone masons and plasterers were imported from Britain. These circumstances explain the fact that buildings in Canadian towns and cities were overwhelmingly frame and the communities vulnerable to conflagrations.[14] In some ways, conditions resembled those in Scandinavian and Russian cities, although in Canada the scarcity of skilled labour might have been more severe and housing demands more sharply affected by waves of immigration.

TABLE 7.3

Home Ownership and Average Number of Persons per Dwelling in Hamilton, 1852-1981

Year	Percentage Dwelling with Owner Occupants	Average Number per Dwelling
1852	26.5	7.2
1861	25.6	5.8
1871	23.7	5.6
1881	30.5	5.4
1891	34.5	5.3
1901	33.3	4.9
1911	51.4	5.4
1921	50.4	3.9
1931	50.9	4.4
1941	48.7	4.2
1951	65.0	3.8
1961	69.3	3.7
1971	57.9	3.3
1981	56.4	2.7

Source : City of Hamilton assessment rolls; Census of Canada

One means available for side-stepping the problem of a skilled labour shortage was to adapt new technologies. By the 1880s, steam technology and the relatively new machine tool industry had combined to provide a sophisticated industry specializing in cheap lumber and more specialized wood shapes. Building contractors mastered the integration of these standardized materials and learned home construction techniques on a steadily improving basis from pattern books and the ability of semi-skilled labour to learn through non-traditional means reduced the problem of labour shortage that had existed earlier in the century.[15] In the early twentieth century, concrete blocks replaced stone work and factory-produced wall board supplanted plastering; again the traditional labour-intensive skills had been by-passed by unskilled or semi-skilled assembly practices. As well, urban contractors had formed city wide associations to negotiate with weakened building trade unions. In sum, it is conceivable - but not as yet empirically demonstrated - that shelter quality improved and labour costs fell as the housing industry and its suppliers coped with the initial problem of a new society lacking a reserve of skilled construction labour.[16]

International financial crises intervened in the evolutionary process, forcing reversals in the scale and capital investment of the construction and supply industries. Depressions interrupted in the 1890s, 1913-15, and 1930-1940. Still, as with land development, operators became larger and more integrated in order to take advantage of bulk purchases of supplies. Both the industry and prospective home owners received an enormous boost at the end of World War II when the Canadian government pursued a policy of using home construction as the major device to bridge the wartime and peacetime economy and accelerated the process of corporate consolidation by favouring builders who undertook large-scale projects and employed mass-production techniques.[17]

Long term financing and blended payments (20 year mortgages with monthly payments on both principal and interest), financing innovations that began on a small scale some time after the middle of the nineteenth century and grew into commonplace practices one hundred years later, helped to spread homeownership. The typical financing measures for those wishing to purchase a house until early in this century appear to have been as follows. The mortgagee who lent the purchaser money required that his investment be secured by having the mortgagor make a significant down payment; in many instances half of the sale price had to come from the purchaser's savings. That in itself imposed a stiff barrier to ownership. Usually the mortgage had a term of two to five years. Payments during this span only covered interest charges; the principal remained due at the end of the term. Therefore, a prospective home buyer needed considerable savings to initiate a purchase and the capacity to save in order to clear an outstanding debt and secure clear title to property. The conservative financial system was one that did not encourage urban dwellers to buy their own houses. Not surprisingly, evidence seems to suggest that contractors experimented with the low down payment and long term mortgage; interested in selling their product a few builders expanded into financial services. Given the choice between immediate payments and piecemeal payments over a longer period, the latter seems the more feasible even though the compound interest means a very high total payment. Nevertheless, the easy instalment scheme grew slowly because of the inherent caution of investors.[18]

Aside from the mortgage arrangements, interest rates have had some influence on decisions about purchasing. On the basis of a study of 706 mortgages negotiated by one real estate firm in Hamilton from 1860 to 1909, it seems that interest rates fell steadily from around 8% in the 1860s to 5% in the early 1900s. The reasons for the decline remain unclear at present, but the Canadian money supply may have been increased by British and American investment. The modest decreases in interest rates may not seem striking enough to influence homeownership levels, but the great stability of the mortgage market contrasted with the soaring rates of the 1850s and early 1860s. At the very least, financial confidence was reflected and consolidated by the trend.[19]

For tenants, the most significant construction and investment strategy changes came as shelter capitalists moved away from owning a set of detached single family dwellings or row houses and erected multiple unit structures : tenements, apartment buildings, and high-rises. The traditional practice of letting out small cottages to tenants, the practice known by research to prevail in Montreal and Upper Canadian (Ontario) cities from the early 1800s to the early 1900s, had several unsatisfactory features for landlords. Maintenance problems posed a series of tenant challenges and overhead costs. The Canadian winter brought rapid and expensive deterioration of vacant dwellings. Tenants could and did use this circumstance to force improvements or even to delay rent payments and rent reductions. Apartment structures offered maintenance savings and a challenge to the occasional ability of tenants to enlist the environment and accommodation surpluses to advantage. Construction of apartment buildings, however, demanded large and immediate outlays of capital; the piecemeal accumulation of rental houses, on the other hand, had not made heavy and immediate demands on capital. To precipitate the apartment construction booms after both world wars required backing from groups of investors or from trust or insurance companies. Corporate consolidation and the integration of housing and land affairs with financial institutions had transpired on all fronts - dwellings for would-be homeowners and dwellings for tenants.

The advance of finance capitalism and the modern corporation, elements of a crude structuralist Marxism, have united much of this discussion of capitalism and housing in Canada. However, this stress can be offset somewhat by the neo-Marxist emphasis on the resistance of the working class -Marx the revolutionary as opposed to Marx the political economist. The political left and labour movements have led the way for housing reforms of varying significance. Rental accommodations have been a major concern of the labour unions from the 1880s to the present. During the former decade, the Knights of Labour pressed for and secured legislation in Ontario that precluded landlords from seizing a tenant's chattels for overdue rent. Today Ontario has rent control legislation and has begun to investigate some recent sales of large apartment complexes to capital rich Saudi Arabian investors. The triumphs in the regulation of rental accommodation have precipitated a new crisis in that capital now has retreated from apartment construction. Contemporary vacancy rates in Toronto, for example, have dropped to an exceedingly low point. Regulation of the private market has generated bureaucracy and litigation; it may have shifted investment away from the rental property business with consequences not yet fully appreciated. As was noted early in the discussion, public housing programmes have had a very minor role in Canadian shelter history.

The ambition to progress from rental accommodations to homeownership is such a strongly entrenched tradition that only a prolonged economic crisis and sustained levels of high unemployment are likely to challenge trust in the private sector or a government subsidized private sector. At the moment, government subsidies and an income tax incentive have been prepared to assist first-time home buyers. For the Canadian middle class and for skilled labour, homeownership has been considered a reasonable expectation. Due to the importance of this ideal of proprietorship and due to the significance of the construction industry to the Canadian economy, no government can stand by idly while the factors that once eased homeownership - stable construction costs, low interest rates, and fairly reasonable land prices - are eroded. In conclusion, strident free enterprise critics of Canadian "statist" tendencies of late erroneously consider the federal government as socialist; in fact the Ottawa government is highly protective of the most fundamental concept of "privatism" - private housing as a business and as an ideal.

THE SOCIAL PATTERNS AND RESIDENTIAL SPACE

In the two preceeding discussions, corporate consolidation has been accented. A spatial counterpart of social segregation can be traced. It must be emphasized that empirical studies based on census manuscripts and assessment rolls are scarce and generalizations stand on the shaky foundation of research on a few centres covering different eras. As well assumptions and methodology have varied.

The phase of urban development that American urban historians and historical geographers have labelled the pedestrian city was evident in the towns and cities of British North America. That is to say, in the era before the electric streetcar, residential location was partly a function of the distance to places of employment; a merchant might live close to some of his clerks and shippers or an industrialist might reside near to a number of his machinists or moulders. Rich and poor, employer and employee, did not live "cheek by jowl", but neither were they so isolated as to have no daily view of one another's dwellings.[20] An examination of city blocks, like the analysis conducted by geographer Michael Doucet for Hamilton in 1851-2, reveals the mix of economic status and religious denomination. There was no exclusive area and no ghetto.[21] Peter Goheen's quantitative review of the same issue for late-nineteenth century Toronto made use of trend surface mapping and factor analysis. Goheen too detected a social and religious mix but observed that the electric streetcar allowed a greater measure of residential choice. The concomitant of this choice, according to Goheen, was to permit the middle class to move into more homogeneous neighbourhoods and thereby to increase social segregation within the city.[22] One problem with this sketch of increasing segregation over time involves the conceptualization of urban space and of segregation. A surface mapping or a block by block consideration fails to consider topography and its important result - drainage. In the years before extensive water and sewer mains, drainage helped to sort out the urban classes; ridges and ravines meandered across blocks and complicated the urban social mix. There was social and religious segregation, but this separation lacked the clearer definition found in the land development practices of the twentieth century.

The concept of a suburb or urban tract of land developed for a particular class has not been an exclusively twentieth-century notion in Canada. One of the large land owning families in Toronto during the 1840s, the Macauleys, established an estate of quite modest cottages for working-class tenants.[23] The narrow lanes and shoddy housing became an inner city slum - "the Ward" - by the early 1900s. Hamilton's "Corktown", Montreal's "city below the hill" (St. Mary's and St. Antoine's wards), and Quebec's St. Roch ward assumed comparable social identities due to their topography and the actions of land developers and investors in shelter.[24] The contrast between segregation in the last century and that emerging in this century has been a matter of developer's deliberation. Consequently, the claim that corporate consolidation has had a spatial counterpart receives a foundation in argument and sufficient supporting examples to stand as a useful hypothesis.

The introduction of extensive industrial concerns into Canadian cities began in the 1850s with the appearance of railway yards and their associated metal working shops for building or repairing railway equipment. At first, Montreal and Hamilton were affected. In Montreal's case, the land-use impact of the railway was prefigured by the Lachine Canal which carried commerce and also powered equipment in a nascent industrial district. The railyards intensified the concentration of working-class dwellings. In a cumulative fashion, the impact of industry was to render adjacent land undesirable; the poor quality of housing confirmed the image of "the city below the hill". By the early twentieth century, land developers were subdividing extensive properties into workingmen's tracts with small lots and incomplete urban services. In the industrial city of Hamilton, several major land developers marketed districts with 100 to 500 lots. A handful of Montreal land developers actually established an incorporated suburban community-Maisonneuve-with an unabashed industrial image.[25] In Winnipeg, the north end of the city, around the city's large railyards for the Canadian Pacific system, became the focus for immigrant and working class dwellings.[26]

If the sheer force of industry on the city and the related calculations of land developers produced exclusively working-class areas, then currently the advance of urban service technology and developer's activities produced distinctly middle-class and elite regions. Extensive sewer construction between 1860 and 1920 as well as the determined efforts of municipal health officers to eliminate privy pits reduced the equation of elevated land with health. Streetcar lines, sewers, and water mains allowed the laying out of entire neighbourhoods for middle-class households. In Hamilton, the syndicate that established the 1700 lot suburb of Westdale in 1920 used restrictive covenants, agreements with builders, and high property prices to create a Protestant and middle-class community. Other cities had comparable areas as well as ones that catered to an even more wealthy clientele, for example Vancouver's Shaugnessy Heights prepared by the real estate branch of Canadian Pacific Railways - one of western Canada's most significant property-industry corporations. The middle-class and elite neighbourhoods were often distinguished from the earlier pockets of affluent housing by four features; the tailoring and marketing of exclusiveness by the developers, the large scale of the undertaking, the distance from large business or industrial enterprises, and the departures from the dominant grid layout employed in most areas of the city. Curved streets, diagonal avenues, and dead end courts have contrasted with the uniformity of the grid in working-class districts.

CONCLUSIONS

Much of the abundant North American literature on urban land use has been descriptive and lacking in a sense of the dynamics of change : Park and Burgess' ring theory, Hoyt's sector theory, and the multiple nuclei model. In addition, another branch of study has adapted neo-classical economics and with it the assumptions of an unmanipulated market place and an abundance of competitive bidders : Alonso's work on rent theory has been particularly important. Finally, the American geographer David Harvey has stimulated a new and dissenting approach that accents Marx's insights on exchange value and manipulated markets. The preceding sketch on the historical geography of urban Canadian property and housing has owed much to Harvey's work. However, Harvey's empirical work supporting his theoretical ventures has an exclusively American setting. Canadian housing issues are not carbon copies of those in the United States. Environment and resources differ; the labour pool and market dimensions always have been much smaller in Canada; the housing crises in Canada have been less evident; banking and finance laws have been distinct. Similarly, the British experience - including much more planning and public housing than Canada - is singular. In sum, the interest in Marx as a guide to urban questions has opened the prospect for research into the study of structural or institutional practices involved in the city-building process. However, the peculiarities of national history must be taken into account. From the perspective of the highly complex culture and varied land-use traditions of India, the history of housing in Canada may seem simply American or western; but, while accepting those broad general descriptions as well as acknowledging the merits of a Marxist framework, this paper has sought to indicate occasional nuances imposed by unique considerations.

NOTES

1 For discussions of Canada as a Tory fragment see George Grant, **Lament for a Nation** (Toronto : McClelland and Stewart, 1965) and Gad Horowitz, "Conservatism," Liberalism, and Socialism in Canada : An Interpretation", **Canadian Journal of Economics and Political Science**, vol.32 (May, 1966); for a discussion of Canadian housing programmes to 1964 see John Christopher Bacher, "The Origins of a Non-Policy; The Development of the Assumption of a Housing Responsibility by the Canadian Federal Government" (Masters Thesis, McMaster University, 1980).

2 For the land question in St. John's see G.O. Rothney, **Newfoundland : A History** (Canadian Historical Association Booklet No.10, 1964); Melvin Baker, "The Politics of Assessment : The Water Question in St. John's, 1844-1864," **Acadiensis**, vol.12 (Autumn, 1982).

3 The P.E.I. land issue is discussed in Frances W.P. Bolger editor **Canada's Smallest Province** (The Prince Edward Island Centennial Committee, 1973), pp.37-114. For Montreal see John Irwin Cooper, **Montreal : A Brief History** (Montreal : McGill-Queen's University Press, 1969). For Quebec City see Louise Dechene, "La rente du faubourg Saint-Roch a Quebec, 1750-1850," **Revue d'histoire de l'amerique francaise**, vol.34 (mars, 1981).

4 Michael Doucet, "Urban Land Development in Nineteenth-Century North America : Themes in the Literature," **Journal of Urban History**, vol.8 (May, 1982).

5 John Weaver, **Hamilton : An Illustrated History** (Toronto : James Lorimer, 1982), passim.

6 Gilbert A. Stelter, "Urban Planning and Development in Upper Canada," in **Urbanization in the Americas** edited by Woodrow Borah, Jorge Hardy, and Gilbert Stelter (Ottawa : National Museums of Canada, 1980).

7 H. J. Selwood and Evelyn Baril, "The Hudson's Bay Company and Prairie Town Development, 1870-1888" in **Town and City : Aspects of Western Canadian Urban Development** (Canadian Plains Studies publication 10, 1981).

8 Michael Doucet, "The Roll of the **Spectator** in Shaping

Attitudes toward Land in Hamilton, Ontario, 1847-1881," **Histoire sociale/Social History**, vol.12 (1979).

9 John Weaver, "From Land Assembly to Social Maturity : The Suburban Life of Westdale (Hamilton), Ontario, 1911-1951," **Histoire sociale/Social History**, vol.11 (1978). Reprinted in **Shaping the Urban Landscape : Aspects of the Canadian City-Building Process** edited by Gilbert A. Stelter and Alan F.J. Artibise (Ottawa : Carleton University Press, 1982).

10 James Lorimer, **The Developers** (Toronto : James Lorimer, 1978).

11 The case for the existence of an oligopoly appears in Peter Spurr, **Land and Urban Development : A Preliminary Study** (Toronto : James Lorimer, 1976).

12 Terry Copp, **The Anatomy of Poverty : The Conditions of the Working Mass in Montreal, 1897-1929** (Toronto : McClelland and Stewart, 1974).

13 Charlotte Erickson, **Invisible Immigrants : The Adaptation of English and Scottish Immigrants in Nineteenth - Century America** (London : Weidenfeld and Nicolson, 1972), pp.279-86. Attempts of the craftsmen to control the building trade are discussed in C. Vance, "Early Trade Unionism in Canada : 1833-1834 : The Carpenters, and Joiners General Strikes in Montreal," **The Marxist Quarterly** (Summer, 1962).

14 John Weaver and Peter De Lottinville, "The Conflagration and the City : Disaster and Progress in British North America during the Nineteenth Century," **Histoire sociale/Social History**, vol.13 (1980).

15 For the experience in the United States see Gwendolyn Wright, **Moralism and the Model Home : Domestic Architecture and Cultural Conflict in Chicago, 1873-1913** (Chicago : University of Chicago Press, 1980), chapters 3 and 8. The Canadian experience seems comparable. See G.E. Mills and D.W. Holdsworth, "The B.C. Mills Prefabricated System : The Emergence of Ready-made Buildings in Western Canada," **Canadian Historic Sites** No.14 (1975); Michael Doucet and John C. Weaver, "Emergent Capitalism and the Property Industry in a Canadian City, 1860-1920 : A Study of a Real Estate and Property Management Agency" (Unpublished paper, December 1982, available from authors).

16 Weaver, **Hamilton : An Illustrated History**, passim. The records of the department of Labour of Canada at the Public Archives of Canada (RG27) contain files on the labour disputes between building trades unions and the emerging contractors' associations.

17 John Christopher Bacher, "The Origins of a Non-Policy"

and James Lorimer, **The Developers.**

18 Hamilton Public Library, Moore and Davis Real Estate Company Records, Pamphlet File, **Patterson Bros., Builders of Homes** (Hamilton, 1887).

19 Doucet and Weaver, "Emergent Capitalism and the Property Industry."

20 Sam Bass Warner Jr., **The Private City : Philadelphia in Three Periods of its Growth** (Philadelphia : University of Pennsylvania Press, 1968), pp.49-62.

21 Ian Davey and Michael Doucet, "The Social Geography of Commercial City, ca. 1853," **The People of Hamilton, Canada West** edited by Michael Katz (Cambridge : Harvard University Press, 1975).

22 Peter Goheen, **Victorian Toronto, 1850 to 1900 : Pattern and Process of Growth** (University of Chicago Department of Geography Research Papers No.127), p.220.

23 **Ibid.**, pp.53-4.

24 Terry Copp, **The Anatomy of Poverty : The Condition of the Working Class in Montreal, 1897-1929** (Toronto : McClelland and Stewart, 1974), pp.15-29. Quebec is discussed in Marc Lafrance and David-Terry Ruddel, "Physical Expansion and Socio-Cultural Segregation in Quebec City, 1765-1840" in Alan Artibise and Gilbert Stelter editors, **Shaping the Urban Landscape** (Ottawa : Carleton University Press, 1982).

25 For Hamilton see Weaver **Hamilton**, p.60. The Maisonneuve situation is described in Paul-Andre Linteau, "The Development and Beautification of an Industrial City : Maisonneuve, 1883-1918", in **Shaping the Urban Landscape.**

26 Alan Artibise, "Divided City : The Immigrant in Winnipeg Society, 1874-1921," in Alan Artibise and Gilbert Stelter, **The Canadian City** (Toronto : McClelland and Stewart, 1977).

EIGHT

Nandeshwar Sharma

Urban Housing

Dimension, Complication and Implication

DIMENSION

Being a very strong urge as the place of living housing in urban context has proved to be a multi-dimensional issue. Urban housing forms naturally (i) a numerical dimension, (ii) a compositional dimension, (iii) a locational dimension and (iv) a dimension as related to qualitative as well as quantitative nature of issues. It forms a numerical dimension in being related to the question of : How many are to be housed? It forms a compositional dimension in being connected with the question : Who are to be housed? It forms a locational dimension in being concerned with the question of : Where are they to be housed? And all these questions must seek the answers in qualitative and quantitative dimensions of urban living.

The section of India's population which is called urban now exceeds 156 million mark. This mark happens to constitute some 23.73 per cent of nation's bulk population. Of even greater interest is the rate to which this section of population tended to grow during the recent most decade. A decennial growth rate of 46.02 for urban population as against 24.43 for India's total and a relative low of 18.96 for country's rural populations may simply be termed as being phenomenal in speed. Maintaining such a speed the urban section of population in India has been projected to counterpart its fellow rural section with a ratio of nothing less than 30 : 70 by the time period the present century rolls itself. This shows the tendency which pushes the numerical dimension of urban housing in the country to be more intense than what it is today.

The compositional dimension of housing urban people is very much related to the bulk which becomes the direct product of numerical dimension. The section of people which demands for housing in urban areas is composed of such number or set of numbers who happen to fall at all rungs of income, taste and affinity in their economic and socio-cultural frame. People rush to urban places to earn their livelihood. They find employments in activities belonging either to organised or to unorganised sectors. They, thus, combine to swell the numerical dimension of urban housing. As they come not from a uniform economic and socio-cultural background they create varied issues of compositional dimension in urban housing. There are to be housed those who earn high income through employment in organised sector activities and who have developed taste and affinity for wide open spaces. There are, on the contrary, to be housed those who manage to have low to very low income through employment or under employment in unorganised sector activities and who just claim a house. It is largely the latter section, often connected to form the class urban poor, that concerns the administrations, policy makers, urban planners and the city dwellers alike. They compose also the major share among those how many to be housed.

The issues, as related to where does the present urban bulk exceeding 156 million mark goes, attain the significance of locational dimensions. The following table 8.1 enlists some of the relevant information to this effect.

TABLE 8.1

Contribution to the Urban Population

Size Class UA./Towns	No. of centres	Contribution to Total urban population	Addition of population	
		1981	1961-71	1971-81
I	216	60.37	52.67	56.83
II	270	11.65	40.94	51.22
III	739	14.35	29.27	28.41
IV	1048	9.52	18.85	24.03
V	742	3.62	-10.38	15.44
VI	230	0.50	-19.70	6.74
All Classes	3245	100.00	37.91	46.20

Source : Census of India, 1981, Paper 2 of 1981, Provisional Population., Rural Urban Distribution.

The information makes the revealment how disproportionately do the urban agglomerations and centres at the class helm share the total contribution to the urban population. This necessitates both the numerical and compositional dimensions of urban housing to complicate the issue to its maximum in urban places and areas of bigger sizes. The situation tends to continue in coming decades unless some checks are anticipated and effectuated. Urban housing, in its locational dimension, is therefore beset with twofold problems of how to contain the disproportionate flow of additional numbers and where to locate how many of whom within individual city encompass.

Indian cities rightly being characterised to be the period pieces in time and to lack the basic unity of lay out and function have developed several numerical, compositional and locational issues of urban housing in its qualitative dimensions. The issue relates not only to the task of providing as many number of houses as to satisfy the numerical dimension alone but also to the task of housing the urban people qualitatively in the light of compositional and locational dimensions. It is with the recognition of this qualitative dimension that the actions as related to environmental improvement find due appreciation in urban housing. The issue of environmental improvement in urban housing has, naturally therefore, acquired a dimension of ever increasing concern.

COMPLICATION

An overview of different dimensions of housing raises many complications of qualitative and quantitative nature in Indian context. There are the complications as related to the questions :

(i) How many houses does urban India need?
(ii) How many houses will urban India need?
(iii) What rate of providing houses has for Urban India been estimated?
(iv) What income level do urbanites in India vary to fall in?
(v) What kind of houses does urban India provide to city dwellers?

All Complications of urban housing may be viewed in terms of having their relations with two issues of (i) housing shortage on the one hand and (ii) housing problems on the other. The former involves the problem of housing those who are unhoused and the latter does so with the problem of housing those who are already housed. The former, thus, becomes a quantitative issue while the latter appears to be a qualitative issue. These quantitative and qualitative issues, when being treated through actions to seek solutions to the problems, tend to bring many more complications, bearing relevance to Urban housing, to the surface.

Any lag with respect to housing the houseless results into housing shortage. This shortage of housing for urban section of population in India has already reached a crisis proportion. The crisis proportion has reached such a dimention of complication that many find a place to live in a virtual impossibility. To be specific in numerical term the housing lag in March 1979 alone was estimated by NBO to the tune of 4.9 million units in urban areas which came to be about one fourth of the total shortage of housing units in India. This estimate for the closing period of the century is kept at 12 million units of houses. And this estimate tells just a broad idea of shortage for the nation as a whole. The real crisis proportion can be visualised only after a detailed estimates for various regions and metropolitan areas and that too in terms of how many houses for whom. The complication to this effect becomes alarming in the sense that in the light of ever increasing population and unabated rush to urban places any estimate of housing shortage proves ultimately infructuous.

The complications as connected with the numerical dimension, i.e., with the question of housing those who are and will be unhoused, do not remain contained within themselves. They as a supernumerary find wide ranging ramifications to complicate the qualitative aspect of urban housing too. The crisis proportion of housing shortages breeds a similar crisis proportion of housing degeneration by causing, (i) a peculiar intensification of undesirable housing and (ii) a still furthered congestion in the individual houses. Thus is added the more complicated issue of environmental improvement in urban housing along with the creation of additional units of houses as per demand of urban dwellers. This situation of the crisis proportion of housing degeneration further complicates the issue of actual estimation of lag in housing units because the peculiar intensification of undesirable housing and the still greater congestion in individual houses combine to increase the proportion of a new section of population what may be termed as the section of those who are neither housed nor unhoused but underhoused.

IMPLICATION

The dimensions and complications as of urban housing have showed widely ranged and far reached implications. They have fetched vast array of the problems of the nature of administrative social, economic, political and planning relevance. There have been additional squatting; larger slums; increased traffic congestion; decreased efficiency of services, amenities and accelerated growth of social evils. Squatting develops in consonance with man's acute struggle for shelter. It represents the case of illegal occupation of vacant land in urban areas and tells the story of the existing gap between ever published lawful provisions and the things in reality. Slums replicate the peculiar intensification of ill housing with a still another story of all round physical, structural, economic, social and folk value degeneration in urban housing. Such a case of illegal occupation and legal degeneration seems poised to drift to a dimension to conform to the dire predictions of being the conditions of habitability and workability the unbearable ones and unless ameliorative steps are undertaken soon the pessimists may well withhold the belief. To this count it becomes imperative to delve into the intriguing questions of, (i) to what extent the complications of qualitative dimension have been tried to meet with (ii) in what way complications of qualitative dimension have been attempted to do away with? and (iii) What positive steps lie in store to overcome problems in due course?

To begin with the question of housing the houseless urban India presents an alarming backlog. With an estimated backlog of 4.9 million units of houses in 1979 an estimate of building 1.2 million housing units to eliminate the shortage within 20 years has been voiced by the planning commission in the Draft Five Year Plan. Present urban India gets, however, on an average just 3.5 houses per 1000 persons annually as against a recommendation of having a minimum of 10 houses per 1000 persons annually (expert body of U. N.). The situation decidedly warrants against any sleakness and warms up for gearing up housing activities. Housing may not any more be treated to be merely a consumptive activity rather should be fitted into productive industrial dimension as it has got its own income, employment generation and redistribution potential. Besides it forms a part of the infrastructure for urban development and can decidedly be used as a tool to help or desist the urban growth. This realisation has not, fortunately, remained unfelt. The seriousness of the problem has been tried to be contained by the efforts of organisations like National Building Organisation, Central Building Research Institute, Housing, Urban Development Corporation Ltd. and government sponsored various housing schemes. They build houses, rent them out or sell them on hire purchase. The result has proved to be far below the expectation. The greatest set back on this score has been observed in the occupation of such houses by those for whom they were not intended. Purchasing capacity of lowest income group people being negligible or even negative, those relatively well-off become the ready buyers or tenants for developers.

Among the problems which urban housing is beset with, the problem of environmental improvement of housing has acquired common man's dimension. Slum clearance, blight removal and urban renewal, as a corollary to it, have become phrases to be ever reckoned with. The houses in such pockets of a city though meaning differently to various sections happen to be both a modus operendi and a modus vivendi for those who dwell in them. The existences of such peculiarly congested sections speak of an obvious paradox where there is the condition of more and more people or houses on less and less land on the one hand and that of appreciable good proportion of vacant land in cities of India on the other. The findings of a Town Planning organisation survey show some four tenths of urban land in the category of undeveloped. For larger cities this share comes to be about one fourth of the total urban land. The inferences drawn on the basis of an acceptable density of 75 persons per hectare, consider many of urban areas in a position to accommodate the number twice their present population. The urge for environmental improvement in urban housing adds a fresh dimension of implication that of developing infrastructure. Past experiences have amply demonstrated that implications of schemes intended to bring environmental improvement in urban housing have been a dismal success. The causes behind have been deep rooted. Only a proper diagnosis followed by actions on the principle of making haste slowly may bring some positive results. The question of environmental improvement in urban housing, is basically related to the idea of providing decent housing to those who are barely housed and of creating decent housing for those who are to be housed afresh. Points of relevant implications to this idea rest with the issues as related to class composition of urban dwellers. There is a class in a position to own houses. There is another class in a position to hire houses on rent and there is still another class in no position to either of the previous. This makes the assessment of the issue that who need what kind of houses to what capacity imperative—Development of Economically Weaker Sections houses (EWS), Low Income Group houses (LIG), Middle Income Group houses (MIG) and High Income Group houses (HIG) follows the consequences of this assessment.

The issues of urban housings and the implications of what has been done and what is being done tend to settle ultimately with the questions of targets and actions. Our experiences to this effect have shown that we are used to reacting to events and not to anticipating and accordingly preparing to face them. The dimensions and complications as associated with urban housing in India provide (i) a city bias to urban housing planning on the one hand and (ii) a regional bias to urban housing plan policy. The city bias urban housing planning policy besides securing effective implementation of measures already in practice to achieve betterment of the chief characteristics of city residential structure, i.e. (i) uneven distribution, (ii) spatial density differences (iii) quality differences, must be oriented to lay greater emphasis on :

(i) provision of sites and services to people who are in need of house instead of creation of housing units to be rented or sold out. Ownership or a secure tenure of land proves to be central to the success of scheme. This will increase direct involvement of persons in need as ownership will prove to be all time a prerequisite to successful self-help operations.

(ii) preference to creation of housing infrastructure to direct production of housing units. Given the condition, environmental improvement is likely to be ensured because infrastructure in the context of urban housing assume as significant a place as house itself. The action will rationalise the use of available resources in being spent more on creation of infrastructure

(iii) popularisation of housing as a part of infrastructure for urban development

(iv) Popularising urban housing to be not only a consumptive facility rather as a productive activity with its own ability to generate income, employment savings and to have redistribution potential.

(v) Provision of low cost technology by introducing cheaper materials, better and simple technology, proper management and spatial design.

(vi) Transfer of housing activity more and more from formal sector to informal sector.
(vii) Optimization of urban land utilization with a purpose to bringing proper proportion of vacant land under urban housing on the basis of the formulation of rational land acquisition and distribution policy.
(viii) Co-ordination between public and private institutions and agencies and between housing agencies financing agencies.
(ix) A balanced view regarding targets and dissatisfaction on the part of potential users.

The success of the city bias urban housing planning measures is anticipated to depend very much on the regional bias planning measures. The nature and degree of urban problems in the present situation is not contained within the individual city bounds rather acquires a regional dimension and implication. The idea of undertaking a meaningful city planning policy only on a regional scale has already begun to gain ground. Regional situation becomes an astounding force for excessive concentration in urban areas. The urban housing planning policy with its regional bias has, therefore, good aspects in effectuating.

(i) Dispersal of population and activities.
(ii) Development of a network of well conceived growth centres as an integral part of balanced regional plans of larger cities so as to contain the excessive flow of people to already excessively concentrated centres of urbanisation.
(iii) Preparing for the development of a hierarchy of townships in the shape of viable growth centres based on careful assessment of development potential of centres in their regional setting.
(iv) Increasing the effective supply of land to effectuate dispersal of people.
(v) Formulation of locational policy for industries, commercial establishments and offices.

Urban housing, in this way, has to be geared up (i) not as a concept of technology alone, but as that of action also, (ii) not as an activity of creation alone, but as that of infrastructural development also, (iii) not as a responsibility of public institutions and organisations alone, but as that of private agencies also, (iv) not as developers' operations alone, but as a self-help operations also, (v) not as a sector of consumptive nature, but as that of productive quality also; and (vi) not as a city biased phenomenon alone, but as one with regional bias also. The dimensions, complications and implications as of urban housing appear to combine to produce an event to which the issue is not just to react alone, but to anticipate and to prepare to face the same patiently and positively.

NINE

Roderick J. Lawrence

Household Technology and Domestic Space

The Development of the Domestic Kitchen in Australia

INTRODUCTION

This chapter explores the interaction of various forms of technology–building design, public services and household appliances–upon the development of domestic architecture in Australia.

It is suggested that there are prerequisites which jointly contribute to the interaction between domestic technology and non-technological factors, such as changes in population and labour force composition, the spatial order of dwellings, and the customary use of these dwellings and their facilities. However, how these kinds of prerequisites are employed by specific groups of people poses a fundamental problem, which Banham (1969) has briefly explored : he employed the parable of a savage tribe to illustrate the close association between possible forms of human shelter and "the predisposing habits of a people". In like manner, Guedes (1979) has stressed that the evolution of building technology should not be divorced from its specific historical and socio-cultural context. While Banham and Guedes have made important contributions to the study of building technology and services, they have not adequately considered several crucial themes related to this subject. For example, although the fourth section of Guedes's encyclopaedia discusses building services and environmental systems, there is very little consideration of how the evolving design of houses interacted with technological factors (such as the development of hot and cold water supply, plumbing, sewerage, gas and electric lighting and power supply), or those economic, social and political factors (such as official health and housing policies and the role of women in society). Yet, the spatial order of the dwelling and the development of domestic technology cannot be dissociated from these factors.

In recent years some historians and sociologists have considered the influence of the domestic environment (including the development of domestic technology) upon household work. Ryan (1975), for example, has provided an historical overview for North America, whereas Oakley (1974) and Summers (1975) have published similar studies for England and Australia, respectively. It is now apparent from diverse studies that, at an international scale, from about the last decade of the 19th century the protagonists of public health and home economics based their lessons upon increased efficiency for housework and a higher standard of cleanliness in the home. As Hayden and Wright (1976, 929) have noted :

> "The fear of germs became, in effect, a way of rationalizing the woman's place in the home where she could exercise some control and ensure its purity. It explains the overwhelming acceptance of the minimal environment, the array of new appliances and the additional work for the housewife, since women believed that they could preserve their family's health, given the right domestic environment."

As houses increased in size, especially in England from the 1920's, an increasing percentage of capital investment was attributed to mechanical services and appliances. Whereas Cowan (1976) has studied the advertising campaigns which supported this increase in domestic consumption, this has also been associated with explicit government housing policies, resulting from health and housing reforms (Lawrence, 1983). This overview has enlarged the framework commonly used to study the development of domestic space and household technology.

In this chapter this diversification is extended by a discussion of some of the findings of an architectural, historical and technological analysis of the development of domestic facilities for preparing, cooking and eating food in Australia since the early nineteenth century. Facilities for food have been chosen for some important reasons (Levi-Strauss, 1966). First, as noted elsewhere Lawrence (1982), the fact that the preparation and eating of food is common to <u>all</u> human societies provides the necessary ingredient for comparisons between different cultures. Second, the activities involved in the preparation and eating of food reveal the socially and culturally defined demarcations (if they exist) between male-female and parent-child roles which are not as evident in the use of other spaces and facilities in the house.

Finally, the development of facilities for the preparation and eating of food is largely mirrored in the history of values and ideas upheld by different groups of people in particular socio-cultural contexts at different times. Given this framework, it is possible to explore the interaction between the development of architecture and technology in specific socio-cultural contexts. Accordingly, this approach enables the analysis of the derivation of domestic architecture and household technology in colonies, such as Australia.

METHODOLOGY

The first settlement of Australia at Sydney Cove in January 1788 was the genesis for the future development of the English penal colony. The development of that colony into a nation need not be described here. However, to understand the derivation of Australian domestic architecture the history of house forms can be interpreted as an indetachable component of a socio-cultural and geographical context. This model can be illustrated by the study of the interaction between the images and ideas of the parent culture - British society - and the specific requirements of the settlers who were transplanted to this completely different place (Lawrence, 1982).

In the Australian context, the important concept to grasp is the adaptation and transformation of specific British cultural predispositions, according to economic, social and political circumstances in the colony. In this respect the content of the colonial culture, and notably its architecture has unique attributes. It is a culture which developed its own institutions, which have regulated the structure, actions and social relations in Australian society. This interpretation contrasts with the widely accepted viewpoint that Australia became a provincial British society following the importation of immigrants, institutions, and material culture from Britain. Such an interpretation fails to account for many other influences : the integration of ethnic groups from both eastern and western Europe, the granting of political rights to most men prior to 1850 and to women after 1894, and the specific economic growth of Australia in which the majority of the population have participated. These and other influences have produced a society and culture different from that in the motherland (Ward, 1963).

Moreover, this interpretation is also quite different from that which is primarily concerned with symbolism, as illustrated by the thesis of Rapoport (1969). Rapoport upholds that the houses of the early English settlers in Australia were reproductions of what had been common in Britain because they had a high symbolic value. Such an interpretation ignores two fundamental themes : first, the kind of "technological transfer" that existed between Britain and Australia within the global context of colonialism; and second, how the Australian experience is related to economic, technological and social developments concerning domestic architecture at an international level.

There is a growing interest concerning the exchange of construction technologies and design principles between the motherland and the English colonies. In one study, Herbert (1978) has examined the development of pre-fabricated building techniques and the evolution of indigenous colonial architecture in Australia and South Africa during the nineteenth century. In this essay the focus will be upon the exchange of ideas rather than equipment or techniques. To establish that focus, the subject ought to be discussed within the wider framework of colonialism, as Gubler (1980, 5) has noted :

> "Colonialism...involves a complex set of interactions between the 'mother country' and the overseas territories. In matters of architecture, this relationship cannot be reduced to a simple shuttle movement : the importation of picturesque exotic styles would correspond to the exportation of the 'mother country's' schemes of composition."

This interpretation is ably illustrated by the provision of reticulated water supply in the majority of residential suburbs in the main Australian cities prior to the same provision in the main towns in England (Freeland, 1972).

Here, the importance of a temporal dimension ought to be stressed, because the culture of both the parent and the colonial societies changed during the nineteenth and twentieth centuries. A study of the evolving relationship between domestic architecture, household technology and economic, social and political factors is crucial, because the parent and colonial cultures served as normative models until the influence from North America became significant during the last half of the nineteenth century, and again after the Second World War.

The approach adopted in this study addresses these themes. It is founded upon a study of documents, such as the serial of housing legislation, the publications of domestic reformers, the writings of architects and other published studies, which have recorded the development of the domestic architecture in Australia. From an analysis of these diverse sources it has become evident that :

(1) the importation of domestic technology into Australia was of equal if not of more importance than indigenous developments in household technology;
(2) the evolution of the design and use of the Australian kitchen was less influenced by social reforms than the development of kitchen planning in Britain or North America;
(3) the transformation of the detached kitchen into the main structure of the house was influenced by social developments (such as the servantless household) as well as new domestic appliances; and
(4) the subsequent rationalization of the domestic kitchen did not occur in Australia until after the Second World War, as the result of architectural ideas, rather than as the product of scientific household management.

In conclusion, it is suggested that the approach adopted in this essay is not only useful for the study of how technological and architectural factors interact in a specific socio-cultural context, but that it can also promote useful information for architects, planners and social scientists.

THE DEVELOPMENT OF HOUSE PLANNING AND DOMESTIC APPLIANCES

There are few buildings remaining from the early period of colonial settlement in Australia which can be cited as examples of how domestic space was organized. As the earliest houses were built from "wattle and plaster" or "split timber and plaster" the reason for the lack of observable evidence is understandable. Moreover, the historical records concerned with town planning and house design in Australia have generally been limited to the presentation of facades much in the picturesque tradition. Nonetheless, Lawrence (1982) shows that apart from maps, paintings and engravings in books there are the official manuscripts which have recorded descriptions of building designs in the colony since the earliest years of settlement. In addition, it is known that the officers, marines, convicts, and the immediate descendants, had been accustomed to an English society attuned to Georgian codes of building. However, many of the earliest settlers, being from the lower classes, knew nothing of the detail of this material culture. Yet, the colonial officials and the free settlers had a common, probably unconscious, taste for privacy as upheld in Georgian England. They accepted the principle that for every family there should be a separate house, with separate rooms for specific domestic activities. This principle meant that the interior of the house should be divided into a series of spatially demarcated rooms, each classified and used for a specific household activity (Muthesius, 1979).

Although the first dwellings constructed at Sydney Cove were only one-roomed huts similar to that shown in Figure 9.1, the houses which replaced them before 1800 reflected the principles of privacy just noted. Freeland (1972 : 73) has observed :

> "In the first one-roomed huts built at Sydney Cove, all living, eating, sleeping, cooking and washing took place in this all-purpose room. From the time houses expanded beyond a couple of rooms, it was the practice to use the house itself for the living and sleeping requirements of the family only. The service spaces – the kitchen and wash houses – were in a separate block at the rear."

From these meagre beginnings the standard of construction and facilities in houses improved rapidly - so quickly that as early as the 1820's the Australian suburban dwelling sited on its "quarter-acre block of land" had been established. These dwellings usually had four or six main rooms, and it was quite common for the kitchen and other service rooms to be detached at the rear. Freeland (1972) has interpreted this demarcation of space as being necessary to combat "the heat from the cooking range, to reduce the risk of fire, to remove flies", which are a curse in the Australian climate, and to accommodate that "quirk of human nature" which demanded that the servants (usually convicts or ex-convicts at that time) be physically separated from the family and their guests.

In Australia, as in other countries at the beginning of the nineteenth century, most buildings including those for domestic purposes had very little service equipment. At that time, a typical house in Australia was heated by open fires, ventilated by non-glazed windows having timber shutters, and lit artificially by a lamp or candle. Furthermore, the cooking equipment was minimal.

For many years in Australia the pioneers had open fires for cooking. From that beginning the initial influence of domestic technology was substantial upon the development of domestic architecture. The first significant innovation in the kitchen, during the mid-nineteenth century, was cast iron, so that "by the forties cast iron stoves and fireplace grates found their way into the kitchens and drawing rooms" (Freeland, 1972, 108). Furthermore, the introduction of mechanical washing machines and water closets during the 1840's was common, but these devices were rarely installed in houses until the later decades of the nineteenth century.

Another important development which had wide ranging effects was a change in the fuels available for domestic consumption. Until about 1850, in Sydney and Melbourne, timber was commonly used for heating water, and in cooking stoves. However, Lewis (1972, 473) found that in Melbourne,

> "from the mid-fifties there was coke being reproduced as a by-product by the gas companies, and then by 1858 Chaplin and McRae of 58 Elizabeth Street were selling a type of briquette, which had been patented in the colony, though it was doubtless derived from overseas."

The study by Lewis has indicated that domestic facilities for cooking and eating were not elaborate in many houses before 1850. In fact, the first domestic stove in Melbourne, to which reference has been noted by Lewis, was a "Brown's Patent Cooking Stove" sent to Georgina McCrae in 1842. However, with a rapid increase in the prosperity of Australia, the number of these appliances multiplied quickly. It became apparent that the influence from overseas countries, apart from Britain, was important, from 1850 as Lewis (1972, 170) has noted :

> "it certainly appears that American stoves were far more popular than English, and by 1856 E.C. Wheelock and Co. of 129 Russell Street, made a speciality of selling such American cooking stoves as the 'Golden Age', 'Vulcan' and 'Crescent'..."

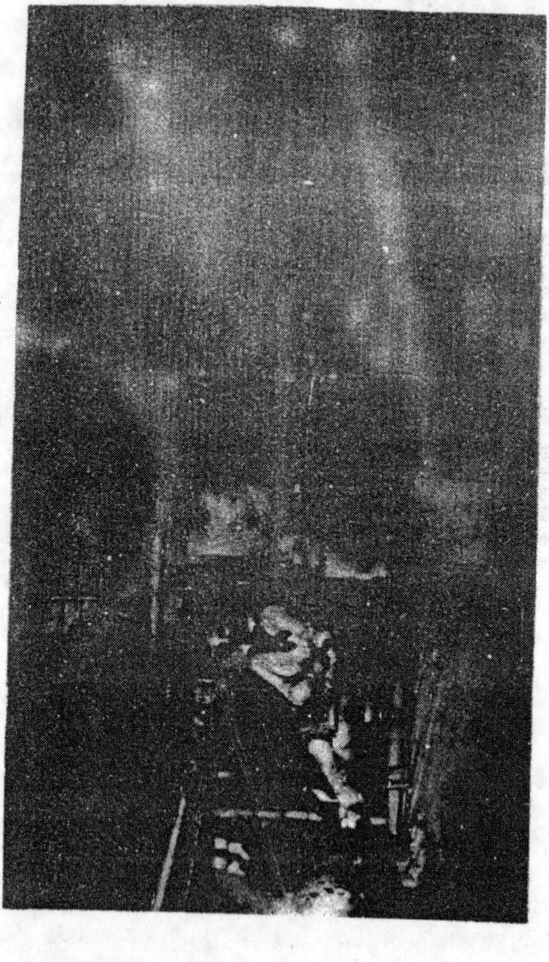

Fig. 9.1 : "The Squatter's First Home" showing equipment used in the earliest dwellings in the colony, published with the kind permission of the Mitchell Library, Sydney.

Furthermore, the local manufacture of cooking stoves and other appliances became common by 1850. Many of the better equipped houses had locally manufactured washing machines and water closets, and by 1873 a shareholder of the local Collingwood Fitzroy and District Gas Company suggested that:

> "the Company should make 'special arrangements with a view to encouraging the use of gas' for cooking and for other purposes besides lighting! By the eighties there were positive developments in the design of gas stoves, reflecting advances already made in Britain."

At the time of the Intercolonial Exhibition of 1866-7, McCallum Brothers of Melbourne showed a variety of locally-made colonial cast iron ovens, which Lewis (1972, 476) has briefly described :

> "F. Wallis of Otter Street, Collingwood manufactured various colonial ovens and a range complete with steamer, boiling tins, grid iron, meat stand, pack rack, saucepans and wrought iron boiler with safety valve all for ?25.
>
> Thomas Nelson of 118 High Street, St. Kilda, showed an enclosed self-acting kitchener, three oven ranges with grill. At the sides of the fireplace instead of a fire lump installation were two high-pressure boilers to provide hot water to the kitchen, scullery and bathrooms."

Moreover, in his monograph Town Life in Australia, Twopenny (1883) has recorded the services and equipment which were common in many houses in Sydney, Melbourne and Adelaide, noting the frequent inclusion of a separate bathroom :

> "Happily every house has a bathroom though it is often only a mere shed of wood or galvanized iron put up in the back-yard. In many of the poorer households this shed does double duty as a bath-house and wash-house, or the wash-house consists of a couple of boards with a post to keep them up, and a piece of netting overhead to keep the sun off..... Nearly all families do their washing, and often their ironing also, at home."

Elsewhere, (Lawrence, 1982) it has been shown that this custom was not common with respect to houses for "the working classes" in England during the late nineteenth century : it is appropriate to recall that the Report of the Tudor Walters Committee (1918) which established design criteria for Local Authority houses built in Britain from 1919, stated that the majority of dwellings built for "the working classes" had no separate bathroom : bathing was commonly done in the scullery or in the kitchen.

In concluding this section, therefore, it is evident that the development of domestic appliances and facilities in Australia was a transformation of "two or three cast iron saucepans.....and a baking camp oven" into a kitchen range. This development was strongly influenced by the importation of appliances from overseas, and by those products which were manufactured in Australia following the designs of imported models. This early trend for the development of domestic technology has been evident from the mid-nineteenth century until today. Yet, what is of particular interest, is that in spite of this custom, domestic architecture in Australia did not imitate the spatial ordering of rooms which contained similar appliances and conveniences in Britain. Therefore, this subject becomes an important theme in a later section of this chapter.

PUBLIC SERVICES AND PRIVATE HOUSEHOLD FACILITIES

An important factor which contributed to relatively high levels of comfort and convenience in the majority of Australian houses before the beginning of this century was the array of public services available for use by each household. While the enterprise of building and buying houses was solely a private activity throughout Australia until 1937, the provision of public services, except for public transport and gas supply, had traditionally been the responsibility of public authorities. Apart from the provision of public transport this division of responsibilities was accentuated by the rapid growth of the suburbs from about 1860, as illustrated in Figure 9.2 with respect to Adelaide. This suburban development was largely due to the introduction of the railway : now suburbs skirted around the railway stations. The railways and tramways services were owned and operated by private companies.

In his study of suburban development during the nineteenth century in Melbourne Davidson (1974) has analysed the contribution of public transport, and the supply of water, sewerage and gas. He concluded that these services usually were developed in advance of house building in the outer suburbs. Davidson's analysis was undertaken using a framework that accounted for population growth, building density and social differentiation. From the Melbourne Census of 1891 he concluded that "medical, aesthetic and symbolic considerations" were significant in the development of suburbs with different social status. This differentiation of areas within a city was characteristic of the other large towns.

Fig. 9.2 : Suburban development spreading north of Adelaide during the last half of the nineteenth century with tramways providing public transport to the city centre, published with kind permission of the State Library of South Australia.

A similar approach to Davidson's study was adopted by Barrett (1971) in his analysis of the evolution of Collingwood and Fitzroy, two suburbs of Melbourne. These studies have been cited to provide evidence of the social stigmatisation of specific residential areas. It is apparent that the spatial expression of this stigma was strong : these areas were often deprived of public services made available to the wider community; consequently they were found to have inadequate cooking facilities and bathrooms by many official housing enquiries. Nevertheless, this deprivation was only applicable to a small number of houses which were not typical of the large majority that had incorporated technological innovations. Elsewhere, (Lawrence, 1979), the built form and ownership of these houses has been studied. It was found that they were usually attached dwellings, built by speculators for rental, giving a lucrative return on the invested capital. The public ideas and meanings which upheld home ownership and traditional suburban development meant that these dwellings were deprived of basic domestic appliances and facilities commonly installed in owner-occupied houses. Thus, domestic technology was a commodity related to social class, rather than being a unilateral product for consumption by all at the same time.

The supply and control of water and sewerage was usually divided among a number of local government municipalities. This patchwork system of provision was replaced by one central authority in most cities during the last half of the nineteenth century. In Melbourne, for example, the Metropolitan Board of Works was not established until 1890 (Davidson, 1974). This public form of control constrasted with that which operated in many English towns at the same time. Elsewhere, it has been observed that in Victorian England, particularly in London, water was a precious commercial commodity for the majority of the urban population (Stedman-Jones, 1971). Apparently, this was not the case in Australia and by 1900 urban dwellings usually had water supply and sewerage (Lawrence, 1983).

Unlike water, the supply of gas to the suburbs of Melbourne (and each of the other major cities) was the responsibility of private companies for many years. In Melbourne, for example, the Metropolitan Gas Company operated from 1880. In the same year the first domestic gas stoves were marketed, and in 1887 gas water heating appliances were advertised to the public as Davidson (1974, 87) has noted :

> "The proportion of new gas connections to stoves grew spectacularly during the decade : by 1885, 12,000 had been installed and about 40 per cent of new connections in 1887 were for this purpose. By 1889 the proportion had risen to 60 per cent. A large proportion of gas stoves were hired rather than purchased. In 1890 the Metropolitan Gas Company had 12,697 on hire."

The trend established by the manufacture and marketing of cooking ranges following the advent of the patent gas cooker in 1894 has illustrated the conservatism with which new domestic appliances were accepted by the public. The patent gas cooker introduced removable burners, and it radically changed the design of these stoves in the following years : Boyd (1968, 69) has stated;

> "The potential influence on kitchen design was immense. Gone was the need for a big brick chimney-piece to carry the one-fire stove. The gas model would sit anywhere with the merest hood of galvanised iron above it. It could be placed beside cupboards or against the sink, convenience alone dictating its location. But for nearly forty years the kitchen resisted the influence. The gas stove, like a surprise visitor, was given a shakedown in the chimney-piece vacated by the fire stove."

Until the late 1930's, when the functional, streamlined kitchen was developed, "builders went through the solemn ritual of building a brick monument to the memory of wood fuel around every new gas cooker". The design of domestic equipment followed a long cycle : Firstly, the principle of the invention was applied to the image of the device it was meant to replace : "thus the first gas stoves in black cast iron were on the model of the firestoves, and later the first electric cookers were on the model of gas". It was several years before a new appliance developed an efficient and self-expressive form. Yet, by the inter-war years, the kitchen stove was entirely enamelled and thermostatic control devices and automatic pilotlights were being perfected.

As the inventions in the field of domestic technology increased during the inter-war years, the kitchen became the centre of the house and the focus of family life. However, several authors, including Boyd (1968) and Ravetz (1968), have discussed the reticence of the public to replace the pantry by cupboard units and the hand beater by a vitamizer. This reticence, coupled with the laborious process by which appliances were designed, inhibited the development of conscious kitchen planning. The time-lag was significant : generally, in Australia, "gas refrigerators (which had first appeared in 1929), gas drying cabinets and some other domestic appliances were (only) in general use in the 1940's" (Boyd, 1968, 251). The wide acceptance of electricity did not occur until after the inter-war years. Yet, a power station in suburban Melbourne was operative from 1890, electric stoves had been imported from the United States in 1907, and electric refrigerators were marketed in 1912.

It is apparent that the development of domestic technology and appliances in Australia during the nineteenth century was related to several factors, which included the provision of water, gas and electricity supply to individual dwellings. Although these services were provided in the largest Australian towns prior to their installation in British towns of the same size, this did not automatically imply that they were used to their fullest potential in the design and utilisation of domestic space. Following Ravetz (1968), it is clear that the public's reticence to incorporate new appliances in the house is not particular to Australia. However, what is of particular interest is that given the acceptance of household appliances and conveniences, the organization of domestic space did change in the Australian house. This subject is the theme of the following section of this chapter.

THE DEVELOPMENT OF THE INTEGRATED KITCHEN

The preceding sections of this chapter have traced the development of domestic technology in Australia during the last century, with respect to imported and local adaptions of appliances and the provision of water, gas and electricity supply. It is now interesting to trace how these factors impinged upon the design of domestic space. It is possible that there were no direct effects on the architecture of the Australian house, and that these developments were simply incorporated into the structure of the existing housing stock, which also served as a generic form for future dwellings. This, however, was not the case; with respect to the development of the domestic kitchen, fundamental changes did occur during the last half of the nineteenth century, which suggest that there was an interaction between technological, architectural and socio-cultural factors.

Elsewhere, Lawrence (1982) shows that the detached kitchen was common in Australia from the first year of settlement. The first substantial dwelling, the Governor's house, had a kitchen in a completely separate building. This spatial demarcation of activities is important in the context of this study. Separation of service rooms from family living rooms was not uncommon in England at the same time (Muthesius, 1979), a demarcation was usually achieved by placing the kitchen in the service wing of the manor house together with the servant's room, or in the basement of the town house. It was also common for English working class families to undertake domestic chores in the scullery and keep the living room for family activities. The solution which the settlers adopted in Australia upheld this organization of space, but its spatial expression was necessarily different.

Until the 1870's, Australian kitchens were always separate and detached from the main living rooms of the house, but at that time an important change in the planning of houses occurred. As Freeland (1972, 131) has noted, the relative position of the kitchen moved closer to the main living rooms of the house until the kitchen "became attached to it, opening off one end of the (back) verandah." At the other end of this verandah was the bathroom, whereas the laundry and water closet still remained in a detached building. On the other hand, Lewis (1972) is of the opinion, and has provided evidence to support it, that it is impossible to generalize. For example, of the four prizewinning designs in the Victoria Freehold Land Society Competition of 1855, two had attached kitchens reached by way of a verandah, while two - the first place winner in each section - had entirely internal kitchens.

Freeland has suggested that these changes in house forms were largely related to the fact that domestic servants were no longer convicts but free settlers, which meant that it was more expensive to employ domestic help. Consequently, the responsibility for housework in most households (apart from those of the landowning and business classes) shifted to the wife and mother. This important social change was very gradual, and by itself can provide only a partial explanation for the changes in house form at that time. Even in 1911 there was still a strong demand for domestic help, as a Parliamentary report stated (Parliament of New South Wales, 1913, 188), although by the late nineteenth century, the wages for domestic servants had risen beyond the resources of the middle-class householder but not the upper classes. This too suggests that the design and function of the domestic kitchen changed gradually, that process of change having begun as early as 1855.

Yet as Lawrence (1982) argues, the role of the servant was only one factor : others included the development of systems of water supply (and the accompanying plumbing facilities, which were more economical if grouped together), different forms of fuel for domestic consumption, and refinement in the design of gas cooking stoves. Thus, the rooms devoted to any of these services and facilities came to be grouped together, and the separate kitchen under the back verandah soon became fully integrated into the main structure of the house, as shown in Figure 9.3. Even though the kitchen was under the main roof, it was still allocated a clearly demarcated space until the open planning principles adopted by architects in this century associated the kitchen with the living rooms.

Fig. 9.3 : The transformation of the detached kitchen, wash room and toilet into service rooms integrated under the main roof of the house, via the back verandah.

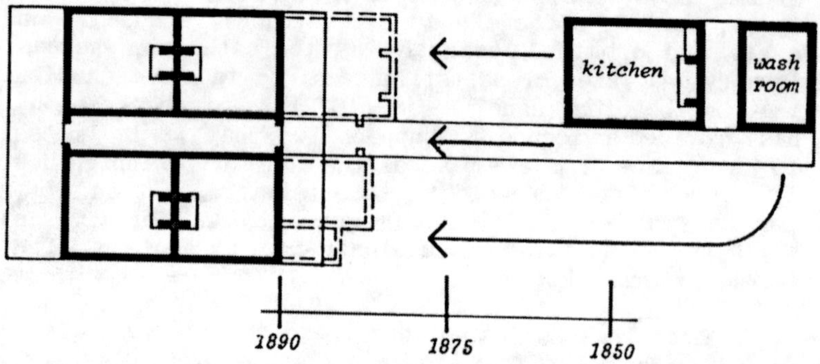

The descriptions of Twopenny (1883) and others provide documentary evidence that Australian social organization of domestic space was a departure from the vernacular English tradition at the same time. The spatial association of food preparation with laundry and sometimes bathing activities customary in England was not evident in Australian houses : Where bathing and laundry were brought into conjunction, the usual location was in a wash-house, detached from the house in the back garden, or accessible from under the back verandah.

During the nineteenth century, the Australian suburban house evolved in the size and design of its built form and use, but did so without losing the modesty of its size of facilities. Butlins' description (1964, 222) provides a summary :

"The average house evolved from two basic types, the elongated three-roomed cottage, set on a narrow strip of land (16-32 feet wide), with each room set one behind the other : or the irregular type, constructed two rooms wide, on a wider allotment, but with an irregular shape, usually two rooms at the rear and one at the front. Subsequent expansion was accompanied in the 'sixties by a continuation of this second type and an increasing irregularity in the first type, usually by the addition of rooms at the rear, doubling the width of the house at

> the back. In the 'seventies, through extension to existing properties and the redesign of new buildings, the modern "box" shape emerged, with the front of the houses tending to be two rooms wide. This so-called "double-fronted" cottage, with a window on either side of a central front door, became the typical up-to-date and fashionable type of structure in the course of the 'eighties."

As the suburban house grew larger, sanitary provisions were gradually improved, and additions for water, drainage and sewerage became common. (It is noteworthy that the larger Australian towns had reticulated water and sewerage before many cities in England.) After the boom period between 1850 and 1890, and until the inter-war years of this century, the small house remained entrenched as the ideal for the Australian. The dwelling remained uncomplicated, usually having four or six main rooms, a small bathroom, and a wash-house for laundry and a water closet, not always detached from the main structure of the house, at the back. After the economic prosperity in the nineteenth century, domestic appliances became conspicuous in many houses.

THE ROLE OF THE ARCHITECTURAL PROFESSION

From its improvised beginnings at Sydney Cove, the typical house in Australia had evolved into a comfortable dwelling. This development was related to a host of factors, including the provision of public services and household technology, and changes in the social structure of Australian society. Keeping in mind Gubler's (1980) reservations about a deterministic interpretation of "architectural transportation" from the motherland to the colonies, it is important not to overlook those mechanisms associated with the development of Australian domestic architecture and household technology.

In his study of prefabricated building techniques in Britain, Herbert (1978) has indicated that the Napoleonic Wars accelerated the development of building technology. Although he has illustrated that the first exports of prefabricated houses from England arrived in Australia as early as the 1780's, it is important not to limit the interpretation of this exchange to general trends in technology and mercantile economy. Concurrently, other influences including the publication of pattern book designs and building journals had an important contribution : Summerson (1948) has listed fourteen monographs that were printed in Britain between 1800 and 1808, publicizing small house and cottage plans. Moreover, some English authors including J.C. Loudon (1833) explicitly wrote about colonial building development; the model house plans in his encyclopaedia are just one example of design recommendations for the colonies :

> "the designs of this book are calculated for what in countries having privileged aristocracy are called the lower and middling classes of society; but which in self-governed democracies like America or in newly-colonized countries like Australia, constitute nearly the whole rural population."

The generic ideas of architecture and planning in Australia had British origins, which remained of primary importance throughout the nineteenth century. However, this custom was confronted by a growing liaison between the architectural professions in North America and Australia after the First World War.

In concluding this section, it should be stressed that there is no evidence to indicate that either British or Australian architects and planners made a significant contribution to the development of domestic architecture in Australia during the nineteenth century. When architects did design houses they were usually private commissions for the upper classes. There were no architectural commissions for housing developments funded by government agencies, trust funds or other institutions prior to the First World War, as there were in Britain and North America. However, this did occur in Australia after the war, and notably during the 1930's with the foundation of Public Housing Authorities by State Governments (Lawrence, 1979). At the same time, other ideas were also widely accepted by the architectural fraternity in Australia, which did have an impact upon the design and use of domestic space. This subject will now be treated in the final section of this chapter.

THE RATIONALISATION OF HOUSEWORK KITCHEN PLANNING

The differences in the history of the social roles of women in Australia and England during the last century have been marginal. In Australia, for example, the main course of women's emancipation did not differ fundamentally from that in Britain (Summers, 1975). Whereas in the nineteenth century in both Australia and England women could not own property or have a voice in politics, they were granted equal political and legal rights just before or near the beginning of this century.

At the same time, the widespread acceptance of contraception, the practice of safe childbirth, and the trend towards reduced family size permitted the transformation of the married woman's life.

However, while emancipation could establish the goal of equal education and employment for women in both countries it did not alter the ascribed role of women as housewives. Until the beginning of this century, the majority of women had one role specifically attached to the "Home and Hearth". Since that time, women have been permitted two roles, one as housewife and the other as paid employee. These two occupations have usually been undertaken by women at the same time, without the benefits that a delegation of household chores could provide.

In Australia, the employment of women outside the home was low and did not increase significantly during the war years. However, since the 1950's, there has been a rapid growth of women in the work force. The result of a government enquiry completed in 1975 has indicated that 39 per cent of all married women have some paid employment, and that over one third of these women have part-time work in a narrow range of occupations (Australian Department of Tourism and Recreation, 1976). This study also established that the employment of women was not confined to the wives of husbands with low incomes.

The influence of the evolution of domestic technology upon the design of houses and the completion of household activities has been examined. During the time-span of this study it could be supposed that as the differentiation between new and old houses has become more pronounced, there would have been a reduction in the amount of time needed to complete household chores. However, the evidence cited by Oakley (1974) and Vanek (1974) does not support that claim.

Some authors, including Ravetz (1968), have documented how developments in domestic technology potentially gave housewives more freedom, but concurrently, raised standards of housekeeping withdrew this freedom. These social trends were also related to the development of the Modern Movement in Architecture during this century. From the Second World War some Australian architects, like their colleagues in Britain and North America, adopted the central themes of a design policy which intended to transform the house, and other building types. The most important effects of this movement did not occur in Australia until after the Second World War (Freeland, 1972; Boyd, 1968).

During the 1950's architects and planners introduced an important challenge to the internal planning of houses. In an effort to meet the economic demands and spatial requirements which lending institutions and local governments imposed, the kitchen was reduced in size. The minimum floor area of the kitchen was determined by the statutory allowable size for habitable rooms, and in designing with this size the kitchen table was removed to a dining alcove and the walls of a small room were lined with kitchen cupboards and appliances.

Fig. 9.4 : Diagram of a kitchen layout planned to reduce steps in the routine of cooking, redrawn by the author from Bunning (1945, 63).

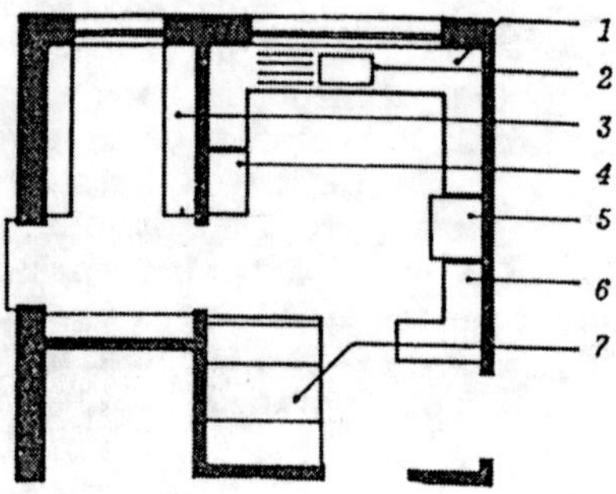

1. Food preparation counter, storage cupboard for pots below and for foodstuffs above.
2. Sink for dishwashing
3. Storage for tinned and unperishable goods
4. Refrigerator
5. Cooking stove and oven
6. Serving counter. Storage for china in cupboards above and below
7. Dining alcove

Furthermore, it is important to note that the arrangement of furniture and appliances in the kitchen related to a functional interpretation of housework as illustrated in Figure 9.4. This approach commonly abstracted food preparation activities from child-minding. It was not assumed that the housewife in the kitchen would combine these two activities. This assumption was in contrast to the overlaying of activities in the dwelling; a spatial ordering of activities which the colonial kitchen had permitted.

The reorganization of family activities in the domestic kitchen and living rooms occurred independently of advances in domestic technology, and the provision of public services in Australia. It was engineered by professional architects and planners who chose to promote the ideology of the Modern Movement in Architecture (Bunning, 1945). This professional ideology employed a functionalist doctrine for the spatial organization of family life. A number of fallacious concepts were expressed. One result was the contraction of the multi-purpose kitchen into a small room, in which efficiency was measured by the number of footsteps required to complete a domestic task. The housewife who also wanted to talk with other members of the household, or assist her children with hobbies or other tasks was ignored.

Another important finding, which has become apparent from this study, if the continual demarcation of cooking, eating and diswashing activities from laundry work and bathing. It has been noted that in spite of economic constraints after the Second World War (which caused a reduction in the total floor area of the dwelling), the social classification of these domestic activities in Australia remained unchanged. This finding has been compared and contrasted with the classification of these activities in English houses (Lawrence, 1982). It is suggested that the differences which have been explored have important historical explanations that have largely been overlooked by architects and planners.

CONCLUSION

This study has traced the development of household technology and domestic space in Australia from the earliest years of colonial settlement. It is apparent that the foregoing analysis of the transformation of domestic cooking facilities from "two or three cast-iron saucepans.....and a baking camp oven", to the functionally planned kitchen of this decade has been the result of numerous factors. Nevertheless, it is evident that the evolution of domestic technology in Australia has not been led by a Catherine Beecher, a Christine Frederick, or even a Mrs. Beeton : The impact and influence of individual reforms, or wider social or political reform movements, has been insignificant, when compared with those influences in England (Ravetz, 1968). Concurrently, the influence of architects, although retarded by comparison with Britain or North America, has been significant during this century. It has been shown that there was a diverse range of factors which interacted upon the development of domestic architecture, and that they cannot be divorced from foreign trends. In conclusion, it is suggested that the architectural, historical and technological perspective which this study has presented can be used in different contexts to provide an enriched understanding of the interaction between domestic technology and culture.

REFERENCES

Australia, Department of Tourism and Recreation 1976 : Leisure : an appropriate concept for women? (Government Printer, Canberra).

Banham, R. (1969) : The architecture of the well-tempered environment (Architectural Press, London).

Barrett, B. (1971) : The inner suburbs : the evolution of an industrial area (The University Press, Melbourne).

Boyd, R. (1968) : Australia's home : it's origins, builders and occupiers (Penguin Press, Ringwood).

Bunning, W. (1945) : Homes in the sun : the past, present and future of Australian housing (Nesbit, Sydney).

Butlin, N. (1964) : Investment in Australian Economic Development, 1861-1900 (The University Press, Cambridge).

Cowan, R. (1976) : "The industrial revolution in the home : household technology and social change in the United States", **Technology and Culture, 17(1), 1-26.**

Cunningham, P. (1827) : Two years in New South Wales, 2 vols (Henry Colburn, London).

Davidson, G. (1974) : "Public utilities and the expansion of Melbourne in the 1880's" In SCHEDVIN, C. & McCARTY, J. (Eds) **Urbanization in Australia : the nineteenth century** (The University Press, Sydney).

Freeland, J. (1972) : Architecture in Australia : a history (Penguin Press, Ringwood).

Gubler, J. (1980) : "Architecture and Colonialism", **Lotus, 26, 5-19.**

Guedes, P. (ed.) (1979) : The Macmillan encyclopaedia of architecture and technological change (Macmillan, London).

Hayden, D. and Wright, G. : "Architecture and Urban Planning" **Signs, 1(4), pp. 923-933.**

Herbert, G. (1978) : Pioneers of prefabrication : the British contribution to the nineteenth century (John Hopkins University Press, Baltimore).

Lawrence, R. (1979) : "The quest for an ideal : housing policies in Australia", **Architecture Australia, 1979, 68(5) pp. 57-60.**

Lawrence, R. (1982) : "Domestic space and society : a cross-cultural study", **Comparative Studies in Society and History, 1982, (January) pp. 104-130.**

Lawrence, R. (1983) : "The sanitary house : an architectural interpretation of health and housing reforms in England : c 1840-1920", **Architectural Science Review, 1983, 26(z) pp. 39-49.**

Levi Strauss, C. (1966) : "The Culinary Triangle" **New**

Society, 22nd December, 1966, pp. 937-940.

Lewis, M (1972) : Tradition and innovation in Victorian building, 1801-1865. A thesis submitted for the Degree of Doctor of Philosophy, Faculty of Architecture and Building, University of Melbourne.

Local Government Board (1918) : Report of the committee...to consider questions of building construction in connection with the provision of dwellings for the working classes in England and Wales and Scotland, cd 9191, The Tudor Walters Report. (H.M.S.O., London).

Loudon, J. (1833) : An encyclopaedia of cottage, farm and villa architecture (Longman and Longman, London).

Muthesius, H. (1979) : The English House (Crosby Lockwood Staples, London).

New South Wales, Parliament, Legislative Assembly, (1912) Immigration and Tourist Bureau Report for the period 1st January 1911 to 30th June 1912.

New South Wales : Joint papers presented to the Legislative Assembly, volume 2 (Government Printer, Sydney).

Oakley, A. (1974) : Woman's work : a history of the housewife (Pantheon Books, New York).

Rapoport, A. (1969) : House form and culture (Prentice Hall, Englewood Cliffs, N.J.).

Ravetz, A. (1968) : "The Victorian coal kitchen and its reformers" **Victorian Studies, 1968, 11(4), pp. 437-460.**

Ryan, M. (1975) : Womanhood in America from colonial times to the present (New Viewpoints, New York).

South Australia (1940) : Parliament, House of Assembly Building Act Enquiry Committee (Second progress report)

South Australia (1941) : Proceedings of the Parliament, Blue Book, volume 2 (Government Printer, Adelaide).

Stedman-Jones, G. (1971) : Outcast London : a study in the relationship between classes in Victorian society (Clarendon Press, Oxford).

Summers, A. (1975) : Damned Whores and God's Police : the colonization of woman in Australia (Pengiun Press, Ringwood).

Summerson, J. (1948) : Heavenly mansions (Norton, London).

Twopenny, R. (1883) : Town Life in Australia (Elliot Stock, London).

Vanek, J. (1974) : "Time spent in housework", **Scientific American, 231 (November), pp. 116-120.**

Ward, R. (1963) : "The Social Fabric" In A. M'leod (ed) **The Pattern of Australian Culture** (Oxford University Press, Melbourne).

SECTION TWO

A MULTINATIONAL PERSPECTIVE ON HOUSING POLICIES

TEN

Michael Harloe

Housing and the Market

INTRODUCTION

This paper is based on current research into the development of housing and housing policy in six advanced capitalist countries, Britain, France, West Germany, Denmark, The Netherlands and the USA.[2] A central feature of all these housing markets has been the growing dominance of owner occupation. This has been widely discussed in the literature. Some analysts tend to regard it as a natural development, a way in which individual choice and preference in housing can really be satisfied (Hallett, 1977; Stafford, 1978). In Britain and elsewhere even reformist left wing politicians have moved towards this viewpoint too, although there is some worry about the trend. But most now accept that owner occupation will continue to expand within a broadly market based system : although at the end of the paper I shall suggest that this may now change.

Most writers concentrate on discussing the likely housing consequences of the shift to owner occupation, beyond references to supposed 'natural' preferences or to the attractive subsidies open to owner occupiers, they do not examine in detail the basic causes of the emergence of this tenure and its growth. Yet this shift is part of a wider process towards emphasis on the market in housing, other symptoms of which include - in most of the countries listed above - progress away from general construction subsidies in social rented housing towards market rents with some personalised assistance for the less well off, and the switch from publicly led redevelopment to rehabilitation led by the private sector.

As a result the consideration of housing policy, at its worst, gets reduced to a set of fragmented, technocratically conceived issues, and, at its best, fails to go beyond rather limited and generalised references to the fact that, for example, inequality in housing reflects the patterns and processes of inequality in society as a whole.

To go further it is necessary to recognise that housing and its evolution over time is characterised by a set of processes that occur more generally in the consumption of certain goods and services and, moreover, that there are strong links between processes that occur in the sphere of production and those which occur in the sphere of consumption. A central concern must be the nature of socialised and individualised production and the consequences that they have for both capital and the working class.

PRODUCTION, CONSUMPTION AND CLASS DIVISIONS

In this short paper it is only possible to list summarily a number of relevant conclusions concerning these factors, a more complete account will be found elsewhere (Harloe, 1981) but even this latter paper only provides at best a set of rather simplified and abstract points about the nature of the production and consumption of commodities, conceptual tools with which to come to grips with the historical and empirical details of housing and housing policy in different countries.

1. The main basis for a capitalist system in the production, exchange and consumption of commodities by individual consumers and producers within the market. The main criterion of access to good is the individual's ability to pay, this in turn depends on access to earnings based on individual skills.

2. Production involves the co-operative division of labour. This offers benefits to capital via rising productivity but costs also, to the extent to which it provides a basis for workers' collective organisation. For workers the incidence of costs and benefits is of course reversed. The balance of costs and benefits at any point in time will depend on the relative strengths of capital and labour.

3. The model of two unified classes is simplistic. At the very least one can distinguish a section of the working class, mainly in large scale bureaucratically organised in-

dustry and commerce, which is organised in trade unions and often has close links with reformist political parties and others who work in low paid and insecure employment (if they work at all) in factories, offices, shops or at home, sharing a position of economic and political weakness with others such as the elderly, the disabled and, in general, those who have little utility for production. Political outcomes may sometimes reflect the interests of the more organised sector of the working class while excluding or even disadvantaging those of the more marginal groups.

4. Similar divisions exist among capital as different branches of capital have differing requirements and interests. So this class is characterised by conflict and co-operation which is often visible in the response of this class and its representatives to specific political issues.

5. Consumption is also characterised by a rather similar set of patterns. Some individualised consumption, i.e., allocation of goods and services on the basis of a definition of 'need' rather than pure ability to pay the price in the market, has been replaced by socialised consumption, i.e., allocation of goods and services on the basis of a definition of 'need' rather than pure ability to pay. This may involve reductions in opportunities for capitalist accumulation, but the reverse has often occurred, for the branch of the economy supplying such goods and services is likely to profit from such supply. Also much state expenditure has been analysed as expenditure which enables capital to be valorised (O'Connor, 1973). Thus the supply of socialised goods and services is often necessary as a precondition for capitalist production, for example to provide a reasonably housed and educated workforce when this cannot be guaranteed out of workers' own earnings.

6. The ways in which socialised consumption is provided are often patterned by these capitalist concerns, thus the main beneficiaries are often key sections of the working class, with the marginalised sector receiving less benefit or receiving benefit on semi-punitive terms (in this case social control rather than productive interests are often dominant). Mechanisms for excluding marginal groups range from simple non-provision to defining the rules of access in ways which are exclusive or even ensuring that those who accept benefits are stigmatised.

7. Socialised consumption offers the working class benefits which their incomes do not allow them to purchase,

less frequently do they provide the basis for collective organisation, although the socialisation of consumption has historically been a key issue for reformist politics. Struggle over socialised consumption involves struggle over its extension and over the terms in which it is supplied. A key issue is who should pay for such provision, how much should the beneficiaries be charged, to what extent should better off beneficiaries subsidise less well off ones, and to what extent should the costs be borne by capital out of taxation or charges.

8. As with production based class struggles, an understanding of the outcome of consumption based class struggles cannot be analysed solely in terms of the immediate politics and economics of the specific good or service involved. Thus narrowly defined conceptions of, for example, the politics of housing are inevitably limited, for the broader state of relationships between labour and capital is often significant.

9. In consumption as production, one can distinguish between differing interests of differing sectors of labour and capital. Thus some producers, who have a general interest in a healthy, reasonably housed, etc. workforce, will support the extension of socialised consumption to the extent necessary to achieve this end, while those producers who will lose profitable opportunities as a result may object. Among the working class, socialised consumption may tend to benefit the organised rather than the unorganised sector and, more generally, variations in consumption may engender conflict and division.

A SKETCH OF HOUSINC UNDER CAPITALISM

As the new working class moved into the towns in the early years of industrial capitalism, their housing was left to the market to provide. Overwhelmingly this took the form of private rental housing. Employment and wages fluctuated, earnings were generally low and mobility was high. Readily available housing at weekly rentals was better adapted to this situation than, for example, owner occupation. Also there began to be available a class of small capitalists which, for a variety of reasons, was ideally suited to supply such housing.

But the private market was never able to supply decent housing at an affordable price for large sections of the still mainly poor working class. Poor housing became a basis for political agitation but it had other consequences too, reducing the level of health and efficiency of the labour force and encouraging the spread of disease which threatened all. (See, for example, Gauldie, 1974; Wohl, 1977; Stedman Jones, 1971; Warner, 1972; Marcuse, 1978; Bullock, 1976; Read, 1976.)

So government regulation began to be introduced. There was resistance to this by landlords but they appear to have been on the defensive, given that substantial sectors of the working class and capital were pushing for change. The importance of the labour movement to this process of limitation of the market provision of basic needs such as housing has been pointed out by several writers (Rimlinger, 1971; Marcuse, 1978; Heidenheimer et al., 1975) who have, for example, noted that in the USA the narrow conception of the role of trade unions and the lack of a working class based political party has been significant in contributing to the relatively underdeveloped alternative of socialised provision. But one might also note that in Germany there was a mass based trade union movement and political party. These were, however, excluded from power, the state intervened less in housing, private landlords remained stronger for a longer period and, at first, much socialised housing was produced by and for trade unionists and those in the labour movement by distinctive institutions (Rimlinger, 1971; Bullock, 1976).

In countries such as France, Denmark, Britain and Germany, even before the first world war there was some support for socialised housing not just by the working class but by capitalists concerned with economic and political consequences of inadequate housing. But the need for new housing to meet the exigencies of wartime production, and in some cases as a counter to actual or feared political instability, led to an upsurge in the production of social housing with state aid in and around the 1914-18 period. (The British case is well discussed in Swenarton, 1980). Rent controls and security of tenure legislation were also introduced. After the war, especially as the short post war period of political instability faded and the world economy began to slump, social housing programmes diminished and governments returned to reliance on the private market. But in many countries a complete return proved politically impossible and some form of rent controls remained, neither was the building of social housing totally forgotten, especially in localities or by institutions under the control of organised labour.

In the inter-war period, in particular in Britain in the thirties and in the USA in the twenties, there were some geographical areas in which the market provision of housing developed rapidly. There were sections of the working class, employed in rapidly expanding growth areas of the economy who benefited from reasonably secure employment and rising real wages. They were able to improve their housing standards and, to an increasing degree, they opted to buy rather than rent their new houses (which were typically located in suburban extensions of the city).

Why should the supply of property increasingly begin to shift at this time from rental to ownership? Some reasons why consumers might prefer this are mentioned later but the shift was actively promoted by producers and associated interests too. A short answer might be that rental housing involved many investors in tying up large sums of capital for a long time, becoming involved in costly and difficult management of the asset and so on. By contrast the development and sale of owner occupied housing involved the developer in no such longer term responsibilities and, provided that other conditions were appropriate, can easily be seen as preferable. When one adds to this the increasing number of controls that governments had introduced on the price, quality, etc. of rental accommodation, compared with the still relatively free conditions in the owner occupied sector, the shift becomes even more understandable. Moreover, as other media (such as the stock market) had become accessible to the small investors (and often gave a better return than housing), landlordism lost some of the attraction that it once had. The larger scale capital began to be associated with the development of suburban estates in the inter-war period would certainly have been looking for returns comparable with those obtainable elsewhere (even if it is clear that some small landlords did 'irrationally' invest) and it is likely that sales to owner occupiers would have been most attractive to them.

The precondition for all this was the development of the economic basis for mass owner occupation. A number of issues are involved here, such as the development of specialised credit institutions able to provide mortgage finance (in many countries these grew by tapping, among other sources, the very same type of capital investment that had formerly gone into rental housing). But above all there had to be a reasonable number of people with secure employment and rising real incomes, thus able to afford the long term commitment to regular loan repayments. If one examines the development of housing in the inter-war period in, for example, the USA, France and Britain, one can compare and contrast the impact of the factors noted above on the growth of social housing and owner occupation. One can see how in areas and countries where there were rising real incomes, owner occupation began to develop quite rapidly; one can see how in Britain, where the labour movement had some impact on central and local development, there was some increase in social housing : in France, where labour was weaker, there was less development; and in the USA none at all - until the New Deal. In this latter country one may also note that the start of social (public housing) in the mid-thirties was a direct response to the plight of key sections of the working class, unemployed building workers and owner occupiers who had lost their jobs and had defaulted on their mortgages.

Since the last war there has been an accelerating shift from private renting to owner occupation. Immediately after the war, about three quarters of the housing stock in France, Denmark, West Germany and the Netherlands was private rented, and here the modern owner occupied market was in its infancy. In Britain, and even more so in the USA, the domination of the private landlord was less marked. But by the mid seventies private rented housing only accounted for 10-15% of the stock in Britain and the Netherlands and probably less than a third elsewhere, except in West Germany, where after many years in which it had continued to develop, it too seemed to be in decline. New rental construction had fallen even more sharply.

Except in the case of the USA there had been a markec increase in the stock of social housing, but this growth was not constant. In fact the major expansion of this tenure appeared to be over by the seventies and, increasingly, new production was for owner occupation. This latter stock was being added to as landlords sold off their properties, and in some countries by the sale of social housing too.

The social composition of the various tenures was changing. Owner occupation was being extended to large sections of the better off working class, aided by heavy government subsidies. Social housing, which had been seen for a time as an attractive alternative tenure for many of the working class who had formerly had to rent privately, was increasingly unattractive in comparison with owner occupation and was tending to house a concentration of those on the lowest incomes who could not afford owner occupation. Private renting, drained of the more solvent demand by the other two sectors, was increasingly in the business of housing low income households who, because of insufficient social housing or restrictive rules of access, were forced to stay in this tenure.

Particularly from the 1960s onwards (though earlier in Britain and the USA) governments acted to promote the emergence of owner occupation as the main tenure and hence to support, with subsidies and other assistance, this distinctive form of the market provision of housing. The principal change was the switch of financial assistance away from social housing to owner occupation (as the latter was usually subsidised indirectly, the main apparent change was to cut back direct subsidies for social rented construction). This switch had distributional effects, accentuated by the fact that owner occupier subsidies via the tax system are regressive. Thus more assistance was diverted to the better off and less to the less well off, who tended to be politically weak too. Other aspects of this change included the switch from large scale redevelopment, which often involved the provision of some social housing for displacees, to rehabilitation based on a system of support for the private market; the move towards restricting subsidised rents (in both parts of the rental sector) to the very poor via systems of inefficient housing allowances; adjusting other rents to market or quasi market levels: and so on.

Of course the pace and the scale of these changes and their details have varied, depending on the situation in which each country found itself after the war, the level and progress of the economy and incomes and political history (see Harloe, 1981 for a fuller account). But now let us turn to consider these developments in the light of the sketch of working class and capitalist interests outlined earlier.

After the last world war European economies were devastated and there was a massive need for new housing, incomes were low and uncertain too. In these circumstances, large scale owner occupation was out of the question even where the dominant political party was ideologically predisposed to this tenure (for example, in Germany). In contrast, the USA soon embarked on its long post war period of prosperity and rising incomes which produced the post war one family, owner occupied housing suburban boom. It was not politically possible, even when governments would ideally have followed this course, to rely on the private landlord. So, just as after the first world war, social housing programmes were expanded and controls remained on private renting, despite the damage that this did to the many small scale capitalists in this sector.

The emphasis placed on social rented housing varied as a result of, among other things, the strength of organised labour. One might compare, for example, Britain where the first post war Labour government followed the most thorough going attempt to replace the private market by social housing; Germany, where the CDU put emphasis on support for the private market and was more reluctant to allot as large a role to social housing (it should be noted that here many who built social rented housing were in fact small landlords); and the USA where, as already noted, organised labour was much less inclined to stress collectivist solutions. In countries such as Germany and France, where the left was excluded for many years from national power, the record of certain socialist local administrations in developing social housing in these years was especially noticeable.

But the pressure for social housing was not simply a response to the strength of organised labour or more generally a move to ensure political stabilisation. For, in the circumstances, the provision of some social housing clearly assisted large scale industrial and commercial capital. First it often aided construction and property interests at a time when the wider market for what they had to offer was very limited. In Britain, for example, several of the companies which later became leaders in the property field 'lived' off council house construction in this period, later such contracts were useful at times when the commercial and private residential market was depressed. Beyond this, there was in several countries a fairly clear link between the provision of social housing and the development of a modern, large scale industrial economy. This was perhaps most so in France, where social housing was built for the newly dynamic industries such as the motor car manufacturers and where many workers were nominated for social housing by their firms (Magri, 1977).

However, there were severe limitations on the extent to which social housing was provided. Although the evidence for this claim needs much more work to substantiate it,[3] it seems that the result of the way in which access was gained, together with the fact that in most countries social housing remained in very short supply - tended to ensure that it mainly housed a relatively restricted section of the working class, and, in particular, that, for many years it was less readily available to the marginal groups which were referred to earlier. Many such groups, the elderly, ex-colonial immigrants and guest workers, the young, mobile and less skilled and so on continued to look to the private rental sector. This weakening of the market for private rental - as more and more of the less poorly paid moved into the other two sectors - further undermined the position of the mainly small scale capital involved in this sector.

To a considerable extent social housing aided a section of the more organised working class. The close link between social housing and the social democratic parties is evident in Western Europe, both in terms of voting behaviour and of the control of social housing organisations. The extent to which there was deliberate exclusion and the extent to which the failure of social housing to extent further was simply a result of its short supply is a matter for further research, but there seems to be some evidence that the latter factor was not the only one.[4]

Turning to the later years of the post war period, rising real incomes and full employment made the large scale expansion of owner occupation possible. This has been accompanied by pressure for the reorganisation of state policies to support this strategy and for the limitation of social housing to a marginal role dealing with those who would not be catered for by private enterprise (which may be essential given the progressive withdrawal of even small scale capital from rental housing). In the USA this was the situation from 1945 onwards. In Britain, given the accession to power of a Conservative government from 1951, it began to happen in the fifties. In countries such as France and Germany, despite the fact that they had governments which were more or less committed to this approach, economic circumstances inhibited its development until the sixties.

Politically it was important that at the time when this process of rapid development of owner occupation began, Conservative governments were usually in power. But subsequent social democratic governments have tended to accept the trend, even to welcome and encourage it, thus withdrawing to some degree at least from their previous emphasis on social rented housing.

When considering why this has been so one needs to recognise the very limited extent to which, in practice, such reformist parties did implement socialised provision and supplant the market when in power. Because of this socialised housing is usually made available on terms which reflect an essentially capitalist concern that its impact be limited. A full account has yet to be written, but it is the case that ownership offer certain material benefits, modest capital gains, freedom from control by landlords and so on. In contrast the social sector tenant has not had these benefits, had faced paying ever higher rents for unattractive property and suffered under bureaucratic and unresponsive management. For those sections of the working class who have had rising real wages, the owner occupation option, especially when aided by subsidies, has seemed increasingly attractive. Especially since the sixties when inflation, prices and rents, began to increase rapidly, the ownership option has been ever more popular.

Given that social democratic parties have hardly challenged the basic legitimacy of the individualised commodity production of housing for profit via effective programmes to socialise land, development and finance, and to redistribute individualised gains and profits over the whole population on the basis of need rather than ability to pay, and given that they have largely accepted the limited scope and nature of social housing, the shift towards support for ownership follows from fairly simple electoral considerations, apart from any reinforcement by changing opinions and preferences of the leaders of these parties. Moreover, once the development of owner occupation is set in motion, the more skilled manual and white collar sections of the working class move into this tenure and, as they provide the political base for the social democratic parties, it is easy to see why the owner occupied sector gains in political strength while the social housing sector gradually loses its former support.

The benefits to property capital and associated business (e.g. lawyers and property agents) from the extension of owner occupation are too obvious to require further comment here. Beyond this there does not seem for very many years at least to have been any serious conflict between expanding property capital and other sectors of capital. Indeed often the reverse was true. Thus it has been pointed out that suburban development of owner occupied housing was at the core of a wider growth and change in patterns of consumption which provided new opportunities for other sectors of capitalism. To give just one example, the growth of relatively low density suburbs stimulated the demand for cars.

The conclusion is that, by the end of the sixties and

considerably earlier in some cases (though possibly a little later in Germany), the focus on the private market in housing in its modern and (from the point of view of capital) most effective form, owner occupation, was without significant opposition, being supported for a variety of reasons by those interests directly involved in its production, by capital as a whole and, to a very large degree, by representatives of the organised working class. In contrast, social housing was beginning to move in the direction of a residual tenure. It was increasingly likely to house marginal sectors of the labour force and, materially and in terms of its social valuation, was taking on the characteristics of welfare housing which it had long previously assumed in the USA, where the absence of any countervailing economic or political reasons for an alternative role had only been present for a few years before and during the second world war.

FUTURE UNCERTAINTIES

But this coalition of interests in favour of the extension of the private market in housing, with the underpinning of extensive public support, may prove to be quite unstable in the new economic situation. In a recent paper, Miller (1978) has pointed to what he calls the recapitalisation of capitalism. By this he means the type of policies now being adopted in response to the growing economic crisis of collapsing profits and business activity and growing unemployment. These policies include cutbacks in public expenditure or at least reductions in expenditure in housing, education and so on in order to meet the growing burden of unemployment benefits, reductions in business and higher taxation, pressure to reduce the social wage and to restrict levels of money wages, as well as the toleration and even the deliberate creation of a high and growing level of unemployment. In housing, although the first move has often been to cut back on the production of social housing. There are signs of growing tension over the continued existence of a highly subsidised owner occupied sector, and the emergence of some divergence of interest between capital employed in the construction sector (which has been hard hit by plunging levels of new construction) and other branches of capitalism which have tended to support policies which have intensified the slump in construction. In some countries, such as Britain and the USA, some criticism has been heard, even from quite orthodox political circles, about the open ended nature of owner occupier subsidies, about the diversion of investment into property rather than into supposedly more productive investment and so on, although the political strength of the millions who by now have a stake in the continuance of the system of government support has, as yet, prevented much action to stem owner occupier subsidies.

So perhaps the continued development of the private market in housing via owner occupation is now more in question than at any time in the last twenty years. So far as working class support for this tenure is concerned, the reality is that the chances of new entrants to the housing market obtaining owner occupied housing is lessening and the burden of repayments on those already in the sector is greater than ever before. But the alternative of social rented housing is not available as new building declines and rents rise. Not one imagines, given the increasingly marginalised nature of much of this sector would it again, at least in its present form, be an acceptable long term housing solution for many of those who aspire to owner occupation. The re-emergence of a large scale housing problem, involving people with low and fluctuating incomes unable to gain access to reasonable housing in either the social or the owner occupied sectors, already seems to be occurring.

Housing policy, after a period in which there seemed to be something of a convergence in its profile in advanced capitalist countries, may become more varied in response. The stronger economies, for whom the current difficulties might be no more than temporary, may soon resume the familiar mix of policies and development, with the owner occupied sector continuing to grow. In other countries, where economic stagnation and mass unemployment continues it is possible to contemplate a more dramatic collapse of the political and economic context in which the development of the private market in housing has occurred. In some cases, especially where the labour movement has significant influence, demands for a reversal of the retreat from the socialisation of the housing market, especially if they are not simply demands for a reversion to large scale, bureaucratically controlled provision may attract more support than at any time since the early post war years.[5] It is even possible that demands for the socialisation of housing production may grow, especially if the obstacles that the continuance of the domination of the profit motive in land and construction pose for socialised housing come to be recognised. In other countries, where such demands are resisted and where economic decline continues, government support may be ever more limited to relatively more privileged sectors of the population and housing conditions for the rest are likely to begin to revert to those characteristic of a bygone age - such appears to be the current British prospect and may well characterise the USA too.[6]

NOTES

Paper presented at the "European Meeting on Applied Urban Research", Erren. Oct. 2-4, 1981.

1 This is a condensed and somewhat revised version of Harloe, 1981.
2 This project has already studied the development of the private rented sector in the six countries, it has now turned to consider the other two main tenures.
3 The argument that the rules of access were, for many years at least, exclusionary is laid out in more detail in Harloe, 1981.
4 Evidence has been collected in the private rental project of the reluctance of some social housing organisations in The Netherlands to accommodate those on the lowest incomes and of a similar reluctance in West Germany to house guest workers and other groups. In France income/tenure /occupational group data show quite clearly that HLM housing has tended to house more skilled manual and white collar workers, not the poorest.
5 It is interesting to note, for example, the shift in The Netherlands in emphasis towards social housing construction and away from owner occupation recently (EEC, 1981) and the new government in France may clearly follow a similar course.
6 For useful analyses of the British situation see House of Commons Environment Committee, 1980, 1981.

REFERENCES

Bullock, N., 'Housing reform and the garden city in Germany, 1890-1915' in **Transactions of the Martin Centre for Architectural and Urban Studies**, 1, 1976, pp. 203-23.

Commission of the European Communities **Report on Social Development**, Office for Official Publications of the European Communities, Luxembourg 1980.

Gauldie, E., **Cruel Habitations**, George Allen and Unwin, London 1974.

Hallett, G., **Housing and Land Policies in West Germany and**

Britain, Macmillan, London 1977.
Harloe, M.,'The recommodification of housing' in Harloe and Lebas (eds.) **City, Class and Capital**, 1981 pp. 17-50, Arnold, London .
Heidenheimer, A., Heclo, H. and Adams, C., **Comparative Public Policy**, Macmillan, London 1975.
House of Commons, Environment Committee, **First Report**, HMSO, London 1980.
House of Commons, Environment Committee, **Third Report**, HMSO, London 1981.
Magri, S., **Logement et reproduction de l'exploitation**, Centre de Sociologie Urbaine, Paris 1977.
Marcuse, P.,'The myth of the benevolent state : notes towards a theory of housing conflict' in M. Harloe (ed.) **York Conference 1977 on Urban Change and Conflict**, Centre for Environmental Studies, London 1976.
Miller, S.M., 'The recapitalisation of capitalism', **International Journal Journal of Urban and Regional Research**, 2(2), 1978 pp. 202-12.
O'Connor, J., **The Fiscal Crisis of the State**, St. Martin's Press, New York 1973.
Read, J.,'Housing and social reform in France, 1894-1935', in **Transactions of the Martin Centre for Architectural and Urban Studies**, 1, 1976 pp. 297-315.
Rimlinger, G., **Welfare Policy and Industrialisation in Europe, America and Russia**, Wiley, New York 1971.
Stafford, D., **The Economics of Housing Policy**, Croom Helm, London 1978.
Stedman Jones, **Outcast London**, Oxford University Press, Oxford 1971.
Swenarton, M., **Homes for Heroes**, Heinemann, London 1980.
Warner, S.B., **The Urban Wilderness**, Harper and Row, New York 1972.
Wohl, A., **The Eternal Slum**, Edward Arnold, London 1977.

ELEVEN

Eberhard Muhlich

New Functions in Housing Policy and New Agencies Engaged in Provision of Living Space

It is well known that, since the beginning of industrialisation, working and living were separated step by step. Except for a few remnants they were, separated because of the development of modern industry and the modern state, subordinated to formal bureaucratic rationality. One of the reasons for this highly bureaucratic steering of working and living is, according to Polanyi, for instance' the fact that labour and land is only in theory allocated by the market. The same reason accounts for the special relationship between the labour 'market' and the housing 'market'. Depending on the type of economic development a nation decided or was compelled to follow, the problems of income distribution erected by the labour market had to be dealt with in some form before they reached the housing market. In many cases the effort was made to hold housing costs at a low level in order to keep wages low enough to allow rapid industrialization.

Today the traditional relationship between the housing market and the labour market is undergoing major changes. There has been long standing tendency towards economic equalisation based on trade unions efforts and political democracy. Today however, the technically speeded-up rationalisation of production processes and a shift in location to cheap-pay countries for certain partial processes together cause a dualisation of the labour market into high-paid and secure jobs on the one side and low-paid and insecure jobs on the other.

This dualisation of the labour market with growing unemployment on the side must also have the same dualising or polarising effect on the housing market, if public means for income and housing policy are shrinking as is apparently the case at present. Following a phase of wide-spread stock renewal which left comparatively little poor housing remaining, a phase of intensive de-investment in growing partial markets is to be expected, especially in weak-growth regions.

In addition, technological development has apparently brought a world-wide diversification and decentralisation of industrial plants, through the possibility of division of the production process into many stages and with distribution of this partial production over the whole world, which stands in contrast to a concentration at the management level. With this, there is not only the possibility of a shift to underdeveloped countries but also a migration of smaller production plants within borders of the industrial nation. A migration especially of the most advanced production of goods and services is being observed at the edges of density areas, but also interregionally into country areas.

Both tendencies together, the internal and external dualisation of the labour market, create the danger of a fast regional and sub-regional segregation of economy and society in areas of disparative welfare. Should it come to the following :

- that the labour market be dualised in the way described as a result of shifting production and rationalisation and through new products;

- that in addition to the differential between higher and lower qualification, a corresponding differential should develop between over-and underemployment which is emphasised even more by curtailing of the education household and by restrictions of access;

- that the basis for calculation of household income should be the increasingly assymetrical relationship between supply and demand on the labour market.

then it can probably be expected :

- that the time has gone when social inequality was on the decrease, that there is less chance for upward mobility, that there is an increase of a hidden unemployment of women and juveniles;

- that social segregation will accompany social inequality resulting in the formation of ghettos of groups of the residential population with highly disparative incomes;

- that the ghetto-formation will be greatly accelerated through decentralisation of production plants to the residential areas of higher qualified employees;

- that the social services will duplicate the social segregation by means of improvement and higher prices in the residential areas of the overly-employed, high-income groups and deterioration in the areas of the unemployed and lower-income groups; above all, it can be expected in the latter that the idle labour of the unemployed and under-employed will be used towards a cheapening of social services in that these will be offered as, "helping them to help themselves"

- that for the rest, workers held in dependency and the initiative of the unemployed and under-employed, inasmuch as it is not eaten-up by the effort of trying to re-integrate, will expand into a twilight of illicit work with the all-too-familiar forms of pre- and early-industrial petty exploitation, petty criminality and insecurity in the case of accidents.

Housing policy would have no legal instrument and no means of meeting with de-investment over a long period in urban areas in which permanent unemployment.and the corresponding income discrimination and social weaknesses instate themselves. Some examples can already be found in the Federal Republic of Germany when investigating those unpopular multi-storried welfare-housing areas of the late sixties and early seventies.

This would mean that already today the sociopolitical dimension of housing policy is dramatically regaining importance, together with the question of housing costs for lower income groups.

But there is an alternative for housing policy. It could help to open a new dimension in the relationship between the labour market and the housing market. As it becomes clear that more and more labour will be redundant, strategies against the dualisation of the labour market and the housing market have to start with the redistribution and reduction of formal working hours in the industrial and administrative system. And those strategies also have to provide compensation for the very probable stagnation or shrinking of formal income. That means the provision of space for an informal economy on the local level, with the informal exchange of goods and services and informal, more or less non-monetary income. Such a modern form of livelihood economy seems to be quite necessary in order to adapt to foreign economic, ecological, social and cultural limits of economic growth. The new function for housing policy will be to provide spatial and organizational base for the expanding informal 'labour market'.

For where else but in connection with housing should the modern livelihood economy find it's place ? How else but in connection with housing should premises be managed for willful work of individuals or neighbourhood groups. Most empirical examples of modern livelihood economy do, in fact, take housing provision, new buildings or renewal of older housing as their starting-point.

The history of housing policy in the industrial countries is distinguished by the fact that the livelihood-economy forms of housing provision, meaning non-expansive, decentral forms, have held most consistently. These have always included the owner- occupied housing of strong-income groups, apartment houses belonging to small-scale and mainly self-occupied people who also live in the house and see it as financial help for their old age, -on the part of qualified industrial workers, white-collar workers and civil servants, the housing co-operatives and also, the informal kind of help given by neighbours and relatives in the country. These decentral and non-expansive agencies for housing provision could hardly, however, fulfill the quantitative requirements of an accelerated industrialisation and urbanisation. It soon became necessary, therefore, to bring up industrial rationality of expansion and centralisation accordingly with regulation of the mortgage-, land-, construction- and, finally, the renting market. First of all, the way was opened for expanding private housing businesses and later on, in order to sustain wages and investment policies, the non-profit making social housing companies. However, the tangible and intangible quality and popularity of centralistic housing provision usually remain behind that of decentral housing provision.

If the not yet established economic policy concept of a double economy should hold its ground in political discussion and should free the way to a dimension of adaptation to external-economical, ecological, social and cultural growth limits which cuts across the traditional argumentation between the liberal and socialist variants of industrial growth, housing policy is then going to be placed in a role as pace-setter. Firstly, because the provision of housing itself is a fitting object for livelihood-economy. Secondly, because self-produced services and goods are mainly produced in the vicinity of housing and for this reason premises and other facilities must be available near living quarters. Thirdly, because a combined agents' form with various functions can be established by the members of a neighbourhood (Agents' Association) for housing provision as for other livelihood-economy functions. To support organisational innovations for the above is certainly the most important function of housing policy in the future this being so fundamental. This can be demonstrated with examples of agents of this kind, one from England and one from The Netherlands.

NEW AGENCY FORMS

The following description of new agency forms for housing provision and infrastructure near housing is based on results from a comparative study of urban renewal in Western Europe. In the search for trend-setting examples of urban renewal, characterised by the economic, political and cultural participation of tenants, we found new forms of agencies in Liverpool and Amsterdam which seem suited to cover the new functions of housing policy.

Residents' initiatives, in the English case example, tenants, in the Netherlands tenants, house-owners, craftsmen and tradespeople, establish an agency, buy pieces of land and buildings and take over their renewal or re-building and management. In the series of traditional agency forms for housing provision, from owner-occupation to rented housing in which the owner also lives, to the housing co-operative or up to the more or less big private or public housing companies - in this series in order of dimension, the new agents' co-operatives are the newcomers right in the thick of it. Developed in two countries in which this middle field has atrophied, these agents fill a gap where traditional house-owners who also live in their houses for certain historical reasons, hardly play a role any more.

In the Federal Republic of Germany, small private landlords have, in the last few years once more demonstrated their competence and performance with lively modernisation activity, with relatively small increases in rents : most landlords are thinking of long-term economical security rather than short-term profits. They are not concerned with sky-high rents which would only cause much conflict in relationships with tenants, with whom they are often living under one roof. However, the growing number of rented apartments being turned into owner-occupied apartments, show that the traditional landlords are retreating. In addition, there is a group of landlords who, for reasons of age, can no longer fulfill their function. The new agents' associations which have grown out of residents' initiatives are not so much, 'stopgaps' for the Federal Republic as that they are not of interest as a 'successor', to be gradually introduced.

As far as the form of residents' initiative is concerned, our English case example, Weller Street Housing Co-operative in Liverpool, goes back to a housing policy compromise made in 1974. At that time, the Conservative Party strengthened its resistance against Council Housing and the Labour Party was against increasing support for the building of owner-occupant houses. The compromise consists of a complete reformulation of the constitution of an old agency form,the Housing Association, to a publicly financed and controlled, non-profit working agent for housing provision. Their activity is directed, above all, toward renewal of old housing stock and alternative new building in old city areas urgently in need of housing.

With these completely newly constituted Housing Associations, British housing policy has a new prop which has been carrying the main weight to renewal in the seven years since 1974. Since then, new regulations in all four fields of intervention in housing policy are in effect : in financing, property market, construction and management. This makes the alternative to the bureaucratic nature of Council Housing and expensive, private owner-occupation viable. Roughly, the new, sub-system of housing policy can be described as functioning as follows : a national trustee association, the Housing Corporation, registers any group of at least seven qualified persons wishing to assign themselves to the task of housing rehabilitation and new development for re-housing without intent to profit as a Housing Association. At first, these were mainly old Housing Associations who wanted to attach themselves to the new system. At the same time it could be a group of specialists looking for independent, satisfying work or a residents' initiative in an old housing area wanting to improve their own housing conditions. The latter are registered as Co-operative Housing Associations and buy the necessary know-how from another professional Housing Associations or form, together with others, a Secondary Co-operative Housing Association to be a common planning and management centre.

Once registered, the activities of the Housing Associations move along a path which, from the Housing Corporation on the one hand and the Town Hall on the other is at once made easier in financing and in support in buying houses but is also relatively narrowly limited. Every property purchase, any planning or execution of renewal or work on new buildings has to be approved and financed step by step. Purchases are made mainly in renewal areas (Housing Action Areas, General Improvement Areas), where the expropriation rights of both the public Housing Corporation and the local authorities are strengthened and supplemented with extra planning and building regulations rights. Expropriation rights were used a great deal to help the new agents start their work quickly and with not too great expense. In Liverpool alone, over 2000 expropriation procedures were instituted up until 1979, whereby the reimbursement sum was reckoned out of the capitalised, publicly laid-down, utility value rent. The Associations receive a subsidy towards the purchasing price or for expropriation reimbursement (Housing Association Grant) which is also meant for lump-sum payments for single management services (purchasing negotiations, negotiations with tenants, renewal planning and implementation) as well as for a part of the cost of renewal itself. The relatively low utility value rent is supposed to cover the remaining renewal costs or annuity arising from the loan given and running management costs (repairs, renting, etc). If the complicated calculations of the relationship between subsidised and lent money are thrown into disorder by growing interest, growing maintenance costs, delayed increase of utility value rent or the like, the Housing Corporation can help close such financing gaps with special subsidies (Revenue Deficit Grant). So, in reality, the professional Housing Associations are private servicing concerns which carry out the renewal of old housing stock with set rules and fees. The difference to the Council is that unable agencies can more easily be disengaged; property which cannot be disposed of reverts to the Housing Corporation.

Things look quite different in those Co-operative Housing Associations initiated by residents. Although in the same institutional and financial frame, they do not bring with them the wish for lasting, more or less satisfying work and income but rather are qualified by their housing needs, usually lack of housing, and have, therefore, a higher conflict-ability with the local authorities and the Housing Corporation. The first Co-operatives for housing area renewal go back to the residents' initiatives before the Housing law of 1974 (for instance, Granby in liverpool, Holloway in London) and took over the new form. Weller Street's Housing Co-operative, which we visited, is an example for the way in which a previously covered-up conflict concerning a demolition and re-building, long overdue, was carried through in the interests of the residents in a productive, negotiable manner. This was by way of the new form and financing and with support from a professional Housing Association (Co-operative Development Service, CDS). Without the new agency form of the Co-operative Housing Association with its political and economical supportive function and without the midwife services of the C.D.S. it would not have happened :

- that the smouldering and undermining conflict which had been going on for years concerning new housing could lead to a search for more suitable land for new buildings in the vicinity and to the lengthy and instructive political assertion of land acquisition;

- that due to the ups and downs of the last four years concerning purchase of estate and finally due to the common planning of a new terraced-housing estate, the Weller Street neighbourhood has re-emerged;

- Those 62 households of the altogether 350 households in the area, which, without any kind of discrimination of access, entered into the apparently rather hopeless experiment, have formed work-groups for the various new functions for their own housing provision and, in the process, have developed a livelihood-economy based on reciprocity which is also suited to other social services. Parallel to the family, the Co-operative has become the second important network for relationships, in which members, according to their own statements, have, for the first time, gained the ability to live and work with others satisfyingly and above all have acquired the language with which to do so.

Our case example in the Netherlands, the Stadsverniewings-corporatie Volkoren in Amsterdam, is a privately initiated and financed project. Successful only thanks to a series of happy circumstances, it wants to demonstrate the practicability and advantages of an agent concept upon the legal embodiments, especially of the land regulations section 1977, of which, the parliamentary coalition consisting of confessional Parties, Workers' Party and Farmers' Party, foundered.

The bill for urban renewal consisted of two main elements. Firstly, renewal should be carried out under control by the neighbourhood. It must procure an organisational form, this being the Stadsverniewings-corporatie, of one kind or another, so as to be able to determine the renewal aims itself and to have the conflict and co-operational ability against the local authorities and state decisional agencies. Secondly, in order that residents' interests can be asserted, which are usually concerned with improvements in housing and premises for small trade at tolerable prices, the well-tried land regulations for urban growth, meaning expropriation at return value, should be transferred to the inner city with its current, controlled rents.

In its land regulations section this bill is therefore very similar to the British Housing Law of 1974. The important difference is, that the suggested new agent form is multifunctional from the start, covering therefore not only housing provision but also the management of trades premises and premises for social services as well as open spaces. The intention, from the beginning, was to bring the interplay or the conflicts between all activities in a neighbourhood under one organisational roof, the agency being the residents themselves. This is in accordance with political tradition in the Netherlands, where differing interests, in this case usage interests, are brought together in a corporative institution with state participation, in this case the local authority and are set under pressure to come to an agreement. Land price regulation is supposed to ensure that interests, as, for instance, between landlords and tenants, do not differ too greatly and do not pull too far apart.

Anticipating these legal fundamentals, this policy has more or less been in practice, only in Rotterdam, since the middle of the nineteen-seventies. A majority of the Workers' Party supports the extensive buying-up of private old housing stock through non-profit-making housing companies. They are trying to generate willingness to buy and also tolerable prices through strict impositions relating to modernisation. The division of the planning authorities into urban area work groups, whose main function is to see 'that life is not impaired', ensures that renewal is kept at a level which residents can pay for.

The Stadsverniewings-corporatie Vollkoren, which we visited, would be suitable for Rotterdam. It is, however, set up in opposition to urban renewal policy in Amsterdam, namely, demolition and rebuilding after the example of the suburbs. It was only in 1978 that the newly voted municipal council distanced itself from the town planning norms for thinning-out, to follow the principles for a conserving, socio-economical area development. Today, 'Vollkoren', is acknowledged in Amsterdam, by the authorities also, as being the prototype for the new approach.

The vollkoren Group, resulting out of a resident's initiative against the demolition of a row of old houses to make way for a new parking-house then took advantage of the devaluation of properties connected with the revision of the usage plans and bought three houses with fifteen apartments. This new agent association called itself Vollkoren because their baker, previously landlord of two of the houses, joined them, selling them his property so as to be able to concentrate completely on his handiwork. He would not have been able to comply with the construction impositions for the renewal and enlargement of his specialist bakery on his own, nor produce the high rents for premises anywhere else.

Until the still hoped-for legislation for urban renewal corporations, 'Vollkoren' is constituted as a Civil Rights Association and is controlled by its members. All residents may participate and have equal voting rights. There is no profitmaking. In the case of dissolution, any property would go to a similar non-profit organisation. In order to retain public subsidies, the municipal housing authorities have the statutory right to inspect the books. The public support received until now has, however, been modest.

Together with the lowered property prices due to planning revision, it was decisive for the financing that a building contractor in concealed unemployment appeared, as preliminary financer and that an architect who was enthusiastic about the agent idea took over the planning and execution cheaply.

The residents, tradesmen and craftsmen are tenants in their own agent's association.

As the apartments were left intentionally under management control of the city of Amsterdam for demonstration effects, each tenant must have a certificate from the housing authority showing right of residence and accordingly, tenants' incomes must not exceed a corresponding eligibility line.

Through the cessation of differing interests between landlord and tenant it becomes quite normal that tenants take over certain simple maintenance jobs or also extra modernisation in the houses, themselves.

SUMMARY

Conventional housing policy, is busy ensuring the necessary living space in a spatially, temporally, constructionally and socially acceptable way within the industrialisation and urbanisation process, at the same time resolving politically, arising conflicts of interests, toward compromise.

There are several reasons to suggest that the industrialisation and urbanisation processes can no longer stretch their external economical, ecological, social and cultural borders just as they would like. Adaptation to a very selective growth but, above all, the development of a modern livelihood economy seem necessary and confront housing policy with new tasks.

A growing need for space in the home and vicinity of the home is to be expected. The conventional patterns of compromise will no longer serve to cover this need for space, nor to meet the new problems of distribution and segregation conditioned by the development on the labour market. Conflicts of interests between demand on the one hand (tenants and owner-occupants) and supply on the other (landlords and mortgage banks, property owners as well as construction agents) cannot, in face of growing demand and falling income, be worked out with the help of inflation, as was the case until now.

On one side it will be necessary to give support to the residents themselves in the development of multi-functional agency forms (housing provision and other services and goods productions of the livelihood economy), to acquire a successor to the traditional landlord. On the other side, it will be impossible to avoid the chance of profit in financing and property sales having an effect on the incomes development of residents, which at present would be tantamount to a price freeze; and tenants will, of necessity, participate in development and management.

If these assumptions are correct, then the English Co-operative Housing Association and the Netherlands' Stadsverniewings-corporatie described above, are exemplary for the new agent forms now needed : both as successors to the traditional landlords and as agents for the establishment of a neighbourly livelihood-economy. They result from initiative groups : squatters in Great Britain and Krakers in the Netherlands, who, over a period of ten years, have drawn the attention to functional weaknesses in the traditional rented housing market with their squatting campaigns and who, with illegal means, have paved the way for a fruitful reform policy. It is to be hoped that in this country also, the conflicts over the weakness of certain sections of the rented housing market, brought into the open by Instandbesetzer - maintenance occupiers, can be translated into reforms.

Now that the manner of functioning of the new foreign agent forms has been described in a comparative study which has just been finished, the following two central assumptions are to be examined in the investigation planned : (a) The need for successors for the various rented housing agents and (b) the necessity of a modern livelihood economy needing especially agents for neighbourhood facilities.

NOTE

Paper presented at the "European Meeting on Applied Urban Research", Erren. Oct. 2-4, 1981.

TWELVE

David C. Thorns

Housing Policies and the Influence of the Growth of Owner-Occupation in Social and Political Change

The policies of the state in Western capitalist societies are shaped by the contradictions and conflicts between different fractions of capital and different class interests. The configurations of interests and conflicts are not static but change over time and are shaped by both internal and external social processes. It is important, therefore, in any analysis of state policy to give some consideration to the structure of state organisation and allocative mechanisms within the arena of policy being considered. It is also important to see the role that particular policies play in respect to the main activities of the state. These activities can be viewed in relation to the need for the capitalist state to create conditions favourable to the growth of capitalist enterprise, to ensure the reproduction of the labour force and to confer legitimation upon activities. (Forrest and Lloyd 1978). A further dimension along which to judge policy is in relation to whether the policy is designed to assist in the production or consumption spheres. Increasingly through the 1960's and into the 1970's the requirements of the capitalist economy for increased output and profit have had severe consequences for the development of what is often called unproductive state expenditures. By this is meant the expenditure by the state upon health, housing, education and social welfare (Castells 1976, Harloe 1980 a & b, O'Connor 1973).

The three countries under consideration, UK, Australia and New Zealand occupy differing positions within the international division of labour which has had implications for the pattern of economic restructuring pursued in the 1960s and 1970s. Britain has been part of the metropolitan 'core' nations whereas Australia and New Zealand have been part of the 'dominion' capitalist group (Armstrong 1978), Ehrensaft and Armstrong 1978).

The governments of the 1960's, of all political persuasions, began to move to a more active interventionist policy to restructure economic activity through deliberate economic planning. One result of this was that the alliance established between capital, the state and labour which formed the basis of the post war welfare policies became progressively eroded. The result was the progressive shift from a full employment, demand management welfare economy to one based more firmly upon monetary control and intervention to aid the re-organisation of productive capital.

It is within this general context of economic restructuring that housing policies need to be located and their results assessed, and the implications for social, economic and political change analysed. In all three cases examined the most significant feature of the housing policies pursued in the 1960's and 1970's has been the centrality of the support for owner occupation. In Britain this is of a more recent origin than in either of the other two societies where both levels of owner occupation and supports for this tenurial system have been considerable for a long period. New Zealand, for example, had over 50% of its households in owner-occupation in 1914 (Whiteley 1979). The policies adopted, however, to achieve owner-occupation have not been identical and it is, therefore, valuable to explore the nature of these policies and the structure of the complex institutional superstructure of credit and service agencies which have grown up around home ownership and which form a major set of interests.

HOUSING POLICY CHANGES

The major shift in housing policy in all three countries has been one in favour of home ownership as the main form of tenure and towards increased private sector activity to attain this end. This has resulted in a reduction in the rental sector. This initially affected the private rental sector but increasingly it has affected the state sector as well, as this sector of the housing market has had its role redefined to one of providing last resort accommodation rather than an alternative to privately provided residential accommodation. It is useful to briefly document the main policy shifts identifiable in the three countries and then attempt to drawn out the areas of similarity and difference.

United Kingdom

The immediate post 1945 years were ones of public sector expansion for renting, however, after 1950 the emphasis changed to one of private construction for sale. Thus by the end of the 1970s private rental made up 10% of all households, owner-occupiers 52% and public rental 35%. Post war housing policy therefore shows the growth of supports for private owner-occupation both at the level of institutional support through the growth of financial institutions and at the level of state activities through regulations and tax concessions. The re-structuring of the 1960s led to reduced state activity in housing and a withdrawal of support for public rental housing and an emphasis upon private urban rehabilitation policies.

Australia

In Australia the public rental stock is small, varying between 6-14% by State. The main thrust of housing policy has always, therefore, been into private owner-occupation which contains 65% of all households. The policy of the new federalism in the 1970s has required individual Australian states to fund a greater part of their housing programmes with the result of escalating costs and a narrowing range of housing opportunities (Cass 1980). The housing policies have, therefore, been individually oriented where the costs and benefits accrue to individuals with the public role being to supply only residual needs.

New Zealand

New Zealand has presently 69% of all households in owner-occupation and as in Australia a small public rental sector (9%). The most significant facet of the New Zealand case has been the existence since the mid 1930s of the State Advances Corporation which provides mortgage finance to first home buyers purchasing new properties (for the most part). This forged an important link between state loans and new construction. Changes in the 1970s have begun to re-shape housing policies through lessening the role of the state in housing and encouraging a more active involvement of the private financial sector. The result of this has been the reduction in housing construction and a limitation of the housing opportunities of the lower income groups.

The policies pursued in each of the three countries examined show how in each case the post war period was one where there was an initial input of state finance into public housing but as the 1950's progressed this commitment weakened. The role of housing policy thus becomes increasingly one of underpinning the private market, encouraging owner-occupation by tax and other incentives and of residualising the state's role in housing to that of accommodating those groups who are unable to buy their own houses. This is underlined by the fact that all three have at the end of the 1970's policies to encourage public authority tenants to buy their houses. A policy which will reduce the amount of public rental housing. Allied with the growth of homeownership in the post war period has been the growth of home financing institutions.

ACCESS TO HOME OWNERSHIP

The development of home ownership housing policies places an emphasis upon the role of market allocation. Housing resources are allocated through a market process in which individuals seek housing within sub-markets. These sub-markets are structured by the supply of finance, the level of construction and the system of town planning in operation(Smith and Thorns 1979). The capacity of individuals to acquire housing becomes a crucial variable and this is shaped by their access to housing finance, the level of wealth accumulation they have achieved through previous home ownership or inheritance and the income level of the household. Within this structure of market allocation there are key actors and institutions which play important roles. These are the mortgage lenders (i.e. Building Societies, Banks, Insurance Companies and Public agencies) and the real estate speculators and other housing and planning professionals (Lawyers, finance managers, housing officers of local bodies, town planners etc.) (Bassett and Short 1980).

There exists considerable diversity in the financing of home ownership in the three countries being examined. In the UK one set of financial institutions, the building societies, control 80% of the home finance market and within this group five societies have, by the end of the 1970's, achieved market domination. The significance in political and economic terms of the Building Societies within the UK can be seen in their privileged tax position and in the close relations they have had with successive governments through the 1970's. In Australia the dominant lending institution is that of the savings banks. The government has not played a prominent role as a direct lender, rather it has assisted the financial institutions through tax incentives for home savings schemes and tax concessions on home loan interests payments. One of the most significant shifts which affected the provision of public housing was the decision to change the basis of the Commonwealth State Housing Agreement in the mid 1950's. The Liberal Country party government under the changes it made to this agreement required 30% of Federal money to the State Housing Commissions to be used to assist co-operative societies develop house purchase schemes. The bulk of this money passed to the terminating building societies which were run by the more affluent who were also the chief beneficiaries (Kilmartin and Thorns 1978). Both Australia and New Zealand have encouraged home ownership savings accounts through tax concessions on interest earned on these accounts and with bonus payments. These schemes contain a considerable element of public subsidy and are a further indication of the commitment in housing policy to owner-occupation.

In New Zealand the pattern of housing finance is much less specialised than in either Britain or Australia. New Zealand had until recently few permanent Building Societies, and this group of institutions as a whole only supplied 7% of home finance compared with 28% in Australia and 80% in Britain. The Banking system also only supplied 10%, again in contrast to Australia where this sector provides nearly 60%. The most significant sources of funds for new construction in New Zealand has been the Housing Corporation which has provided around 50% of all mortgage funds for new construction. The second most significant source of funds for new housing is solicitor's funds. These are mortgages raised by solicitors usually from the funds of their other clients, or from estates, trusts and other investments. In respect of the total housing market (including existing housing) the Housing Corporation is less dominant providing overall about 17-18% of the market. The banks, building societies, insurance companies and finance companies all supply around 8-10% of the market and the remainder is supplied by the solicitor's market (Burtt 1979). Government policy since the mid 1970's has been aimed at reducing both the role of government in housing finance and the role of the solicitors and to replace them by corporate financial institutions. This can be seen as part of a wider re-organisation of the economic and financial structure of New Zealand towards corporate organisations with strong links to trans-national capital in both the manufacturing, development of natural resources and financial spheres. The development of the home finance industry creates an important set of interests within the structure of capital which are committed to the preservation and extension of this particular tenure structure. This is particularly true for the Building Societies in the British context as their business is almost entirely tied up with home loans. Thus the Building Societies have been a significant pressure group in the debate regarding both the sale of council (public) housing and the financing of the occupants purchase of their formerly publicly owned properties.

WEALTH TRANSFER

Housing unlike some other commodities has both a use value as a means of shelter and an exchange value (capital value). This means housing can perform both a welfare role and an investment role for both occupants and financial institutions. It is important, therefore, to consider the effect that tenure status may have upon the creation and distribution of the wealth stored within the housing stock (Murie and Forrest 1980, Saunders 1979).

The most significant periods for change within the housing system in respect of shifts in wealth occur during periods when the rate of house price inflation has been in excess of the general inflation rate. During these periods there is a real increase in the value of housing relative to other assets thus the accumulation of wealth in housing is at a greater rate than in other areas of investment. Consequently redistribution of wealth will take place. The 1970's in all three countries were periods when these conditions prevailed for periods of time. There was an initial boom period in the early 1970's and a later one beginning around 1978 particularly in the UK and in some Australian cities but largely absent in New Zealand where this upsurge did not appear until the 1980's.

The increased wealth experienced during these periods by owner-occupiers represents transfers of wealth from other groups. It is, therefore, important to attempt some assessment of which groups are being exploited by owner-occupiers. There are three groups which need consideration. These are firstly those entering the home ownership market for the first time and thus required to pay the new inflated house prices. This group is faced with a growing 'deposit gap' and the necessity to commit an increasingly proportion of their household expenditure to house purchase, at least in the initial years after purchase. The people whose income is insufficient to allow them to accumulate the new higher level deposits are the group who are becoming the housing deprived and are trapped into often unsatisfactory rental housing. The second group are those saving with a financial institution and receiving interest rates which are less than the inflation rate. The funds of this group in real terms is declining at the same time as they are in fact subsidising home buyers. Some of this group will be current tenants saving for home purchase. However, this may only be a relatively small number of the savers. The third group are the renters who live in property with, for them, only a use value, thus they have no means of benefitting from the capital appreciation of the property.

The gains which have accrued to home owners have not been even across all home owners. There have been regions and sub-markets which have made spectacular gains while others have barely kept pace with inflation. Data from the analysis of rates of gain in the countries under consideration suggest that it is the existing, particularly the long established owner occupied households who purchased their housing prior to the booms of the 1970's, who have benefitted most. Further it is those who live in the most affluent, desirable suburbs in the prosperous regions of the country (e.g. London and the South East, Sydney, Auckland) that have received the greatest gains. It has, therefore, been a process of wealth transfer to those already affluent which has reinforced existing class positions and inequalities rather than weakening them. Those who have lost in the sense that their access to housing has become more restricted have been the low income households, particularly those which are single earning family households, one parent families, particularly those which are female headed and aged pensioners who arrive at this status without being owner-occupiers (Cass 1980). The market changes of the 1970's would, therefore, appear to have enhanced the opportunities and accumulative potential of the more affluent existing home owners and decreased the opportunities of those renting and saving for a house by raising both the cost of housing and the cost of house purchase (through higher interest rates).

The increased economic attractiveness of home ownership as a source of income through capital appreciation together with the shifts in all three Governments towards private rehabilitation as opposed to comprehensive urban renewal has a further consequence for the rental sector. This is to increase the attractiveness of selling inner city and inner suburban housing by landlords who are mostly small scale operators with only one or two properties (Kilmartin and Thorns 1978, Kemeny 1980). These landlords are more likely to be attracted by prospects of capital gains than by long term rental income. Therefore, inner city properties become sold, and then rehabilitated either by speculators or residents which raises the value of properties in the area and thus encourages further sales. This process of 'gentrification' (Hammett and Williams 1979) leads to a shrinking of one area of traditional private rental. This coupled with policies for sale of public rental creates severe problems for the low income groups in the population who have problems collecting sufficient money to allow them to move into ownership and who are, therefore, having to wait a long time for public rental. Thus there has been an increase in all three countries of waiting lists for public housing and of homelessness and rental overcrowding.

SOCIAL AND POLITICAL CHANGE

The housing policies of the three countries examined all exhibit strong commitments to owner-occupation at both the level of state policies and at the level of practice with a wide range of schemes to facilitate the growth of this tenure form. The position of owner-occupiers within the class structure has been a source of considerable theoretical debate. Traditional Marxist writing has seen owner-occupation as irrelevant to class relations determined by the relations of production. Such writers dismiss any attempt to view owner-occupiers as a class base. Owner-occupation they see as performing the role of deflecting attention from the class struggle around the means of production and in helping to develop false consciousness by creating the illusion that owner-occupiers have in fact made, through their tenure change, a significant modification of their social class location. This view of the role of tenure has been taken up by other writers who have adopted a more Weberian position. From this starting point property based distinctions assume more importance and it is possible to see owner-occupiers possessing a 'middle class' location within a set of property classes. (Saunders 1979). Owner-occupiers are located between those who derive all their income from the ownership of property, the landlords, and those for whom housing is simply a cost, those renting. Owner-occupiers in contrast to these other groups are able to accumulate income from the operation of both the property market (capital gains etc.) and from the labour market. They, therefore, do occupy a separate position which has the potential to be a basis for class formation.

The argument for a domestic property class necessitates the existence of real benefits to owner-occupiers which are not available to tenants which consequently provides each group with a distinctive set of class life chances. During the 1970's conditions in the housing market were such that these possibilities existed and wealth was transferred to and accumulated by owner-occupiers at the expense of renters and savers. The gains, however, within the ownership category were uneven, which points to the necessity to explore intra class as well as inter class variations. (Thorns 1981, Murie and Forrest 1980, Williams and Forrest 1980).

The extent to which owner-occupation is a significant class base requires the wider context to be examined and the intersections which exist between positions within the domestic property market and the labour market explored to see the extent to which they are mutually reinforcing. The owner-occupiers who have over the 1970's sustained the most gains appear to be those in the higher income occupational groups in the highest cost sub-markets. (Thorns 1981). Access to potential gains through owner-occupation would appear to be far from open, consequently housing market returns are likely to reinforce rather than determine class position.

Differentiation within the group of owner-occupiers regarding capital gains serves to show the complexity of the relationship between tenure status and class formation (Williams and Forrest 1980). Tenure as a factor shaping class relationships may be significant at the class margins where the shift to ownership may lead to individuals adopting more individualistic responses to social changes. This would in part be brought on by the heavy debt burden that accompanies house purchase. Owner-occupiers become caught up in a system of expectations of capital gains from an expanding ownership market. (Agnew 1978). They thus form a potential political base for the continuation of policies to expand and reinforce this tenure form.

Owner-occupation has a marked effect upon labour mobility. Workers who have acquired their own houses during the 1960's and 1970's and are resident in areas which are now facing economic stagnation or decline are likely to be in possession of an asset which is now worth less in real terms than when it was purchased. The costs to these workers of selling their houses - and moving to areas where jobs are available are likely to be high. Prices for house purchase are higher in those areas where economic activity is strong and weakest in the depressed regions. The owner-occupier faced with this situation is much more likely to remain, accept unemployment allowances and attempt to develop the local informal economy (Pahl 1980). These responses are not ones likely to produce a strong class base for political or social action. One consequence of the transformation of the housing tenure structure in England and Wales and the continuation of the dominance of owner-occupation in Australia and New Zealand is, therefore, the tendency towards working class fragmentation. This is the result of regional variations in property and labour market changes which bring real gains to some sections of the middle and working class. Those members of the working class, for example, who obtained housing before the 1970's in the areas where economic activity has been strong during the 1970's have made substantial real capital gains from their possession of domestic property. This accumulation separates them from those workers who have entered the market during the 1970's and often found themselves in a marginal situation and from those who are in rental accommodation. The marginal owner-occupiers are those who either bought old housing, often in the inner suburbs, as the private rental market contracted for those who bought housing in the regions and the cities which are now declining. The fragmentation of class consciousness is functional to the interests of capital and the state during a period of economic re-structuring which requires a redistribution of resources from the welfare state sector to that of capitalist private production. It is thus important to these interests to increasingly portray owner-occupation as a tenure form providing individual private gains.

CONCLUSION

This paper has attempted to review some of the major changes in housing policy in three western capitalist countries which have historically had different patterns of tenure and procedures for housing allocation. The changes that can be identified have partly been a response to the fiscal crisis which has affected all three countries to varying degrees during the 1960's and 1970's and partly as a response to sets of interests which have provided a coalition to support the growth to domination of private owner occupancy as the main tenure form. This coalition is based on financial institutions involved in the financing of the domestic property markets, particularly significant are the Building Societies, Savings Banks, Insurance Companies and

Public Authorities), the real estate professionals (agents, speculators and home builders), and individual owner occupiers who have sustained real gains as a consequence of the tenure structure changes and house price inflation. This coalition of interests has affected the role of the state in public housing policy in such a way that through the 1960's and 1970's the role of the state has contracted to a residual role in housing provision with public housing being seen as a last resort for those groups unable to move into the ownership market. The promotion of ownership is advocated on the grounds that it improves choice for the consumers of housing and allows for a more effective and rational distribution of housing resources than would be achieved by bureaucratic state allocation. The structure of the housing market, however, demonstrates the limitations of this position, in that all housing opportunities are shaped not by choice but by sets of constraints which relate to the individual's economic capacity and the availability of a range of housing in the region in which the household is located. (Smith and Thorns 1979, Clarke and Moore 1980). The strength of a viable public housing policy, as practised in Britain from 1945-50 and in New Zealand from 1937-49, was that it provided a set of real alternatives to all those seeking housing and who for a variety of both social and economic reasons opted for rental rather than ownership. It further provided a greater range of controls over the housing market than currently exist where the intervention of the state is increasingly at the fiscal level rather than in the supply and construction of housing. This means that state policies are applied by private financial institutions, who then become through their crucial position in the supply of housing finance, the main controllers of access to housing resources.

NOTE

Paper presented at the "European Meeting on Applied Urban Research", Erren. Oct. 2-4, 1981.

REFERENCES

Agnew, J.A., Market relations and locational conflicts in cross national perspective in Cox, K. (ed), **Urbanisation and Conflict in Market Societies**, London 1978.

Armstrong, W., New Zealand : Imperialism, Class and Uneven Development, **Australia and New Zealand Journal of**

Sociology, Vol. 14, No.3. 1978.
Bassett, K. and Short, J., **Housing and Residential Structure**, London 1980.
Burtt, D., Sources of Housing Finance in **Housing Finance Seminar Proceedings**, National Housing Commission, Paper 3/79, Wellington 1979.
Castells, M., **The Urban Question**, London 1976.
Cass, B.,, **Housing and the Family**, Social Welfare Research Centre, University of New South Wales, Sydney 1980.
Clark, W.A.V. and Moore, E.G., **Residential Mobility and Public Policy**, Beverly Hills 1980.
Ehrensaft, P. and Armstrong, W., Dominion Capitalism : A first Statement, **Australia and New Zealand Journal of Sociology**, Vol. 14 1978.
Forrest, R. and Lloyd, J., Theories of the Capitalist State : The Implications for Policy Research, **Papers in Urban and Regional Studies**, Vol. 2 1978.
Harloe, M., Housing and the State : Recent British Developments in Karn V.W. and Ungerson C. **The Consumer Experience of Housing**, London 1980.
Jessop, B., The Transformation of the State in Post War Britain. In Scase R. (ed) **The State in Western Europe**, London 1980.
Jones, M.A., **Housing and Poverty in Australia**, Melbourne 1972.
Kemeny, **The Myth of Home Ownership**, London 1980.
Kilmartin, L. and Thorns, D.C., **Cities Unlimited** Sydney 1978.
Pahl, R.E., Employment, Work and the Domestic Division of Labour, **International Journal of Urban and Regional Research**, Vol. 4 1980.
O'Connor, J., **The Fiscal Crisis of the State**, New York 1973.
Saunders, P., **Urban Politics**, London 1979.
Smith, B.N. and Thorns, D.C., **Constraints Choice and Housing Environments**. National Housing Commission, Wellington 1979.
Thorns, D.C., The Implications of Differential Rates of Capital Gain from Owner Occupation for the Formation and Development of Housing Classes. **International Journal of Urban and Regional Research**, Vol. 5 1981.
__________, Industrial Re-Structuring and Change in the Labour and Property Markets in Britain. Forthcoming **Environment and Planning 1982.**
Williams, P. and Forrest, R., The Commodification of Housing : Emerging Issues and Contradictions in the Growth of Home Ownership, **Mimeo**. Australian National University, Canberra 1980.

SECTION THREE
THE IMPLEMENTATION OF HOUSING AND URBAN REVITALIZATION POLICIES AT THE LOCAL LEVEL

THIRTEEN

Jan van Weesep

Dutch Housing Policies

Problems and Prospects

INTRODUCTION

Most western countries aim to provide all their inhabitants with adequate housing and a safe and suitable residential environment at an affordable price. To this end, most countries acknowledge the necessity of some form of public intervention in the housing market. In The Netherlands this public involvement has developed from modest production incentives and indirect controls for public health and safety into an elaborate system of intervention : the government sponsors the construction of public housing units and extends construction subsidies to private investors; it controls rents and maintains a system of operating subsidies and rent supplement payments; and it controls the allocation of homes to safeguard a proper distribution of the available housing stock.

In spite of the introduction of these instruments the national housing goal has not been reached. Several population groups are faced with a persistent and growing housing shortage; in spite of changes in the subsidy systems, most benefits of the housing program accrue to the highest income groups; as a result of the financing techniques and recent efforts to stimulate housing construction, future governments will have to struggle with a rapidly inflating housing budget; cost increases are quickly raising the housing costs for some groups beyond a reasonable share of their income. These problems and prospects are rapidly turning the present housing situation into a highly-charged political issue.

GOVERNMENT INTERVENTION UNTIL 1960

The Second World War signalled a fundamental change in the construction and housing involvement of the government. The wartime situation saw the imposition of several temporary emergency controls; after the war most of these were retained to deal with the severe housing crisis that had developed. New construction had come to an almost complete standstill and many homes had been destroyed. The Census of 1947 estimated the housing shortage at 300,000 units. But the war had also left a crippled economy, and economic reconstruction became the government's first priority. To this end, stringent controls were imposed on investments, wages and prices. Low rents were deemed essential to the effort, and thus the rent controls introduced upon the outbreak of the war were prolonged. The government opted for a modest residential construction program, to ease the shortage gradually and to not have to divert investment funds from the production sector (Nota Volkshuisvesting 1972). But even this modest program would not stand a change of success without some compensation for the reduction in revenue due to rent controls. Soon the government resorted to giving low-interest government loans to housing societies for construction of low-income housing and to offering construction cost-reduction subsidies to private investors. Non-subsidized private construction slowed to a trickle. The construction market changed dramatically from its pre-war state : essentially, a free market with very limited public intervention. Only during and immediately after World War I had the instruments of low-interest loans to housing societies and construction subsidies been used to combat a similar crisis, but as soon as was possible this policy had been abandoned (see Figure 13.1).

The construction stimuli proved to be very successful, as the target of an annual number of 55,000 units was surpassed each year after 1952. Occasional rent increases permitted by parliament improved the cash-flow for investors, and the total annual production increased to above 80,000 units by the end of the fifties. A proper regional distribution was safeguarded by a construction quota system for each region based on the magnitude of the regional housing shortage (and later, in an all-out effort to eradicate the housing shortage, on the regional production capacity). But the shortage did not diminish : in 1960 it proved to be exactly as large as in 1947. The changing demographic structure, the decrease in the average family size, earlier marriages, and changing values and aspirations, fuelled by increasing personal affluence, led to a rapid, continuous drop in occupancy rates (from 4.33 in 1947 to 3.88 in 1960, and to 3.0 in 1978), and thus in increasing demands for new construction. As a result the housing shortage became a political issue, both in the public opinion and in parliament, especially when the yearly production targets were set.

Fig. 13.1 : Housing completions by financing sector, 1910-1980.

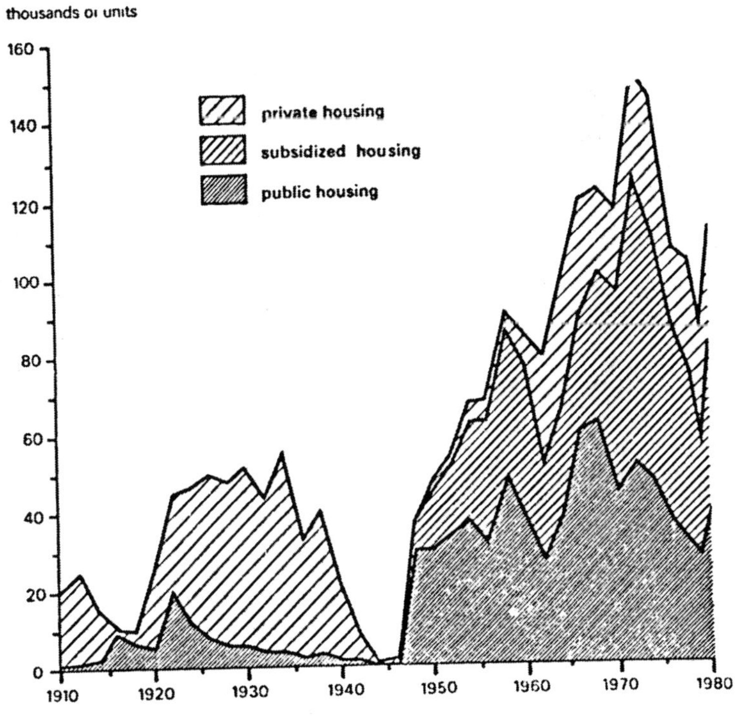

Source : Central Bureau voor de Statistiek.

The rents for existing homes were increased occasionally, but the rents for new homes, set as a percentage of the construction costs, increased more rapidly. In order to keep these rents affordable - and to defuse wage-increase demands - the lump-sun construction subsides increased, until by 1960 they amounted to 63% of all government housing subsidies (Conijn 1980). The gap in housing costs, however, continued to grow. Lack of mobility meant that the housing costs for newly formed households tended to be higher than those for established ones (i.e., lack of filtering of the housing stock).

The allocation of homes was regulated by the local governments; the local regulations were based on national legislation and guidelines from the Ministry of Housing (Adriaansens & Fortgens 1978). Not only were price and allocation of public housing units determined, but all sectors of the rental markets apart from the most expensive were controlled. The instrument for control was the issuing of the residence permit, which could be withheld from any household seeking access to a dwelling for which it would not qualify. Municipalities determined the criteria, administered waiting lists, and set priority rules. The owner-occupier sector was much less controlled than the rental sector. Only newly completed dwellings could be controlled; most directly, subsidized ones. But since the municipality generally acts as the land developer, also the non-subsidized sector could be influenced, commonly through the sale of building lots to residents only. The housing business had turned into a massive bureaucratic system.

ATTEMPTS TO RETURN TOWARD A FREE MARKET

At the end of the fifties, the left-centre coalition that had held political power since the end of World War II ruptured and was replaced by a series of centre and centre-right coalitions that governed the country until 1972. For the public involvement in housing, this power change did not lead to an abrupt policy shift, but the long term objectives were different; namely, to minimize public intervention in housing and return to the free market. This was considered to be attainable only after the housing shortage would have been resolved. To reach this goal, the government production stimuli, the pricing and subsidy systems, and eventually the allocations were all changed.

The construction subsidies were changed from lump-sum contributions to a yearly subsidy over a number of years, until the charged rent equalled the fair market rent. Facilities for the owner-occupier sector were improved. The low-interest loans to the housing societies and the municipalities to construct low-income public housing units were changed to market loans. After an initial increase in government expenditure reflecting the rapidly growing production output, these changes did result in a decrease in the budget of the Ministry of Housing, relative to all public expenditures.

The production soared : it reached 100,000 units completed in 1964 and went as high as 150,000 units in 1972. Private investment flowed freely toward housing, but when this began to falter around 1968, the government immediately increased the number of permits for subsidized dwellings, a policy that had to be resorted to more frequently in later years. The result of the construction boom was a slowly increasing vacancy rate (Figure 13.2), reflecting a diminishing housing shortage in many regions (but not in the cities, nor in the densely developed Western part of the country). It also gave rise to the monotonous residential areas with an increasing proportion of high-rise multi-family structures.

Fig. 13.2 : The number of vacant habitable dwellings, 1966-1979.

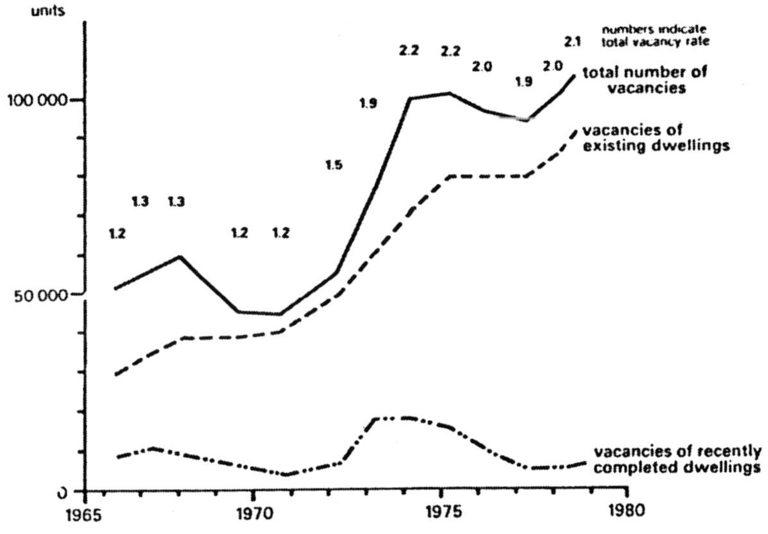

Source : Central Bureau voor de Statistiek

In the areas where the housing shortage had diminished, the rents were decontrolled from 1965 onwards; only to dwellings that were still subsidized and to public housing units the controls remained in place. Along with the price de-regulation the allocation of these houses was decontrolled. But many municipalities in these areas successfully restricted access to the local housing stock to local inhabitants; they could do this on the basis of private contracts as land-developers and of spatial planning legislation that was introduced to limit rapid sub-urbanization (Nauta 1979).

The end of the sixties marked a gradual change in government policies. The government was forced to step up the public intervention to maintain the production increases. The subsidies that had dropped from 4% of the budget in 1960 to 1% in 1968 had to be increased; they grew by an average of 30% per year between 1970 and 1979. The negative side effects of the de-regulation were countered by the introduction of a limited, temporary rent supplement program in 1970. For relatively expensive housing built since 1960, the inhabitants were paid the difference between the charged rent and a percentage of their income (varying from 11%-18% depending on their income position). In the first year of the program 31,000 households (that is, 1.3% of all renters) took advantage of this, and by 1974 this number had increased to 125,000 (that is, 4.7% of all renters). In 1971 a differential program for rent increase was introduced, allowing for extra rent increases for existing homes of good quality, in an attempt to reduce the cost-gap between existing homes and newly completed dwellings, and then to promote filtering. But while the centrist government increased its intervention in the housing market on pragmatic grounds, its 1972 left-centre successor expanded it even further as a matter of principle.

RECENT CHANGES IN HOUSING POLICIES

Two main problem areas were identified (Nota huur en subsidiebeleid 1974). First, while the housing shortage remained acute in the Western part of the country and in the cities, newly completed public housing units stood empty because the low income groups for which they were intended could not afford them. The housing costs could not be brought down due to rising construction costs and, especially, interest rates. An expansion of the rent supplement program was more in line with government policy, since this subsidy can be directed more precisely to the lower income groups. From a temporary adjustment subsidy, the rent supplement program became an essential part of the subsidy system in 1975 (Lucassen & Priemus 1977). Immediately the number of households receiving such payments soared, from 125,000 in 1974 to 318,000 (=11.3% of all renters) in 1975. The budget likewise increased, from 110 million guilders in 1974 to 235 million in 1975, and reached 906 million in 1980

TABLE 13.1

Public expenditures for housing, selected programs, 1973–1980 (millions of guilders)

	1973	1974	1975	1976	1977	1978	1979	1980
Rent supplement program	72.5	110.0	235.0	510.0	596.7	799.0	873.8	906.0
Operating subsidies								
public housing	387.0	491.8	597.1	792.5	968.3	1099.3	1179.3	1241.0
private housing	237.9	297.7	385.0	462.6	453.4	529.0	534.6	475.0
Subsidies owner-occupier units	166.0	210.0	277.0	322.2	402.5	416.4	506.8	483.2
Urban renewal, rehabilitation, home improvement, infrastructure, location subsidies	161.5	256.6	531.4	698.1	776.1	790.4	1213.4	1364.0

Source : Ritzen 1977; Hubner 1979; both publications compiled the data from the budgets of the Department of Housing. The most recent data are underestimates of the real expenditures since they do not include additional programs added in the budget year to compensate for the drop of private investment in construction.

The other area that was addressed by the government was the system of operating subsidies that compensate the investor entirely for his negative cash flow (still allowing a competitive return) in the initial years of operating and then allowing a better than reasonable profit to develop afterwards due to the annual rent increases. The initial rent of public housing subsidies was determined at five per cent of the construction cost. For all other dwellings the rent was set at a maximum of 6.5%, at which the investor would have the competitive return over the economic life of the building. Receiving anything less than this amount in rent, his investment would be covered by an operating subsidy as long as the minimum rate of five per cent was charged. The negative cash flow (or reduced profits) at the beginning of the operating period could be covered by government loans; the result of this is that the private investor is dependent on subsidies and rent increases for a much longer period and the subsidies for rental housing while substantially lower during the initial years increase rapidly in the long run.

The effects of this system showed up clearly after 1976. The initial annual subsidy for a public housing unit in 1978 dropped on average to 777 guilders in 1978 (was 4263 in 1975); for a private rental dwelling it had dropped to 497 guilders (was 3868 in 1975); and for an owner-occupier dwelling it had dropped to 2241 guilders (from 4439 in 1975) (Woningraad extra 1978). But this drop resulted in immediate rent increases for the new dwellings and in rapidly growing long-term commitments for the government regarding operating subsidies and rent supplement payments, stimulated by the escalating construction costs (Figure 13.3) and high interest rates. In the long run the government subsidies would only decrease if sufficient rent increases could be charged to keep up with inflating construction costs. Given the consistently high rates of inflation and the high interest rates, this does not seem guaranteed. Instead, the government budgets are growing rapidly and will continue to do so, in spite of a considerable drop in new construction (Figure 13.3). The changes did imply a shift from operating subsidies to user oriented subsidies. This was considered to be a major improvement, since the subsidies did not redistribute income from higher income groups to lower ones (Table 13.2).

At the same time that the changes in initial rent calculation and subsidy systems were introduced, a number of other changes were made. Instead of a return to the free

TABLE 13.2

The share of housing subsidy programs accruing to various income groups, 1975. All households have been ranked by income from low to high and ten equally sized groups are distinguished (millions of guilders)

	Income groups										
	1	2	3	4	5	6	7	8	9	10	Total*
Rent supplement program	41	36	41	19	12	8	3	3	5	2	170
Operating subsidies	45	39	50	50	115	80	122	145	178	113	937
Subsidies owner-occupiers	0	1	2	3	5	15	18	34	32	30	140
Imputed rent benefits	36	76	73	92	132	177	199	241	394	861	2281
Transfer taxes (costs)	-4	-4	-9	-29	-25	-62	-41	-80	-118	-187	-559
All programs combined	118	148	157	135	239	218	301	343	491	819	2969

* The study was based on samples. The total is not equal to the actual expenditures according to the budget, but the proportional shares are approximately correct. The results can be interpreted as an indication of the proportions of the benefits accruing to each group. It should be noted that the amounts in the table are estimated based on the sample and thus subject to sampling error. Due to varying sample sizes for each group, the standard errors are unequal.

Source : Ritzen et al., 1977.

market by lifting restrictions in specific regions, some generally applicable changes had to compensate for some of the problems that had developed over time. Allocation restrictions were lifted for all expensive dwellings, both rental and owner-occupier units, throughout the country. The government still determined the initial rents of all public housing units and subsidized units - both of new completions and of extensively rehabilitated dwellings - and to these the maximum allowed annual rent increase was applied for five consecutive years. After that period rents would be determined in negotiation between owner and tenant, subject to the general guidelines. Depending on quality, a fair rent can be derived from a table listing quality points for a large number of characteristics and zero-points (no increase) for serious deficiencies. Finally, some major changes were made with respect to the policy for the owner-occupier sector.

The left-centre government saw homeownership as a mechanism to increase the housing options for all income groups and aimed to develop low-income owner-occupier dwellings. A new category was introduced that could only be bought by households with a low income. The major concern was to keep these units available for low income households, i.e., not to provide the initial occupants with windfall profits upon selling the home. Various restrictions have been introduced in the form of a private contract between the initial buyer and the sponsor of the homes (the building societies and other non-profit developers of public housing, using the same government-provided construction loans as for public rental units) which keep the home in the low price range for ten years.

The reaction to the changes was severe; rapidly the private investment funds for residential construction dried up and the construction rates dropped considerably (Jacobs 1978). At the same time the public expenditures for housing did not decrease in spite of the drop in construction; this is explained by the frequently expanded programs for public housing and the increasing interest rates. The rising interest rates cannot be charged to the renter by increasing the rent beyond the norm; since they are to be paid by the non-profit owner in full (for lack of tax deductions), they in fact have to be borne by the government in the form of higher operation subsidies. Affected is not the demand for new rental units, but the public expenditures.

Figure 13.3 : Development costs of new public housing units, 1953-1978.

Source : Centraal Bureau voor de Statistiek.

PROBLEMS

The period since World War II has witnessed major changes in the price of housing and in the subsidy system. The government intervention changed in response to the changing situation and varied with the political ideas of the alternating coalitions. The price of owner-occupier dwellings has increased throughout the entire period, until recently. Till around 1974 the price increases were more or less equal to the increases in construction costs and wages. But then they exploded, and for a number of years they rose some thirty per cent faster than the cost of new construction and wages. In 1979 this trend changed sharply; prices at first stabilized and then decreased. In comparison with the price of re-sales, the cost of new housing constructed with government subsidies has lagged behind, giving the owners substantial appreciation profits, and thus reducing their housing costs. At the same time, this ran counter to the government objective of providing subsidies to keep owner-occupier units affordable for lower income groups. Sale restrictions on the less expensive dwellings in this category have somewhat improved the situation. The housing costs of owner-occupiers have somewhat increased due to the high interest rates since 1973. But the tax regulations provided a hedge against rapidly increasing costs, and non-moving owners are hardly affected; for those that did move, the capital gains more than compensated for the higher financing costs. In all, the cost increases of owner-occupier units has only substantially affected the costs for new homeowners and has drastically reduced the possibilities for entering this sector (Van der Schaar 1981).

The renters have had comparable experiences. One to slowly increasing rents from 1950 till 1967, the rents decreased relative to the inflation rate. Since 1967, however, the rents have increased faster than the cost of living index. Not accounted for are the rent increases due to substantial home improvements and rehabilitation. Also, secondary housing costs have inflated rapidly due to sharply increasing energy costs. Thus the housing costs for non-moving renters remained reasonable, but those who took up residence in a newly completed dwelling had to face the consequences of the increases in construction costs. These rents have increased since 1969 at a faster rate than the cost of living increases, resulting in a growing gap between the rents of the older stock and the cost of new rental units. Since the lower income groups are disproportionately represented among the renters in the public housing units, they face a greater than average increase in housing costs; there, the maximum rent increases are applicable, and the public housing stock has been rehabilitated to a larger degree than the privately owned rental stock (Van der Schaar 1981).

Figure 13.4 not only sketches the development of rents and construction costs relative to the cost of living and wage increases, but also demonstrates the difference in experience and relative position of older and younger households. Older households, used to the relative cost structure of around World War II, have seen their incomes grow rapidly compared to the cost of living and rents. For younger households, the relative positions of costs and income around 1960 (or later) are more applicable. From this section of the figure, it can easily be inferred that their increase in affluence has been much less favourable. Of course, these relative positions only apply to non-movers. Any household that moves to a new home will be affected by the much higher initial rent sum and by subsequent increases. Also, since extra rent increases can be charged for high quality dwellings once these become vacant, it can easily be seen that a substantial tenure discount accrues to non-movers. This is the basic reason for the failure of filtering policies.

The recent problems in the housing market have forced the government to adapt its policies. The strong emphasis during the second half of the seventies on owner-occupier dwellings has made the construction program more vulnerable to the changing economy. The gloomy income expectations and the increased interest rates have decreased the number of housing starts considerably. This led to increasing unemployment rates of construction workers and forced the government to increase its public housing construction program of rental dwellings. There are, however, budget limits, and at the same time the government faces an exploding budget for operating subsidies, even without the necessary changes in the construction programs. But these have to be increased frequently to compensate for the disappointing rate of private investment in housing. There is still a considerable housing shortage, and the demand requires a minimum annual construction program of 100,000 and a maximum of 125,000 units throughout the eighties. Without such construction rates the situation would rapidly deteriorate. Public response to the continued housing shortage and to the gloomy prospects has been very negative. The squatter movement which grew rapidly throughout the latter half of the seventies is but one signal of this public disenchantment, but it has drawn much attention. Because of the often violent clashes between the squatters and their supporters versus owners of buildings and the police, it has certainly turned the housing question into a highly charged political issue.

PROSPECTS

It will be difficult to design a policy that will solve the housing crisis without major conflicts between population groups. The government will not be able to expand its budgets for housing subsidies indefinitely. Re-targeting of the present subsidies seems to be the only solution, but of course this will lead to conflicts with severe political repercussions. From Table 13.2 it can be derived that the present subsidies, even disregarding the income benefits from the tax deductability of mortgage interest payments, accrue mainly to higher income groups. Also the housing costs are unequally distributed (Figures 6 and 7). Both among renters and among homeowners the housing costs of the higher income groups are substantially below those of the lower income groups, when expressed as a percentage of spendable income; at the same time the quality of their housing is higher.

Fig. 13.4 : Development of selected indices, 1940-1980

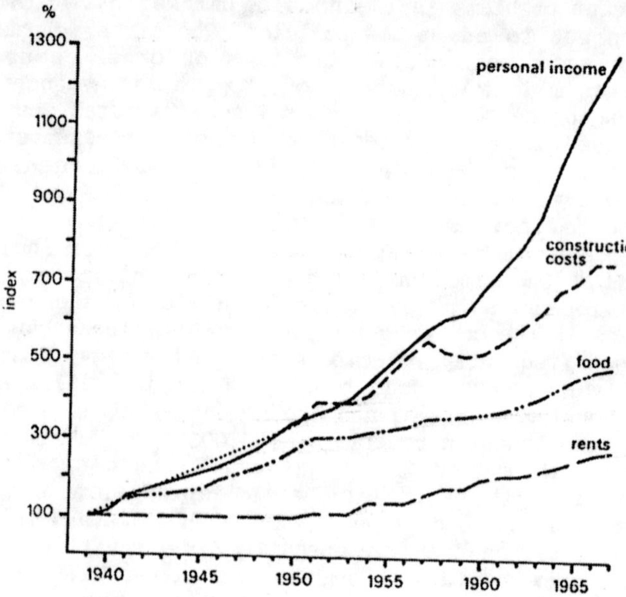

(1939-100)

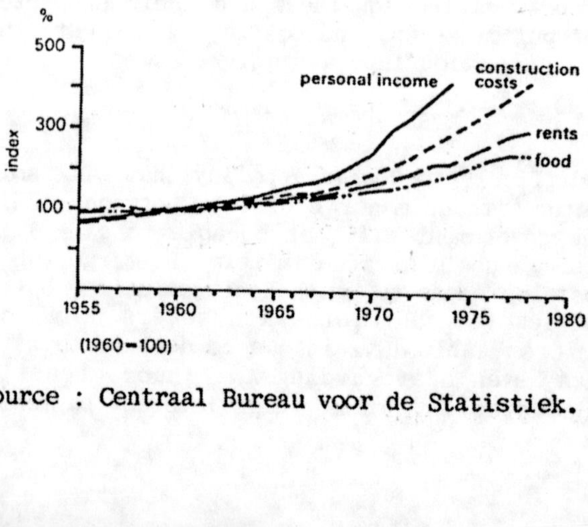

(1960-100)

Source : Centraal Bureau voor de Statistiek.

Fig. 13.5 : Net rent quote by income group, 1977.

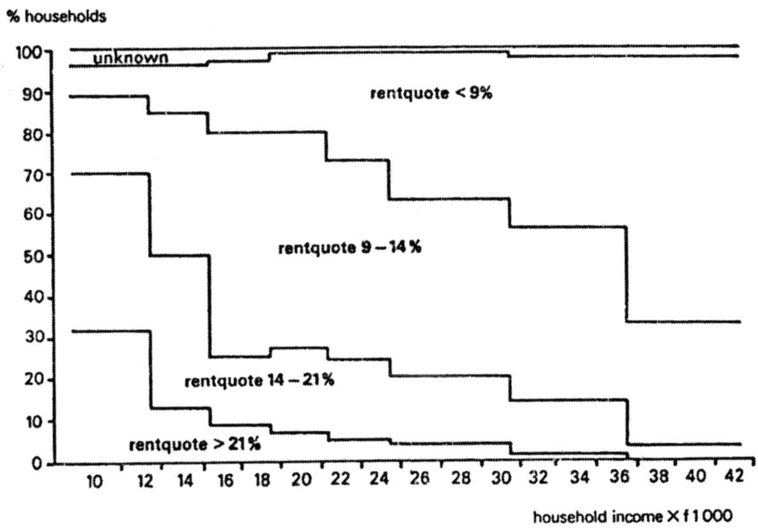

Source : Van der Schaar 1981.

Fig. 13.6 : Mortgage costs before tax deductions as percentage of income, by income group, 1977.

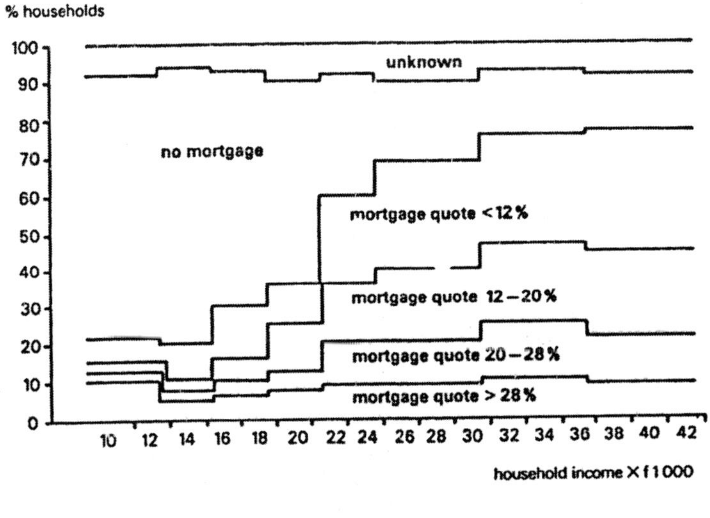

Source : Van der Schaar 1981.

Redistribution of housing costs through further changes in the subsidy system and through taxation policy could take place, given the existing distribution of housing costs. This could generate substantial funds for better targeted aid to households presently suffering from the housing shortage and the high costs for housing. Cost reductions in new construction are also of great importance. A reduction in housing quality standards, or a more diversified construction program which takes advantage of the different housing needs of the various stages in the life-cycle, would only result in the desired effect if filtering of households can be guaranteed. A reduction in interest rates paid for housing investment could only succeed if the freedom of investment were to be restricted; this, however, could easily increase the flow of capital to foreign destinations and would negatively affect foreign investment in the Netherlands. It is easy to see that the housing question will continue to be one of the most hotly disputed issues in the politics of the Netherlands.

NOTE

Paper presented at the "European Meeting on Applied Urban Research", Erren. Oct. 2-4, 1981.

REFERENCES

Adriaansen, C.A. & A.Ch. Fortgens, 1978, **Volkshuisvestingsrecht**, Kluwer, Deventer.

Conijn, J.B.S., 1980, Achtergronden van de stijging in woonsubsidies. In : **Economische Statistische Berichten** 1980, Nr. 3284, pp. 1376-1379.

Hubner, T.K., 1979 De volkshuisvesting in de rijksbegroting 1980. In : Stedebouw en volkshuisvesting 60, Nr. 12, pp. 605-608.

Jacobs, A. 1978 Huur en subsidiebeleid schuld van terugval bouwproduktie? In : **Bouw,** Nr. 26, pp. 36-37.

Lucassen, C.T.J. & H. Priemus, 1977, **Individuele huursubsidie, evaluatie vaneen instrument van volkshuisvestingsbeleid.** R.I.W. Instituut voor Volkshuisvestingsonderzoek. Staatsuitgeverij, s-Gravenhage.

Nauta, A., 1979, **Inventarisatie toewijzingsregels.** Deel 1 : Methodische inleiding op het onderzoek. Rapport 6024, Stichting Bouwcentrum, Rotterdam.

Nota huur en subsidiebeleid, 1974, Tweede Kamer der Staten-

Generaal, Zitting 1974-1975, 13025. Staatsuitgeverij, 's-Gravenhage.

Nota volkshuisvesting, 1972, Tweede Kamer der Staten-Generaal, zitting 1971-1972, 11784, Nr. 1. Staatsuit geverij, 's-Gravenhage.

Ritzen, J.M.M. et al., 1977, **Profijt van de overheid.** Sociaal Cultureel Planbureau, Cashier 12. Staatsuitgeverij, 's-Gravenhage.

Schaar, J. van der, De sectorindeling en visies op de volkshuisvesting. In : **Gebouwde omgeving; gebruik, beheer en inrichting.** Staatsuitgeverij, 's-Gravenhage, 1981 pp. 155-208.

FOURTEEN

Erwin Zimmermann

The Implementation of Public Housing Policy in Switzerland

INTRODUCTION

The research note presents selectively some major findings of an ongoing research project on implementation of Swiss Federal Housing Policies during the years 1965 to 1976. Despite serious doubts about the existence of clearly stated policy goals, (Mayntz, 1980) implementation research is concerned with identifying policy and implementation failures and with pointing out the reasons which might be responsible for such failures. This is what we have done during the first by now concluded phase of our research.[1] Three specific kinds of analyses have been undertaken in order to catch the entire policy process :

(1) A qualitative analysis of the policy formulation and adoptation process and its content.

(2) A quantitative analysis of determinants of effective policy implementation in the twenty-five Swiss Cantons.

(3) An empirical analysis of all public housing operations in the Canton "Vaud".

The presentation of the findings we propose here is highly selective and we do not intend nor pretend to demonstrate their empirical validity in any considerable detail. It is however our intention to stimulate substantive exchanges among European housing policy analysts.

GOALS AND OBJECTIVES OF SWISS HOUSING POLICIES

Swiss National housing policies[2] became quite important during the Second World War. Rent controls like other price stops are intended to prevent massive monetary inflation in times when housing production levels are low.[3] Progressively, however, other measures are set up to protect tenants against unjustified resiliations of leases by land lords. By 1942 housing construction sharply declines and unemployment increases. For the first time in its history the Swiss Confederation intervenes by the means of special capital outlays in order to increase the volume of housing construction in general. The Federal policy is to stimulate the building industry, to create jobs for the unemployed and to avoid important housing shortages. During this period, subsidized housing construction exceeds by far that financed exclusively by private capital.

At the end of the War, housing construction by private promoters becomes again very important and opposition to State intervention into the housing market grows. Subsidies for low income housing construction projects are abolished by 1949 and general rent controls by 1954. Rent controls remain effective for old housing built before 1946. Legally permitted maximum rent levels are however, raised at several occasions. But despite the considerable private housing construction activity, increasing urbanization in the mid-1950s leads to important housing shortages in urban areas, especially for families with moderate and low incomes. As a consequence, a new federally subsidized housing construction policy is initiated by 1958, but fails to a large extent in getting implemented.

Private housing promoters and the political right blame the still remaining rent control measures for insufficient returns on capital investments and thereby for existing housing shortages. They argue in favour of a complete liberalization of the entire housing market. By contrast, tenant associations and the political left maintain that, given observed shortages, rent controls are necessary to protect tenants against unjustified rises. They further consider that the free housing construction market is unable to cover housing needs for low income families and for elderly and physically or mentally handicapped persons.

Under these conditions, any federal housing policy of the 1960s has to accommodate the two opposing political tendencies. Indeed, each of the two political coalitions is sufficiently strong to oppose successfully any policy which would fail to take into account the main interests of both parties. A national Commission of housing experts and politicians is set up in 1958 and succeeds after long years of laborious consultations with economic, social and political interests groups in elaborating the basis of a new global housing policy. In its essential characteristics the political compromise put forward by this Commission enters the Federal Housing Act adopted by the Swiss Parliament in 1965. We have analyzed elsewhere in detail the policy formation process (Bassand, Chevalier, Zimmermann, 1981) and want to limit ourselves to a brief description of the three kinds of policies stipulated in the 1965 Housing Act (see Figure 14.1).

FIG. 14.1 The Swiss Housing Policy in 1965–Goal and Policy Objectives

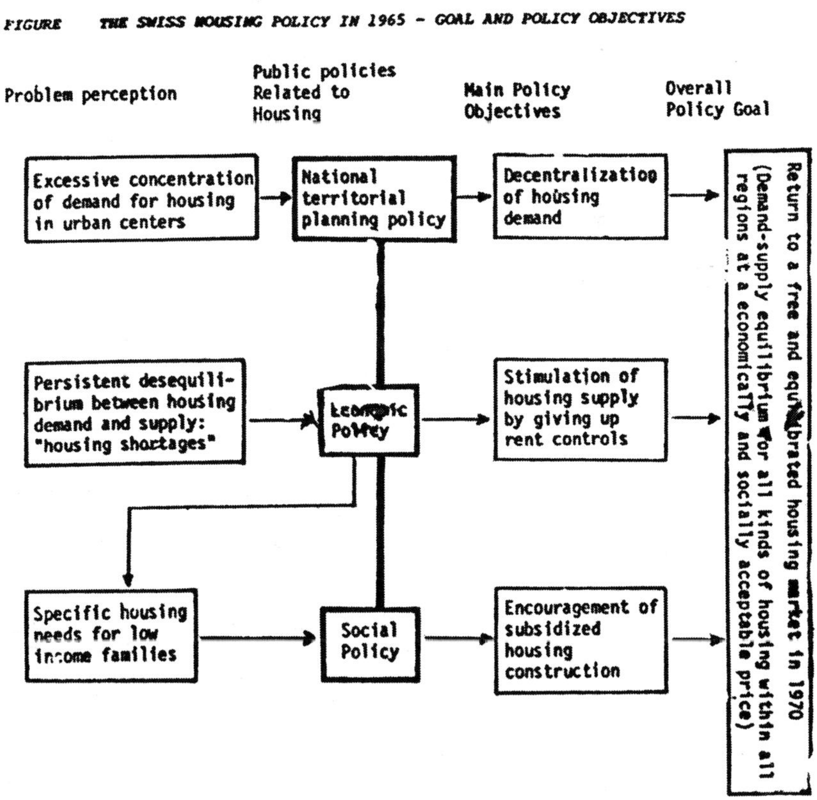

The overwhelming policy goal aims at returning to a free and equilibrated housing market by 1970. National territorial planning, economic and social housing policy are to contribute their specific shares to the realization of this goal and form a rational and well integrated set. The policy stands as a logical and not a political necessity. In fact, however, the political compromise between the right and the left presides over the problem perception and the formulation of policy objectives. The terms of the political exchange are quite simple : the left agrees that rent controls be loosened and progressively abolished by 1970 in exchange for a low income housing construction program as a concession from the right.

For reasons of limited resources, we have chosen to focus our research exclusively on the Low Income Housing Construction Policy as initiated by the 1965 Federal Housing Act and terminated in 1976. This policy recognizes explicitly that the free housing construction market is unable to satisfy socially legitimate needs for adequate housing as far as low income persons and elderly and handicapped people are concerned. Policy incentives are formulated in such a way that low income housing construction can be carried out by the usual promoters operating in the free market. This is done by subsidizing returns on capital investments.

Furthermore, promoters with moderate own financial resources may contract federally secured mortgages with private or parastate banks. The availability of land is to be increased by the means of national territorial planning. In exchange for these favours, public housing operations are subject to a few limiting conditions : (1) total construction costs cannot exceed a certain legally fixed maximum amount per apartment, (2) apartments are to conform to minimal surfaces for rooms, (3) a tenant's income may not exceed the sextuple of rents and in no case be higher than 24,000 Swiss francs (Base = 1965), and (4) rents are strictly related to effective costs and cannot be raised in accordance to the upward trend in the free market.

If the low income housing construction policy is to be implemented by the usual promoters of the construction market, Cantons[4] play a very important role in complementing federal policy incentives. For the Federal Housing Act to be effective, Cantonal legislators have to enact their own legislation. Policy incentives and constraints can be strengthened but not weakened. Furthermore, federal subsidies may only be obtained if a Canton's financial contribution to a public housing operation equals at least the amount of the federal contribution (e.g. principle of "fifty-fifty matching funds). Quite a few Cantons have been slow in coming up with their own low income housing construction laws, but only one Canton (Appenzell IR) has never adopted such legislation.

In conclusion, the policy program and policy implementation structures are such that successful policy implementation will mainly depend on two kinds of actors : (1) the attractiveness of policy incentives for housing construction promoters and (2) Cantons and municipalities favourable to low income housing construction. The findings of this macro-implementation process are now presented in this following section :

THE MACRO-IMPLEMENTATION PROCESS IN THE TWENTY-FIVE CANTONS

This section addressed the macro-policy implementation process of federally subsidized low income housing construction for the years 1966 to 1976. The following two questions shall be answered : To what extent can low income housing construction efforts been explained by objective measures of needs for such housing ? How did the public and private sectors react to local housing shortages ? Specifically, I will propose a model to explain the differences in construction volumes for low income housing in the twenty-five Swiss Cantons.

In only one Canton federal subsidies have not been used at all[5]. Appenzell IR refused, indeed, to set up a Cantonal Housing Act necessary for obtaining federal funds. But federal housing funds have profited very unequally to the various Cantons. Depending on the Canton we chose to consider they have allowed to build 1.1 up to 21.3 apartments per 1,000 inhabitants (mean = 7.1 apartment units). How can we account for such striking differences ? The first and most obvious hypothesis is the following : low income housing construction levels can be explained by objective indicators of needs for such housing. This hypothesis, however, empirically is disconfirmed. Low rates of vacant rental apartments — indicating a shortage of housing in general—, and the ratio of "rents-to-wages" for workers do not have any statistically significant relationship with low income apartment units effectively built ($r \leq /.20/$).

We can therefore conclude that the federal housing

policy has failed to be implemented according to needs for low income housing. But, how can we explain this finding ? Figure 14.2 illustrates graphically what we might call the implementation paradox.

Fig. 14.2 : A Hypothetical Model of the Implementation Process in the Twenty-Five Cantons

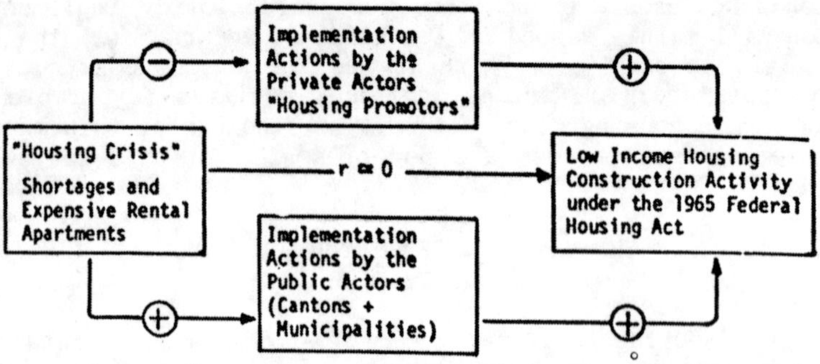

Starting with the right hand side of the figure, let us recall that the low income housing construction activity depends on implementation actions by both the private and the public actors : First, Cantons and Municipalities may be more or less willing to come up with the necessary matching funds for obtaining federal subsidies. Second, private housing construction promoters may respond in smaller or larger numbers to the public incentives and therefore be more or less numerous to build low income housing. We expect, indeed, policy implementation to be most effective in Cantons where both public and private actors have very favourably responded to federal policy incentives.

Let us now ask the question about the factors which lead public and private actors to a more or less favourable response. Our hypothesis is the following :

> The intensity of the "housing crisis" helps to explain implementation actions of both types of actors, but the effects of the underlying housing market conditions are just opposite. We are faced with a implementation paradox.

The following politico-economic theory should apply : (1) For private promoters of housing construction in general the "housing crisis" presents the following advantages : the more intense housing shortages, the higher the rents and profits, and the lower risks for capital investments in housing construction. Under the 1965 Housing Act profit-making possibilities are reduced. By law, only "normal" returns on investments are permitted and potential profits are de facto limited by a mandatory submission to rent controls for the period during with public subsidies are effective. Therefore we expect that private promoters will be least attracted by policy incentives in areas where the local housing market is tense. (2) For public actors (Cantons and municipalities) the situation is quite different. Their actions are subject to local political control. Housing shortages and high rent levels tend to mobilize "citizen-voters" in favour of public housing policies and local political authorities will be put under pressure accordingly.

In short, we have good theoretical reasons to expect that the opposed reaction of public and private actors to identical housing market conditions might help to explain why needs for low income housing remain unrelated to the volume of such housing effectively built. Figure 14.3 shows the results of an empirical estimation of our "path analysis model". The results are to a large extent self-explanatory and confirm quite clearly the implementation paradoxe hypothesis. First, involvement of private promoters and their financial resources is essential in determining the volume of low income apartments built (path 11). But such involvement is much less likely in Cantons in which the local housing construction market is heavily invested by profit oriented building societies (path 8). The existence of such societies is, however, most prominent where rents in relation to wages are relatively high and prospects for high returns on housing investments good (path 4). Second, the importance of general public investments in housing by a Canton and its municipalities determines federally subsidized construction volumes (path 12). These public investments, in turn, depend on a favourable orientation of local political parties (path 9) and of "citizen-voters" towards public housing policies (path 5). The canton's fiscal capacity acts as an important constraint on housing expenditures and has a quite considerable impact (path 10). Let us now turn to a few selective findings on micro-implementation processes in the Canton of Vaud.

Fig. 14.3 : Implementation Process of The Swiss Low Income Housing Policy during the Years 1965-1976 an Empirical Estimation of a Causal Model (Path Analysis)

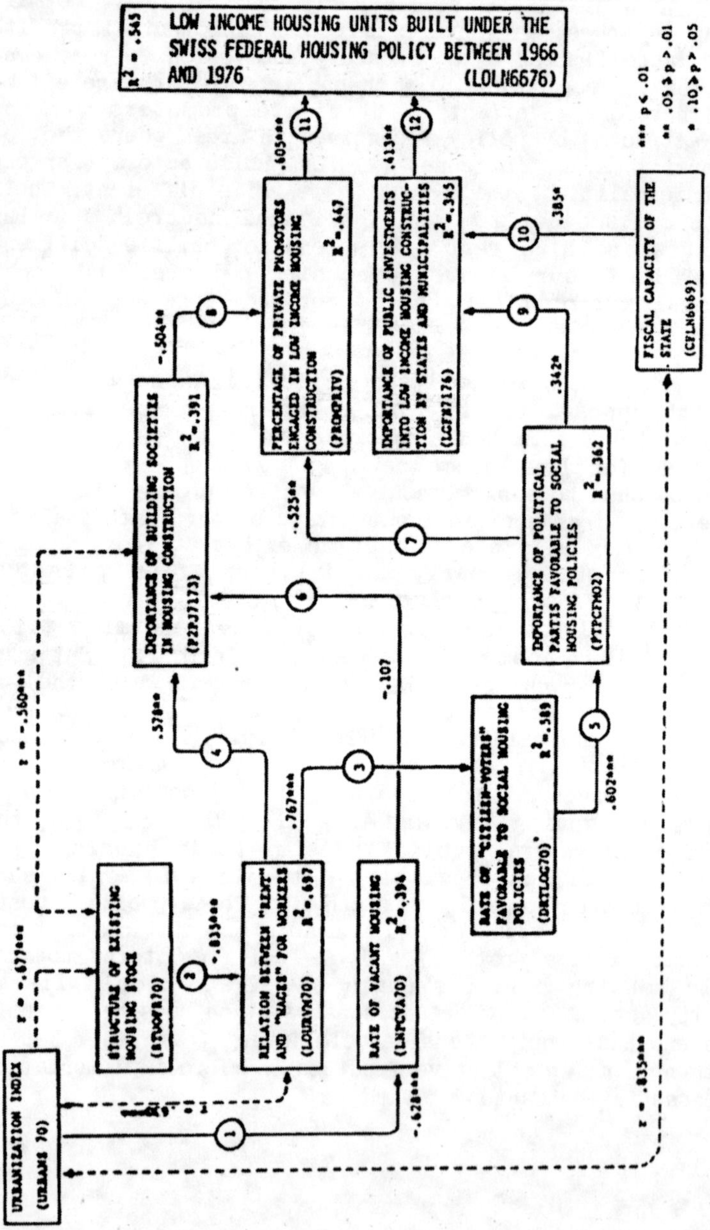

MICRO-IMPLEMENTATION PROCESSES OF LOW INCOME HOUSING OPERATIONS IN THE CANTON "VAUD"

Micro-implementation processes have been analyzed on the basis of seventy federally subsidized housing construction units in one Canton (Vaud)[6]. This Canton is not necessarily representative. Its median position on housing market characteristics and low income housing construction volumes offers, however, a good opportunity for studying in some detail a variety of micro-implementation processes. This part of our empirical research on housing policy implementation led us to extensive statistical analyses from which we want to summarize here only a few major substantive findings. First, we find that the principal promoters of housing in the free market, such as large building societies, housing investment funds and insurance companies have not chosen to respond to public policy incentives as stipulated under the 1965 Swiss Federal Housing Act. These economic organizations did, indeed, not at all engage in subsidized low income housing construction activities. It is common knowledge that wealthy corporate investors often invest only "own funds" and do not rely on any mortgages from banks. In any case, the financial position of these organizations is such that they do not need public securities for bank mortgages. But more importantly, moderate expected returns on investments as well as various public controls over housing operations discouraged them from participating in public housing construction. Second, promoters of public housing construction are found among corporate actors who are able or willing to invest only minimal own financial resources into housing construction : small industrial and commercial firms, housing construction firms, housing and building cooperatives, and last but not least public entities such as larger cities and municipalities. For all these public housing promoters, the realization of profits on investments is not a predominant objective. They are as much motivated by work opportunities (construction firms) and/or low rent housing for themselves (housing and building cooperatives), for their workers (industrial and commercial establishments) and for their constituencies (Municipalities). Third, the chosing of the legal status by public housing promoters as joint-stock companies or cooperatives is not indifferent for the realization of their interests. Municipalities adopt most often the special status of public entities accountable to local governments and legislators. Three types of housing promoters were distinguished : (1) Public entities, (2) Housing Cooperatives and (3) Joint-stock Housing Companies.

All there three of them have participated to almost equal parts in low income housing operations. Fourth, the three types of public housing promoters have a very unequal propensity to build public housing within urban agglomerations where needs for such housing are most evident. The most profit oriented "joint-stock housing companies" refrain from public housing investments in urban areas. Because of legal restrictions on total costs of public housing operations, and high land values in urban areas, investment returns and profitability of urban public housing operations are severely constrained. Fifth, housing operations realised by three types of public housing promoters can be differentiated in terms of the size of building units, housing equipment standards and rent levels as shown in figure 14.4.

Fig. 14.4 : Public Housing Promotors and Selectiv Caracteristics of Low Income Housing Operations

TYPE OF PROMOTOR	*PUBLIC ENTITIES*	*HOUSING COOPERATIVES*	*JOINT STOCK HOUSING COMPANIES*
TYPE OF BUILDINGS	Very large housing units	Small and median size buildings	Large high rise buildings
HOUSING EQUIPMENT	Excellent	Good	Minimal
RENT LEVEL	High	Low	Median

Based on these and other criteria, we have come to the conclusion that public housing realized by housing cooperatives is best suited to the specific needs of tenants with large families and moderate incomes. Constructions by public entities offer some special advantages to elderly and handicapped persons. Joint-stock housing companies show the least satisfactory results. It appears that federal policy incentives have selectively attracted public housing promoters with very limited own financial resources. It can also be shown that not all of these promoters have given equally satisfactory results in terms of the quality of public housing operations which were realized.

CONCLUSIONS

The Swiss federal low income housing construction policy has been successful in that more than 40,000 apartment units have become available for persons and families in need of such housing. How many such apartment units would have been effectively needed remains undetermined. Let us recall only two implementation failures : (1) Public housing units were not built in regions where housing shortages and needs for low income housing were most intense. This implementation failure is a direct consequence of homogeneous policy incentives which were indifferent to local housing market conditions. (2) The absence of the usual promoters may or may not be considered as a failure as such, but it is clear that policy incentives for "marginal" promoters such as housing cooperatives have been too weak to fill in this vacancy.

Are we not rather dealing with policy than implementation failures? Why has the Swiss low income housing construction policy failed to take into account even the most obvious variations in local housing market conditions and characteristics of prospective implementers? Whey were selective and discriminatory incentives not put to work?

The research conducted until now has heavily relied on objective indicators of policy outcomes. The explanation of these outcomes and their shortcomings has been based on several assumptions about interests and resources of private, para-state and public policy implementers. The implementers' interests and resources, as well as collective action around public housing operations have not yet been studied. To do this is the main-objective of the second stage of this research design on implementation of public housing policies, where the bottom up perspective is to become largely predominant. Hence, networks of public housing promoters are to be carefully investigated by the means of in-depth interviews with all individual and corporate actors associated in low income housing operations. Results should provide a better understanding of the application and effectiveness of various negotiation strategies and the combination of specific resources necessary for successful collective implementation action. We also intend to confront individual actors with a variety of policy incentives in order to determine their most likely action. Results of this second part of the study should become directly useful for designing new public housing policies.

NOTES

Paper presented at the "European Meeting on Applied Urban Research", Erren. Oct. 2-4, 1981.

1 Michel Bassand, Gerard Chevalier and Erwin Zimmermann,

La mise en oeuvre d'une politique d'incitation : La politique federale du logement, Research Report, C.E.A.T. - I.R.E.G., Swiss Federal Institute of Technology, June 1981, p. 336. To be published in book form by Georgi-St-Saphorin, Switzerland in June 1982.

2 For a quite detailed historical background on the Swiss housing market and related public policies, see Kleps (1969) and Bindella (1975) as well as numerous publications by the Swiss Federal Office of Housing in Bern.

3 Switzerland's general reputation for wealth contrasts sharply with its very low rates of owner occupied housing compared with other highly industrialized and modernized nations. This rate is around 40% in 1940 and has been decreasing ever since : 37 per cent in 1950. 34 per cent in 1960 and 28 per cent in 1970.

4 In Switzerland "Cantons" correspond to "States" or "Lander" in the federal political systems of the USA and Germany.

5 It should be pointed out that the 40,354 public housing apartment units built between 1966 and 1976 in Switzerland constitute only about 6 per cent of all constructed apartment units.

6 The 70 low income housing operations generated a total of 3199 apartments units. For most of the empirical analyses, housing operations have been proportionally weighted by the number of apartment units they contain.

REFERENCES

Bassand, M., Chevalier, Ch. and Zimmermann, E., 1981, **La mise en oeuvre d'une politique federale du logement, Research** Report, C.E.A.T. - I.R.E.G. Swiss Federal Institute of Technology, June 1981, p. 336.
To be published in book form by Georgi, St-Saphorin, Switzerland in June 1982.

Bindella, R. (ed.), **Schweizerische Wohnungswirtschaft in Gegenwart und Zukunft.** Haupt-Verlag, Bern, Switzerland 1975,.

Kleps, K., Wohnungsmarktpolitik in der Schweiz. Bern, Switzerland : Haupt Verlag 1969,.

Mayntz, R. (ed.), **Implementation politischer Programme.** Meisenheim : Athenaum Verlag 1980,.

FIFTEEN

Frederick A. Lazin and Sam Aroni

The Implementation of Low-Income Housing Policy in the United States

The Case of Section 8 Existing Housing

By the mid-1970's many American scholars, politicians and government bureaucrats consider the federal low-income public housing program a dismal effort.[1] The program failed to build a sufficient number of units to meet minimum needs of eligible persons and frequently constructed poorly designed drab high rises which become segregated enclaves of poor socially marginal minorities fostering social malaise. Public support for the program dissipated and white and black communities throughout the country increasingly opposed new construction for families outside of unattractive areas of inner cities. By the end of the decade rising management and maintenance costs of existing public housing added a further liability to the program.

Citing these and other shortcomings then President Richard Nixon issued a moratorium on new construction in public housing on January 5, 1973. The White House and the United States Department of Housing and Urban Development (HUD) emphasized that the suspended subsidized housing programs were "inequitable, wasteful and ineffective and worst of all ... do not serve the intended benificiary - the poor".[2]

In place of the suspended subsidy programs for low-income housing the Nixon and Ford administrations proposed Section 8 Housing Assistance Program which provided direct rent subsidies to persons whose income was not more than 80 per cent of the median income of the area to rent standard housing in the private market.[3] Rents could not exceed a Fair Market Rent (FMR) set by HUD and tenants had to pay up to a maximum of 25 per cent of their income with the subsidy covering the difference between their contribution and the market rent. Eligible tenants could remain in their present apartments.

The shift in emphasis from a construction to a rent subsidy reflected the central hypothesis of the Nixon position on the housing problem; that it was one of income and not housing per se : "... the principal root cause of families living in substandard housing is plainly and simply a lack of income to afford standard units, either newly constructed or existing.[4]

Critics of the proposed new approach challenged the assumption that the basic problem of 'shelter' for low-income persons was one of income and housing. There was no way, argued the National Association of Home Builders (NAHB) that the "maximum use of the existing housing stock will enable low - and moderate - income families to obtain housing.[5] "... there just is not enough standard housing in the country today to meet the needs of all who need adequate housing."[6] Moreover the likelihood of low vacancy rates nationwide combined with the FMR restrictions, they argued, would undercut the potential effectiveness of rent subsidies in the existing markets.

The moratorium on public housing can also be understood in the context of the New Federalism. Then President Richard Nixon wanted to redress a perceived imbalance of federal relations in the United States. He beleived that the federal government had become too powerful vis a vis the States and local governments, being too involved in "local" affairs. The failure of public housing was seen as proof of the ineffective federal effort to deal with problems which local governments and/or the private sector could handle better. In the case of public housing, however, the evidence suggests that the problem was one of an ineffective national role rather than a federal domination of the program. Since 1937, the local housing authority (LHA), responsible to elected municipal government, has implemented the federal public housing program; it finds sites, arranges for construction, recruits and assigns tenants and manages and maintains units in accord with federal guidelines, supervision and funding. In practice, HUD and its predecessor agencies have been supportive of local efforts to implement the program in accordance with local interests and values regardless of conflicts with federal objectives and guide lines.

A case in point is the experience with racial discrimination and segregation. Despite Constitutional bans and federal regulations to the contrary many LHAs through the 1970s operated the program to prevent racial integration. In a classic case of a "constiuency relation" HUD, who funded and supervised the program, supported and defended the LHAs against critics despite a clear violation of federal law.[7]

Section 8 too provides the LHA with a key role in implementation.[8] It receives an allocation of rent certificates from HUD which must be used in its jurisdiction, screens and processes applicants, issues certificates and inspects units to be leased. In contrast to Section 23, a rent certificate program in operation since 1965, which had the LHA sign the lease, in Section 8 the recipient signs the lease with the landlord. Section 8 therefore grants both the LHA and the private market (landlords) pivotal functions in implementation. Their cooperation and involvement is required to achieve the goals of the program. They have the potential to influence the success or determine the failure of a federal program. The purpose of this paper is to evaluate the effect of the roles given the LHA and private sector on the implementation of the program in Los Angeles, California. It is assumed that in practice, the LHA and market, more so than HUD determine the character and outcome of the program.

The paper is based on a case study on the Existing Section 8 program in Los Angeles from its inception in 1975 thru June 30, 1980.[9] Despite limitations a case study has advantages when compared to research grounded on national samples. Although not necessarily a typical city, the study of Los Angeles illustrates in depth and detail the problems of implementation; of actions and practices taken to overcome the obstacles created by social, economic and political conditions at the local level. In fact, the uniqueness of Los Angeles, in particular its housing market and minority mix, serve to illustrate many of the important issues and problems facing federal low-income housing policy today.

THE FINDINGS

In contrast to previous construction subsidy programs proponents of Section 8 hoped that it would serve more persons, be cheaper, quicker, provide greater opportunities of choice of location, result in less concentration in racially and economically impacted areas and influence interested landlords to make minor improvements in marginal units.

At first glance the Section 8 program and approach in Los Angeles can be viewed as being successful. Public housing had become potitically unfeasible to build since the early 1950's when "the growing opposition to public housing resulted in an ammendment to the California Constitution which required voter approval of all public housing projects."[10] The continued hostile climate of public opinion in California during the 1950's and 60's opposed construction of public housing even for the elderly. In contrast rent subsidies were acceptable and more successful in the City of Los Angeles (HACLA) constructed 8690 units of standard public housing from 1941 thru 1955 and leased over 5000 units of Section 23 from 1965 until the Nixon moratorium in 1973. From 1975 through mid 1980 the HACLA had approximately 12400 units of Existing Section 8 under contract with HUD. In a few years therefore using Section 8 it operated more units than public housing had built in several decades.

A closer examination of the results of the program, however, question the apparent numerical success. Shortcomings are evident and similar to findings of Section 8 throughout the country.[11] First the HACLA had considerable difficulty "leasing up" that is, in utilizing funded certificates to rent existing units. It failed to achieve HUD objectives of renting up each project (a bloc number of units) within a year and having an overall 95 per cent occupancy level.[12] In April 1979, for example, of 12400 authorized units only 10023 were under lease. Thus almost 20 per cent of the allocated certificates were either not being used or the recipients were still looking for units. Throughout the operation of the program, therefore, thousands of rent certificates went unused.

A related problem which persisted from the outset was the leasing of large apartments. The majority of the participants in the Los Angeles HACLA Section 8 program were elderly and or handicapped and small families; few large families participated. The following table illustrates the discrepancy between need (active applicants) and apartments in the program (units under contract).

Even more indicative of the problem was the admission by HACLA in 1977 that of 1760 and 376 certificates it issued since October 1975 for non elderly 3 and 4 bedroom apartments only 241 (13.7%) and 17 (4.5%) contracts respectively had been signed and of these 50 per cent were in place.

TABLE 15.1

HACLA section 8 applicants of units under contract (early 1977).

Status	type and size of family			
	total	elderly handicapped	small family	large family
Active applications	15008	3,837 (25.0%)	6,082 (41%)	5,089 (34%)
Active Certificates	3,174	1,163 (36.6%)	1,230 (38.8%)	781 (24.6%)
Units under contract	3,914	2,668 (68%)	1,012 (26%)	235 (6%)

Third, the program served too few people. Almost from the outset there was a waiting list of 28000 applicants. Early in the program and continuing through 1980, with a few exceptions for the handicapped and elderly the HACLA ceased accepting new applications, thereby denying the estimated hundreds of thousands of eligible persons the opportunity to participate.

Fourth, many of the leased units were marginal and substandard and had not been upgraded, despite HUD regulations that repairs to units not meeting HUD's Housing Quality Standards be performed before "a contract is signed."[13] HUD estimated that as of March 1980 as many as 53% of the units may have difficiencies.

Finally the program did not foster any meaningful or significant movement out of recially or economically impacted areas. The figure of 55 per cent in place units suggests the opposite with most people remaining in their original apartments.

There are several interrelated explanations for the shortcomings of the program in Los Angeles. These include the interplay between market conditions and program requirements, and policies and practices of the HACLA and HUD.

A major impediment to greater success of a program designed to have low-income persons rent units in the private sector were market factors including low vacancy rates, rising rents and the reluctance of landlords to accept low-income families. From the outset, on the basis of low vacancy rates one could predict with some certainty a poor performance by Section 8 in Los Angeles. In testimony before Congress proponents of the proposed legislation emphasized the need for at least a 5 per cent vacancy rate to make the Section 8 Existing program feasible.[14] Yet from the outset Los Angeles had an overall vacancy rate for rental housing well under 3 or 4 per cent and estimated to be under 1 per cent by the spring of 1980.[15] The slow down in new construction of rental units, the high conversion rate to condominiums and the poor condition of at least 20 per cent of the vacant apartments further exacerbated the situation. All of these factors limited the potential workability of the program in terms of number of households served and the possibility of economic or racial integration within large areas of the City.

The FMR similarly limited utilization of many vacant apartments outside of impacted areas because they were too expensive. The FMR involves both rent and utility costs and represents the average rent or authentic mean. HUD (Washington) computes the FMR for each county for units by bedroom size and for elevator and non elevator buildings. HUD permitted a LHA to grant a 10 per cent exemption above the FMR for 20 per cent of its units. A rate exemption of 20 per cent required special HUD approval. The HACLA received HUD permission to exceed published Section 8 FMR for selected locations in the city.

In the opinion of some in the HUD Los Angeles Area Office the FMR is the average rent for a particular unit size and basically realistic, that is, it works in lots of areas especially those impacted with racial minorities. Others argue that the FMR "is out of date before you print it" because of inflation. Moreover some HUD specialists doubt whether HUD can accurately determine the FMR for a county and question the accuracy of sources on which Washington computes the FMR. If not accurate, out of date or unable to be properly determined then an entire program rests on questionable information.

Finally, landlords prefer as tenants elderly persons rather than families especially in the case of low-income and minority persons. The extremely low vacancy rates, moreover, reduces the economic risks of rejecting families. A larger vacancy rate might move them more flexible.

A possible intervenor was HACLA. Its actions and policies might have offset some of the limitations imposed by market conditions. For example, it could have made a maximum effort to recruit landlords with vacant apartments. In practice HACLA had no outreach program to help eligible clients find suitable apartments—only the handicapped and non-ambulatory elderly received such services. Nor did it recruit potential landlords in a systematic way. With respect to support services the HACLA failed to satisfactorily perform inspection of apartments and recertification of tenants. Unlike Section 23 in which it leased and managed units and sublet them to eligible persons with Section 8 it had less incentive to provide outrearch services. Moreover the HACLA argued that HUD provided insufficient funding to allow it to adequately perform outreach and support functions essential for the proper operation of the program.

Finally HUD too proved to be an ineffective catalyst. HUD who set up the program, funded it, provided guidelines and monitored operations failed to alter or improve the situation. Its actions were limited to repeated criticism and chastisements of HACLA shortcomings, which short of resulting in readjusting meaningless figures, had little positive effect on the operations of the HACLA. HUD did not use its financial resources to effect changes in the HACLA operations of Section 8. Thus the only losers are the eligible persons who will never participate in the program.

RECOMMENDATIONS AND CONCLUSIONS

What recommendations can be made to insure greater success of Section 8 and the overall federal effort to improve the housing conditions of low-income persons : to serve more persons especially larger families, to increase opportunity of choice and to upgrade existing apartments ? First, while not abolishing the current Section 8 Program the government might reinstate section 23 which had the LHA lease and manage apartments in the private market and sublet them to eligible persons. This may increase incentives for the LHA to find housing and implement the program. Despite the element of institutionalization for participants — the LHA signs the lease—the eligible would benefit by an increase in available housing. In practice the American housing market and society make meaningless the formal freedom of Section 8 whereby a participant chooses where to line.

Second, regardless of what programs are pursued HUD should provide adequate funding to enable the LHA to provide satisfactory outreach services to recruit landlords, assist eligible tenants, and inspect apartments. This might enable all concerned to cope better with market conditions.

Third there should be greater emphasis on production or construction subsidies including public housing to help offset limitations of the market and the shortage of vacant standard rental housing which is affordable and accessible to low-income families. Rent subsidies failed to adequately meet the housing needs of low-income persons because vacant units within the FMR limitations were not existent. The shelter problem was as much one of housing as of income. Public housing is possible and desirable means of providing this housing. Even in Los Angeles with its past opposition of public housing, the City has referendum approval to build thousands of units throughout the city with as many as 20 units per site. Production subsidies are also needed to spur private and non-profit construction of low-income housing.

An unanswered question remains whether different HACLA policies and practices could have altered the limitations imposed by the market. It is important to remember that Section 8 was designed to offset negative market conditions by increasing the resources available to low-income persons to obtain decent housing in the private market. But the reality of the market limited implementation in Los Angeles. In practice HACLA policies did little if anything to offset these limitations and thereby improve the success of the Section 8 intervention : there was virtually no outreach to recruit tenants or landlords. It might be that the HACLA lacked the resources to do so. But even if the efforts were made they may not have overcome the limitations imposed by the market : there were too few vacancies, there was little new construction and landlords were unwilling to rent to families under existing conditions. Perhaps more federal resources in the form of larger subsidies are needed to enhance the Section 8 intervention.

What is clear, however, is that Section 8 like its predecessors public housing and Section 23 is a local program. In practice HUD forfeits its influence and supervisory role over the LHA's operation of the program. HUD delegates its authority to the LHA and in doing so allows it to determine policy output and outcome. Evidence of the forefeiture is evident in the case of Housing Assistance Plan (HAP) of the Community Development Bloc Grant (CDBG) application of the Housing and Community Development Act of 1974. This legislation sought to combine several existing community development categorical grants under one application and to end the divorce of "responsibility for overall community development from the responsibility of providing housing."[16] In filing a CDBG application the municipality must also submit a Housing Assistance Plan (HAP) which states housing needs for low-income persons, existing conditions and programs designed to achieve stated goals. Subsequently the city also files annual Grantee Performance Report (GPR) on its progress in implementing the HAP.

A review of the City of Los Angeles's CDBG applications and GPRs from 1975-1980 indicates a failure by the City to deal adequately with low-income housing in general and an ineffective utilization of allocated federal funds for low-income housing including Section 8, in particular. HUD, who processed, reviewed and approved both documents criticized the City's record and pressed to improve the situation or risk having CDBG funds cut. However, year after year despite delays which resulted in revising meaningless figures and statements of housing goals which remained in the opinion of HUD experts "ludicrous", HUD funded the applications. In fact, when an administrative complaint was filed with HUD, challenging further CDBG funds for the City because of its failure to provide low-income housing HUD defended the City and its housing record.[17]

A major improvement on implementing the goals of federal low-income housing policies whether they be public housing or rent subsidies requires a strengthened federal role in implementation. The current political climate in America as well as the balance of power in Washington mitigates against such a direction. Federal low-income housing programs, whether construction or rent subsidies, will remain local in character with local authorities and private interests determining their outcome. What happens in more unitary systems? Is implementation of national housing policies delegated to local authorities and if so what is the nature of the delegation? Does it result in a shift in policy making from the centre to the periphery? In the case of Section 8 in the United States the implementation process transfers policy making or the determination of policy outcome to the local sector, thereby giving it a veto over national housing policies.

NOTES

Paper presented at the "European Meeting on Applied Urban Research", Erren. Oct. 2-4, 1981.

1 Henry Aron, **Shelter and Subsidies** (Washington D.C. The Brookings Institution, 1971, pp. 108-126;

Catherine Bauer, "The Dreary Deadlock of Public Housing, : **Architectural Forum** (May 1957);
Leonard Freedman, - **Public Housing** (NY : Holt, Rinehart and Winston, 1969); Fred Lazin, "Policy Perception and Program Failure : The Politics of Public Housing in Chicago and New York City, "**Urbanism Past and Present**, IX (Winter 1979-80) pp. 1-12.

2 **Hearing on Oversight on Housing and Urban Development Programs**, part I, Before Subcommittee on Housing and Urban Affairs of the Senate Committee of Banking, Housing and Urban Affairs, 93rd Cong., 1st Sess. (1973), p. 3. The moratorium also suspended Sections 23, 235 and 236.

3 30 per cent of the participants within a single jurisdiction had to be lower income, that is, below 50 per cent of the area median income. The program was part of the 1974 Housing and Community Development Act (88 Stat 633).
Richard L. Cole, "The Politics of Housing and Community Development in America" in David Caputo, (ed.) **The Politics of Policy Making in America** (San Francisco, : WH Freeman and Co, 1977), p. 100 and Alexander Polikoff, **Housing the Poor** (Cambridge, MA. : Ballinger, 1978), p. 71.

4 **Hearings on Administration 1973 Housing Proposals**, Before Senate Committee on Banking, Housing and Urban Affairs, 93rd Cong., 1st. sess. (1973). P. 10.

5 **Hearing on Housing and Community Development Legislation - 1973**, part 1, Before Subcommittee on Housing of the House Committee on Banking and Currency, 93rd Cong., 1st sess. (1973), p. 897.

6 **Ibid.**, P. 871.

7 Frederick A. Lazin, "The Failure of Federal Enforcement of Civil Rights Regulations in Public Housing, 1963-1971, "**Policy Sciences** 4, (1973), pp. 263-273 and Philip Selznick, **TVA and Grass Roots** (NY : Harper and Row, 1966), pp. 145-155, 183-184, 210, 290.

8 In the original Nixon proposals HUD and not the LHA would have administered the program. See Polikoff, pp. 68, 69.

9 Fred A. Lazin and Samuel Aroni "The Existing Section 8 Program and the Housing assistance Plans : A Case Study of the City of Los Angeles and HUD, 1975-1980" (unpublished manuscript). This paper does not examine the operation of the Section 8 New Construction and Substantial Rehabilitation Programs.

10 Shlomo Hasson and Samuel Aroni, **Public Housing in Los**

Angeles : A Social Study (Los Angeles : UCLA, SAUP, 1979), p. 25. The first referendum was held in 1975.

11 Margret Drury et. al., **Lower Income Assistance Program** (Section 8) : Nationwide Evaluation ... (Washington D.C. : Office of Policy Development and Research, HUD, 1978). Grace Milgram, **The Section 8 Leased Housing Program : Where are we now?** (Washington, D.C. : Cong. Research Service 1979) : Office of Program Analysis and Evaluation (OPAE) HUD : **Section 8 Housing Assistance Program : Existing Housing, A field Study** (Washington, D.C. : HUD, 1976). See Lazin and Aroni for a complete bibliography.

12 Letter from Don Phillips (HUD LA Office) to Homer Smith (HACLA), June 29, 1979.

13 HUD LA Area Office "Coordinated Review of the Housing Authority of the City of Los Angeles, CA" (March 31, 1980, p. 118 (mimeographed).

14 **Hearing on Housing ... Legislation - 1973**, pp. 559, 575.

15 **Los Angeles Times**, May 19, 1980.

16 Statement by REp. Thomas L. Ashley in **Daily Congressional Record** September 5, 1973, p. 189.

17 Polikoff, pp. 74-76. The findings of this study confirm his point that the link between community development and HAP is illusory because the city is not required to implement the HAP.

SIXTEEN

Horst-Juergen Wienen

The Integration of Parameters of Action for the Local Government of A Big City in the Ruhr Area into the Economic, Political and Institutional Environment

INTRODUCTION

Symptoms and causes of turbulences on the housing markets of agglomeration areas

The "Instandbesetzung", i.e., the occupation of abandoned houses for the purpose of rehabilitation in Bochum and other places, the number of new dwellings decreasing every year, particularly in the agglomeration areas of the Federal Republic of Germany, the poor housing situation of the students of our Ruhr University, the regional asymmetry of housing subsidization which has adverse consequences for agglomeration areas, but also the order of the City Council Commitee of May 30, 1980, to check by a current control of results to what extent the population target figure underlying all special projects calls for a correction, underline at an ever increasing rate the necessity to integrate municipal housing policy into the entire economic-legal and social systems.[1]

Thus, our Office can refer to a report of 1967 on the economic policy of the cities in general[2] so that this time again, the special aspects of housing policy will be stressed. At that time, it was still absolutely questionable whether the cities could at all engage in economic policy. Other writers proclaimed the simple thesis of the "generally recognized" aim of a maximum increase of the social product, a concept which - considering present-day understandings of environment protection problems - seems too simplified a way of thinking. In the field of maintenance and improvement of infrastructures (bases or preconditions for economic activity), though, housing appears as a target of municipal economic policy, being defined quite generally as "shaping measures undertaken by the State or the institutions derived from it or actually competent, in respect of the economic process, economic structure and economic system".[3]

Where is Bochum situated ?

Fig. 16.1

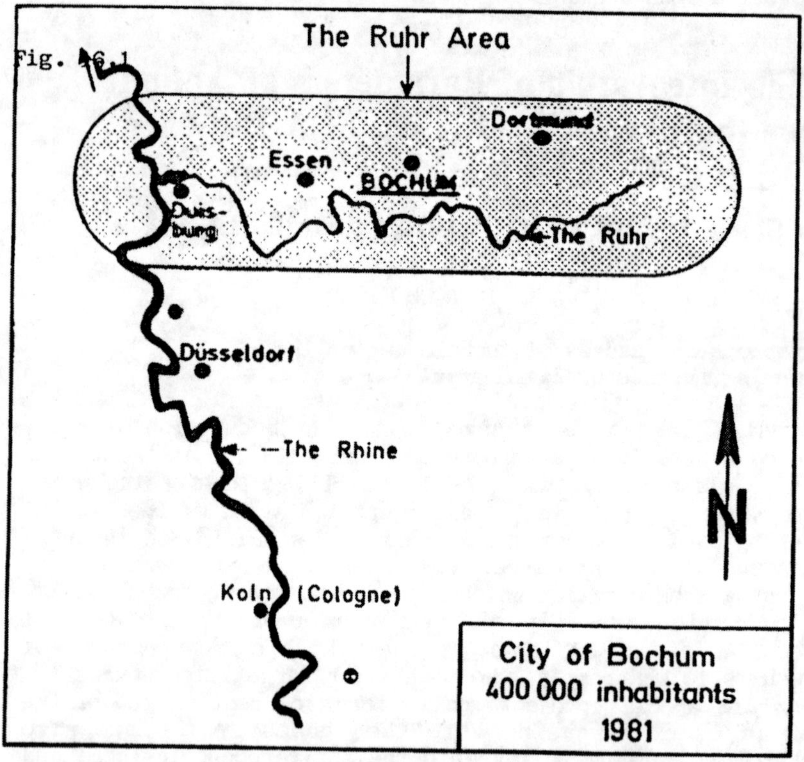

Besides an analysis of the situation related to other than municipal organs of decision and to those of the City, the following paper is to discuss the parameters of action of the Council and the Administration in respect of the economic, legal and social-political systems. Thus, it is to continue a work which, in 1977, was concerned with the housing requirements of the elderly, i.e., a special group of demand.[4] Like the results of the investigation of that time, this paper, too, is to serve as an aid of decision in the complexity of problems.

By showing the interrelations and the approximate quantitative orders of magnitude, it is possible to take pending decisions on a safe basis. In a similar way as at that time in the case of construction of apartments for the elderly, the general municipal housing policy, too, must be coordinated with other targets of municipal development planning.

In any case, problems will continue to exist in the forseeable future in the cities of the agglomeration areas, hence also in the Bochum area and thus within the municipal district of Bochum. Despite a very impressing effort in the field of house construction, the latest offical figure (random housing census 1979) showed a calculative surplus of 1.7% of households against dwellings in the Ruhr area cities (excluding Hamm) whose status is comparable to that of a county borough. The number of 1,492,600 main and second dwellings (WE = dwelling units) campared to 1,516,900 households (HH).[5] Although this is based on a random census with the inevitable errors of such census, we are certainly far from having reached the figures scheduled in the Lucke-Plan of the Sixties. At that time, a surplus of appr. 3% of dwelling units over the households was laid down as a precondition for a liberal housing market.

Another statistic characteristic figure is a cause of preoccupation : According to the "latest" official figures, the number of persons per dwelling unit in the so-called county boroughs of the Ruhr district is much higher in the other county boroughs. Whereas in this part of the Ruhr district, 100 dwelling units are "crowded" by 242 persons, the other county boroughs can offer these dwelling units to only 234 persons.

To this global disequilibrium must be added structural disparities, i.e., regarding the different types of dwelling units or households respectively, because the dwelling units available do not always comply with the requirements of certain types of households. A change in the habits of demand, e.g., an increasing disintegration of senior members from existing family units, cannot be converted, without any difficulties, into the corresponding buildings within a short time.

Generally speaking, the housing demand will continue to rise if the most important factor determining the demand, i.e., the household income available, too, continues to increase in the future. A floor area of 45 square metres per inhabitant, which has actually been reached already in Zurich,[6] could be reached in about 20 years when the income is expected, by optimistic assumption, to rise at an average rate of 2.5% per year. At any rate, the floor area per inhabitant in the Federal Republic of Germany underwent an increase from appr. 15 sq.m. per inhabitant in 1950 to appr. 31 sq.m. per inhabitant in 1978; thus, it was more than doubled. Even if the real income should no longer increase, which would be an extreme case, the floor area per caput will rise till the year 2000 to an average of 35 sq.m. because the average household will be reduced in number as a result of the continued disintegration of the "large" family already mentioned before. Consequently, the housing market does not show any tendencies of saturation; the only question is, as a matter of fact, the speed.

This applies to Bochum, too. Here, the floor area per inhabitant changed from 21.1 sq.m. in 1970 to 27.2 sq.m. at the end of 1979. The figures for 1980 are still under preparation. But certainly, the provision of housing has again increased during that year.

Differentiation of partial housing markets

It is necessary not only to make a difference between the agglomeration areas on the one hand and the rural areas on the other, but also to subdivide the housing market into different partial markets :

- privately financed housing market
- market of state-financed low-cost housing
- company-owned dwellings
- dwellings of housing cooperatives
- other types of dwellings

It is the dwellings owned by institutions which is the very characteristic of the large cities in the Ruhr district : About 70% of residential premises here are held by private or non-profitmaking enterprises, in the large cities outside this region only about 60%. Of course, dwellings owned by companies or housing cooperatives can be either of the privately-financed type, or they belong to the category of state-financed low-cost housing.

Since, for financial considerations of the Federal Government, no recent assessment of all dwellings has been made,[7] there are only approximate estimates regarding the classification of the appr. 182,000 dwelling units in Bochum. More than 70,000 dwelling units are state-financed low-cost housings; about 10,000 dwelling units are company-owned dwellings and thus subject to special allocation terms. Approximately 40,000 dwelling units are owned by housing cooperatives or by the local non-profit making building societies, the major part of them, with appr. 30,000 dwelling units, being the state-financed low-cost dwellings.[8] A more exact statistical survey will be provided only by the next large-scale census the inquiry part of which might be terminated by 1982 and the results might be available by 1984.

All further considerations of this paper refer exclusively to the two housing markets of privately financed dwelling units and state-financed low-cost housing. Here, too, are to be found the decisive causes; they are

- economic
- legal
- emotional-psychological
- political or the result of power structures

Part of them refers to both partial markets, the other part only to either market of the two considered.

Has the State been too niggardly?

One cause which would otherwise rather suggest itself, namely the lack of public subsidies, should be disregarded from the beginning. Subsidies last year amounted to around 20,000 million DM[9] and the prospects for the current year are not bad at all when, according to the calculations of our Office for Housing Matters, appr. 100,000 DM of public subsidies will be raised for each dwelling unit. How, then, can we find an explanation for the fact that despite these tremendous amounts, there are obviously some things which are not as they should be?

The causes and consequences are to be dealt with on the following pages :

CAUSES AND CONSEQUENCES ON THE TWO IMPORTANT PARTIAL MARKETS OF "STATE-FINANCED LOW-COST HOUSING" AND "PRIVATELY FINANCED HOUSING"

Regional asymmetry in the field of state subsidies

Cause No. 1 is the asymmetry of state subsidies practised over long years. That is to say above all, less subsidies have been paid to the agglomeration areas than to the flat countryside.

Example Bavaria

According to the Federal Ministry for Landscape Planning, Building and City Construction, the formation of property in the agglomeration areas in Bavaria between 1975 and 1977 was subsidized with around 107,000 DM per inhabitant, whereas the rural population received more than double this sum, i.e., 227,000 DM per caput.[10]

Example North-Rhine Westphalia

According to investigations carried out by the Academy for Landscape Research and Landscape Planning, the average amount paid per year and per inhabitant in 1969/1975 for housing construction and construction and city building was (in DM per caput)

in agglomeration areas	78
non-agglomeration areas	91

In comparison to the record year 1973 with 336,200 dwelling units, the increase on a federal level was reduced to only 59,800 dwelling units in 1979. The deficit in the construction of new dwellings for renting was concentrated practically to the large cities only because 80% of the households on the countryside live in homes of their own. The tendency in the large cities is that that there is a housing shortage whereas the situation on the countryside is satisfactory.

Additional increase in demand as a result of the demo-social situation

Cause No. 2 is the additional increase in demand as a result of certain phenomena which become more and more apparent and are a typical characteristic of the agglomeration areas.

- The already mentioned disintegration of the large family who was predominant in the pre-industrial age. Young people leave the "shelter" of their parental home from the age of 18 at the latest and look for an apartment of their own. The larger apartments are blocked by aged persons when, after the move-out of the children or the death of the husband, there is no sufficient amount of smaller apartments available on favourable terms, which would better meet the needs of aged persons.

- Housing deficits will be caused by demolition in cases where reconstruction would be too expensive.

- A continued immigration into the agglomeration areas of foreigners by family members joining the foreign workers and the concentration to certain areas of the appr. 3 million foreign workers already living in the Federal Republic of Germany is to be observed.

This demand is increased further by the fact that presently the generation of the years with high birth rates has reached the phase of founding a family, and they try to find as fast as possible a roof over their heads which is independent from their parents' home.

Lack of building capacity

Cause No. 3 is the consequences of a hoarding of dwellings which could be observed in 1973/1974, also in Bochum.

- The city fathers saw no point in allocating building plots; they saw themselves supported in their attitude by the exodus from the cities to the noise-free environment which was prevailing at that time but has been stopped by now. Today, even building plots allocated cannot be developed by the communities for lack of funds. In Bochum, sufficient building plots have been allocated or buildings are constructed according to the general planning rules without zoning ordinances.

- At that time, in the Republic appr. 400,000 construction workers lost their jobs, migrated to other branches of industry, and this caused a shortage of personnel during the boom from 1977 onward. In Bochum, too, the building industry is employed to capacity; an expansion is possible only by recruiting workers from other industries for the main and ancillary building industries. A factor indicative of this fact, although with multiple limitations, particularly under the aspect of the scab work widely practised in the building industry, is the unemployment statistics. In Bochum, the number of unemployed persons in the main and ancillary building industry was only 423 at the end of 1980, plus 518 employment applicants, both groups counted in their place of residence.

Ever increasing building costs due to inadequate rationalization of building technology

Cause No.4 is that too little consideration is given to the possibilities of improving the rationalization of building services. It is true that the percentage of pre-fab houses is increasing, but only at a low rate. Exceptions confirm this finding. Quotation of an expert : "If the VW beetle would still be built in the way it was done 30 years ago, as it is the practice in the building industry - brick by brick - it would cost at least 50,000 DM!"

Further price increases as a result of state-ordered quality improvement

Cause No. 5 is that stricter state regulations are established which lead to a steady improvement of the quality of new housing. The multitude and variety of works of public charity comprise noise protection and insulation measures as well as the sizes of cross-section rooms, the number of rooms and the cross-section of electric cables. Calculations for the Land North-Rhine Westphalia show for a dwelling which costed in 1977 round 119,000 DM a real price increase, due to such quality improvement, of appr. 36,000 DM (additionally!). It is certainly an advantage that new dwellings are furnished in optimum quality. However, everybody should realize that everything has its price.

Increasing prices for building plots because of a shortage of supplies

Eventually, the prices of building plots have an influence on the costs per square metre of floor space although the plots available are exploited more effectively for building houses, so that the prices of plots have no such great effect as, e.g., 10 years ago. This situation is due to the following causes :

I. Lack of zoning ordinance and non-realization of existing zoning plans.

Cause No.6 is to be attributed to the fact that particularly in the agglomeration areas, it is sometimes not at all an easy task to enforce zoning ordinance. But even existing zoning plans require in many cases an allocation procedure which may take years. To such inevitable delays must be added the scarcity of funds of municipal authorities already mentioned before.

II. Hoarding of developed building plots ("hoarding of building gaps").

Cause No.7 is the consequence of the runaway prices for plots which are the reason why gaps are not filled in anticipation of further price increases. "Building gaps are held like golden watches, like decorative accessories to property of other kind!" These were the words uttered recently by a top official of ministerial bureaucracy. Building gaps frequently represent additional property to their owners and are in many cases retained for heritage. In some cases, they serve also for maintaining the required distance to neighbouring estate, e.g., when using a plot for trade purposes, the more so since the regrettable decree on distances is not too well suited to facilitate economic encouragement in agglomeration areas.

Apart from the increase in prices to be expected according to concrete experience from past years, the proprietors benefit from clear tax privileges. The fact that proprietors are allowed to keep fully developed plots, i.e., plots that are ripe for building, for a few DM of annual tax, is much to be questioned.

Summarizing the above, the shortage of building land, hoarding of developed plots (building gaps), deficit of building capacities, along with the regional asymmetry of promotion and the additonal demographically founded demand made prices climb faster than scaffolding.

CAUSES AND CONSEQUENCES ON THE MARKET OF STATE-FINANCED LOW-COST HOUSING

Steadily increasing discrepancy between the rent allowed and the cost rent

Cause No. 8 is the steadily increasing discrepancy between the rent allowed and the cost rent which raised the demand of public subsidies and caused a reduction of new low-cost housing as a result of the funds available for subsidies.

The cost rent in Bochum is at present between 15 and 20 DM per sq.m. of floor space; by state subsidies, it is brought down to the allowed rent of 5.90 DM per sq.m. of floor area. However, this is an intial rent which rises in the course of years in proportion to the gradual suppression of subsidies. Since the tenants are often not aware of this built-in raise, the rent increase should in the future be included as " sliding-scale rent" in the lease contract.

Additions to the state-financed low-cost dwellings decreased as follows :

1970	appr. 80,000 dwelling units
1978	appr. 39,000 "
1979	appr. 40,000 "

The number of new privately-owned dwelling units was reduced in a similar way, although not quite so much because of the demand of subsidies being only half the rate; from 1960 to 1978, the number of all state-subsidized low-cost dwellings went down from 263,000 to only 89,000.[12] Since 1976, privately owned dwelling units quite generally exceed the number of rented dwelling units in the Federal Republic of Germany.

Conditions in Bochum are reflected by similar development statistics. In 1970, there were still almost 2,400 new dwelling units, in 1979 only slightly more than, 1,100 (after a climax of 4,400 in the year 1973).

Misappropriation

Cause No. 9 are those households that qualified long years ago, by the then permitted income, for a low-cost dwelling, but which meanwhile do no longer belong to the group of entitled persons because of their high income, however, as a result of the existing legal situation, must not leave the state-subsidized low-cost dwelling. Thus, they are blocking these dwellings at the expense of the households entitled today. These people are called "Fehlbeleger". Although no precise statistical data are available as a consequence of the lack of a recent largescale census already mentioned in various instances before, there is a quite good research result of Infratest (opinion research company in Munich) for the Federal Building Ministry which shows that 22% of all social dwellings are "missubsidised" (or misappropriated), especially those in houses from the beginning 50s until the 60s. A solution of this question would of course be an important contribution to solving the problems of the local market.

CAUSES AND CONSEQUENCES IN THE FIELD OF PRIVATELY FINANCED HOUSING

Decreasing expectations of return on investment

Cause No. 10 is to be found in the hesitating attitude of investors. Considering the return on investment, which is the classical investment incentive, nearly no return at all is expected by the most important building investors, the life insurance companies. It is almost impossible for them to reach the legally required 3% minimum return on the capital paid in by their customers. The reasons for this situation are to be found partly in a drastical increase of repair costs, partly in the great appeal of financing investments as a result of the high-interest policy practised already for some time by the German Bundesbank (the Federal Reserve Bank), which policy is accountable also for the general rise in rates of interest for credits required to finance building projects. This increase in interest rates, too, has a cooling effect on the economy and reduces building activities but not strictly because the long period of high interests caused lack of demand and building prices fell; this, actually, gives to many a landlord the incentive, not to care for the high interest, especially when expecting them to go down soon.

In this context, people often argue that the portion of rent expense, averaging 15.5% of the net household income, is too low. However, this figure is questionable because it is an unsuitable average value considerung the extreme range of dispersion.[13] The major part of the population in the agglomeration areas pays (at least) one quart of its income. But 25% of this income are not sufficient in the case of a privately financed rent of 20 DM per sq.m. of floor space. In rural areas, a much smaller portion is required for high-standard accommodation.

Problems involved in private rent legislation

Cause No. 11 is the problem of rent legislation on the privately financed housing market.

> An exaggerated protection of tenants is considered by proprietors and their pressure groups to be identical to a freezing of rents. It is very difficult to raise the rent because this is subject to strict formalities : It is necessary to produce an expert opinion or

three so-called "reference dwellings" for which higher rent is being paid; otherwise, the only recourse left might be that of legal action since the legal provisions preclude giving notice to leave for the purpose of raising the rent; hence, it is nearly never claimed by the landlors.

This is inconsistent with the development observed in practice and proclaimed by the Federal Minister for Housing. The difference between the rents charged by old tenant contracts and those of new contracts has remained the same since 1966, with about 20%; it should however have grown if the claimed exaggeration of tenant protection were true. This finding is further supported by the fact that only about 10% of proprietors feel themselves handicapped by the reference rent law in respect of rent increases. 25% of the proprietors think that the rent index indicating the local reference rents is really a help for them. These results were disclosed by an investigation made by lpsen (Kassel University).

Penetration into the (modernized) old housing stock by the high-income classes at the expense of large groups of populations

Cause No. 12 is the new trend found with the high-income classes, to move into the old houses near the city centres, after previous modernization with state subsidies (combination of small flats, installation of sanitary facilities, insulation glas, etc.). Older houses and thus cheap dwellings for the low-income class in the large cities are available at an every declining rates; the consequence is that the number of urgent cases applying for a state-financed low-cost dwelling is going up in the housing offices. At present the aforementioned cause is of less importance in Bochum but it could become more noticeable and worsen the local housing situation at the cost of tenants.

In this context, the key-word of modernization should not be misinterpreted in the way that the population in improvement areas and zones of modernization should be regrouped to the benefit of the high-income groups of the population. The explicit aim of the local government is and continues to be avoiding any kind of shifting by modernization. Thus, established communities are preserved and not destroyed as has been happening occasionally in other cities during the past years.

APPROACHES TO SOLUTIONS BY THE STATE

No pat solution because of the bundle of causes

As shown, the peculiar situation on the housing market in agglomeration areas - also denoted as new housing famine - has many causes. Pat solutions to these questions must fail to be successful, be it the call for re-establishing market economy which resembles the prayer wheel, be it still more centralized, state-controlled economy. What can help only, is a well balanced bundle of coordinated steps which have lead already to the appropriate legislative initiatives by the Federal and Land Governments.

Stimulation of capital flow

However, Government alone cannot provide assistance for lack of additional capital and with its present instrumentarium. What it could do, is to stimulate the flow of capital from private investors, i.e., to guarantee the necessary economic background. Such private capital will, of course, not flow unless there are sound prospects of getting a return and unless psychological barriers are eliminated, in particular an uncertainty about the future. As to the last mentioned point, one aspect is undoubtedly that tenure legislation must be simplified. A simple (unbureaucratic) approach would be, e.g., the sliding-scale rent for which the contracting parties would agree on certain rent modifications already at the time of concluding the tenancy agreement. Another suggestion would be to permit increases in rent within 7 years from first occupancy.

It should not be forgotten to mention that besides the Government and private investors, the Bundesbank has a strong influence, particularly on the housing market, by using its instrumentarium to control the level of interest rates and thereby indirectly the direction of national capital flow. We cannot forecast to what extent its policy in the near future will be influenced or even bound in this respect by the decisions taken in other countries. However, its national economic autonomy should not be questioned in this connection.

Solving the problem of misappropriation

The problem of misappropriation—although, on a Federal level, it might relate to only some ten thousands of state-financed low-cost dwellings or own houses—must be solved, but not by means of the "misappropriation charge" requiring much administrative work.

One of the suggestions discussed was to raise generally the rent to the local reference rent. But other proposals, too, which do not necessarily blow up the administrative system, are worth being discussed.

CHECKING THE PARAMETERS OF ACTION OF LOCAL GOVERNMENT

Although the possibilities of influencing the housing market on the local level should not be overrated, it would not be right to throw up the sponge right at the beginning. Various methods have not been used in Bochum, some of them not even checked.

Sufficient building capacity in the coordinated and approved zoning plan

The zoning plan as one of the criteria determining city development on the basis of city planning considerations has been established in accordance with the Federal Building Act, and after coordination with planning on the Land level, it was approved by the Council of Bochum City. The zoning plan is final and binding. As far as residential building areas represented in the plan, it shows sufficient capacities. This may be seen also from the explanatory report belonging to the graphic representation of the plan.

Any intention to extend the capacity would lead to a conflict with planning on the Land level, and would also affect zoning, particularly in view of the sometimes prevailing trend to gnaw the green spots because this seems to be the easiest way for building houses. By the way, it should be stressed once again how questionable an instrument is the binding construction key planning when it is to stimulate building activities. It is possible, though, to use a well-known proverb : You can take a horse to the water, but you cannot make him drink.

Realization of developed, city-owned plots by building or selling

Another parameter is the utilization of developed plots owned by the city. No immediate building or sale should be advocated here. Municipal estate policy has to consider other development targets. Thus, e.g., it is absolutely necessary to keep plots for people displaced by construction schemes in order not to cause undue delays in carrying out important infrastructure measures. Possible may be hereditary tenure as well.

Suggestions to large building societies of the city-related and non-city type

Although success seems to be not quite certain, the attempt could be made to suggest to the large building societies that they may direct their economic consideration to renouncing perhaps to part of their normal return. This may even be part of the obligations of some societies towards the economy as a whole.

Moral suasion, by local government, of private property owners to build or to sell their plots

On a local authority level, too, contributions can be made towards removing the psychological barriers mentioned before in the analytical part. Although success is not certain from the beginning, it is worth considering the question how private owners could be stimulated to build or sell their estate. Perhaps, it will be found that many an owner of estate has displayed no initiative for lack of information on the possibilities existing - be it only that of assisting other people. Lack of information seems to prevail also in respect of the encouragement of providing "students' dens".

Orders to build after preceding "official" pre-applications for building permits

For good reason, local authorities in Germany have so far issued practically no orders to build. Orders to build and expropriations are enforceable only if adequate return can be expected - and just this is not the case! But considering only the procedure, it is at least expedient to first have a pre-application for a building permit filed and put through; otherwise, it might turn out, after having decreed the building order, that no legal preconditions for the building project exist. Because of this procedure of "official" pre-applications for building permits alone, the legally existing means of a building order is obviously not a very suitable instrument on the local level to contribute to solving the mentioned problems.

Local government subsidies for interest on building loans

In view of the financial problems which the Ruhr area cities are facing, it seems an absurd idea to make building loans more attractive by local government subsidies for interest on such loans in order to increase building activities. Nevertheless, this point should yet be mentioned to make the list of possible parameters of local government initiative complete.

Law for avoiding misuse of dwellings and law for guarding of dwellings

Before the release of the "law for avoiding misuse of dwellings ("Zweckentfremdungsverordnung") the local authority was only able to do steps against speculation by announcing the release of a local "law of maintenance of houses", a so-called "Erhaltungssatzung" based on article 39 h of the Federal Building Law. The now already a longer time being applied "Zweckentfremdungsverordnung" gives besides of the now to be approved destruction of houses the instrument into local hands to approve or disapprove the unification of dwellings and the use of dwellings for non-housing purposes.

Thus, there is the opportunity of the conservation of the stock.

Similarly the same is true with respect of the law for guarding of dwellings. The local authority may influence the general level of rents because too high ones (as compared with the local rental table) are to be persecuted.

Influence on the local rental table ("Mietpreisspiegel")

In the local rental table there is—referring to the legal rules—put down the average rent for the different types of dwellings. In Bochum all institutions involved (city of Bochum, association of tenants, landlords etc.) found these general prices without difficulties and without special scientific research. Maybe that as a result of the latest proposals just now under legislation procedure there will be a less direct or no more way of influence by the local authority.

Premiums for moving

The already mentioned misappropriated may move when they get payed their removal and a premium on top. Some German cities do pay these amounts. As there is no information whether people do move because of the money they get or whether they would have done so even without it (and take the grant thankfully and laughing : the German term is "Mitnahmeeffekt") this measure is not to be recommened easily.

SOME FINAL REMARKS

We see, actually, the economic, political and instituional environment the local authority is confronted with. When using this term instead of "local government" it will be shown to the reader some doubts with respect to ours political system which guarantees by constitution the so-called self government on the local level. The framework we are acting in has to be put doubtlessly by the state. The question is : Are cities able to act within this framework with any success? The answer is : Yes, there are good chances, cities should take them.

NOTE

Paper presented at the "European Meeting on Applied Urban Research", Erren. Oct. 2-4, 1981.

REFERENCES

Children of foreigners in Bochum, Special report of the Department for **Statistics and Urban Research**, vol. VI No. 25 (August 29th,) 1978).

Peter Christ : "Housing famine - and no prospects" in "**Die Zeit**", No. 14, dated March 27th, 1981.

"The demand for housing will continue to increase" in the "**Frankfurter Allgemeine Zeitung**" of December 20th, 1980.

Foreigners in Bochum, Special report of the Department for **Statistics and Urban Research**, vol. IX No. 4 (March 5 th, 1981).

R. Gunzert : Wirtschaftspolitik der stodte und Statistik, in Special Report of the Statistics Office of the City of Bochum (Appendix to the Month Reports), No. 10 (December 20th, 1967), Page 81 and following.

The housing situation of the foreign workers of the Ruhrkole Inc. (management of the research project : Hermann Korte), Bochum 1981.

Municipal Survey Research : Housing requirements of aged persons (reviewed by W. Heckmann, Th. Schutz, E.-O.

Sommerer) in : **Contribution to municipal development planning**, edited by Department for Statistics and Urban Research, Publication 19 (1977 a).

Municipal Survey Research : The situation of the foreign workers (reviewed by W. Heckmann, E.-O. Sommerer, Jurgen Lower) in : **Contribution to municipal development planning**, edited by Department for Statistics and Urban Research, Publication 18 (1977 b).

Ruhrgebiet Communal Association, 1% random housing census 1978, Results for the Ruhr area (copies from the manuscript), Essen 1981.

Karl Schiller, "Wirtschaftspolitik", in : **Manual of Social Science**, Volume 11, Stuttgart, Tubingen und Gottingen 1965, page 210 and following.

H. J. Wienen : Allocation, by areas, of subsidies and constructions measures of the Land North-Rhine Westphalia 1969/1975, in : **Agglomerating and public financing**, Research and Assembly Report of the Academy for Landscape Research and Landscape Planning, Volume 134, Hanover 1980, page 97 and following.

SECTION FOUR

PROBLEMS AND ISSUES CONFRONTING HOUSING POLICIES : POLICY INPUTS AND RESIDENTIAL EVALUATIONS

SEVENTEEN

Tor Bysveen

Analyzing Moving Chains in Oslo

THE PRIMARY OFFER OF HOUSING AND THE SUBSEQUENT CHAINS

The primary offer of housing in an area is made up of five factors.[1]

(a) The extent of new building
(b) Households who move out of the area, leaving vacant dwellings behind
(c) Deaths in one-person households, leaving vacant dwellings behind
(d) One-person households moving together, leaving vacant dwellings behind
(e) Dwellings being demolished, changed in their use or united into one.

The primary offer of vacant dwellings in a certain period is given with a + b + c + d - e. But it is not sufficient to know the extent of the primary offer. As families evolve through stages of their life cycles, their housing aims change. Some of them are established households looking for a better dwelling. Others establish their own household, or the family grows and presssure is felt for more room. As families move out of dwellings the same dwellings reappear vacant. They attract other families and vacancy chains are created.

Hans and Grete have a daughter and live in an old two-room flat in the centre of town. Through an estate agency they get information on vacant dwellings in undetached houses. The old flat is occupied by a young couple who has until recently been living at the woman's parents' house. The parents do no longer want a lodger, and this small flat is reunited to their dwelling.

Fig. 17.1

As our example indicate, the primary offer generate chains. We have studied the chains generated by new building. In our estimate of the primary offer of dwellings in one year in Oslo, new building count fcr 20%. 4 out of 5 households who manage to accomplish their demand for housing, move into a dwelling in the existing housing stock.

A STUDY ON CHAINS GENERATED BY THE BUILDING OF NEW HOUSES

The data are collected through intereviews with the occupants of 428 new dwellings, and with 404 households who moved to an existing dwelling as a direct result of the occupation of new dwellings.

The average length of a chain (number of dwellings) is the multiplier, the total number of moves caused by the initial arrival of a vacancy. In this study the registered multiplier was 1.9. But there are losses caused by interviewing failures, even where the chains actually proceed. Had it been possible to follow these losses to a satisfactory conclusion, the multiplier would have been somewhat higher. Our estimate is a multiplier of 2.3.

Before commenting on the principal findings we shall compare our multipliers with the multipliers in some other studies.

Multipliers for 6 studies of chains generated by the building of new houses

Authors	Country	Registered multiplier	Corrected multiplier
F. Kristof[2]	USA	2.40	no correction
J. Lansing, C.W. Clifford and J.N. Morgan[3]	USA	2.68	3.50
C. Watson[4]	U.K.	1.54	1.87
A. Murie, P. Hillyard, D. Birrell and D. Roche[5]	U.K.	1.43	1.54
H. Spohr[6]	Den.	1.86*	3.20*
T. Bysveen O. Foss and S. Knutsen[7]	Nor.	1.94	2.29

* The use of data registers for movers, enabled the project to continue the chains even where households denied to participate in the interviewing. The multiplier was then 2.46, and this multiplier is the basis for the corrected multiplier.

The highest multipliers are found in the American studies. A high multiplier gives many households an opportunity to change their housing, but will often be based on a situation where new houses are built for those who already have convenient dwellings. A short multiplier means that new houses are built for those who do not have a dwelling of their own, or who live in dwellings in slum clearance areas.

THE MARKET IMPACT OF DIFFERENT BUILDING

The market impact of house building as measured by the multiplier in our study is found to differ according to characteristics by the dwellings. Parallel to the other reports we found that the building of large dwellings and high-priced dwellings, generate a strong market impact.

In the foreign studies the multiplier caused by production in the private sector is higher than production in the public sector. In our view the public sector produces houses for those with the most pressing need for housing, while the private sector to a greater extent could produce for those who are better off. Murie et al. stress that "as households in the public sector sequences were more likely to be older and "poorer", it could be argued that the American fascination with length of chains is less relevant than who benefits and to what extent?"8

However, in our material new houses built by the housing cooperative also generate a strong market impact. The public housing sector in Norway is dominated by the housing cooperatives. Their position are strongest in the great cities, where they have been advocates for social housing. Let us add that in our country the municipal authorities themselves seldom build houses, but usually act through the cooperatives. The members of the cooperatives have free disposal of their own dwellings, but are subject to certain restrictions if they want to sell. The main restriction is a prohibition to sell at full market value.

Historically the housing cooperatives have an ambition to build houses for low- and medium income groups, and especially for those with no housing or a bad housing situation. The high multiplier found in our study may indicate that the cooperatives are in no position to fulfil this ambition. Another indication is the long seniority necessary to obtain the new dwellings. In a pressed housing market as in Oslo, the necessary seniority for new dwellings in the housing cooperative could be 10-15 years.

The average income of the occupants in the chains diminish with rising position in the sequences. This indicates that a process of filtering by income is at work. Looking at the monthly costs, a theory on social effects of filtering gets strong opposition. Almost 2/5 of the households who bought their dwellings in the existing stock have monthly costs in the same, or higher, price range than the sellers have in their new dwellings. Our data suggest an assumption that "the poor pay more" in the housing market, rather than an assumption that a filtering process secures a reasonable social distribution of housing in the population.

A SHORT NOTE ON FILTERING

There are diverging views on filtering in the literature. Grigsby mentions filtering as a phenomenon where a household can achieve a higher quantity of housing and more space for the same price as before moving, or the same quality and space to a cheaper price. In this way the dwellings could be filtered down in the income groups.[9] But at the same time there is a process where the households who change dwelling try to achieve better quality and more space. The household filter upwards in the dwelling stock.

White look upon filtering as a position element, and argues for a housing policy that will generate high multipliers, "subsidized housing will not have as large a multiplier effect as new housing units built for medium and higher income groups".[10] He also stress that "subsidizing new housing will not, in general, be the most effective path to the national policy goal of improving the overall match of families' needs with available houses".

Sands and Murie et al., highly oppose filtering as a distribution system of housing. In a study of housing turnover in New York State, Sands points out that "the vacancy chains generated by the most expensive new housing, had little effect on the housing need of low income families".[11]

Murie et al., reject a housing policy based on filtering. They argue that "filtering is an idealized concept of the operation of the housing market under certain conditions. As those conditions do not obtain in practice filtering ceases to be a representation of what happens in the housing market".[12]

DIFFERENT ACCESS TO RESOURCES GIVES DIFFERENT CONTRIBUTIONS FROM PUBLIC EXPENDITURES.

Our results in the study of chains points out that in a pressed housing market as in Oslo, the households with low resources like small income and savings are taken care of through the municipal authorities efforts to give them housing.

The households with high resources have either high income and savings, or a long seniority in the housing cooperatives. They could build or buy a house of their own in one of the surrounding municipalities. Studies on intermunicipality moving show that families with children and high resources in fact leave Oslo.[13]

The "losers" are the households with medium resources. They cannot afford a house of their own and they have short seniority in the cooperatives. Their housing markets are the housing cooperatives and in the block of flats, especially in the existing housing stock. As our conventionalized figure shows a family in this group get the smallest contribution from the public expenditure on housing.

Fig. 17.2 : The distribution of public expenditure on housing to households with different resources, for the housing market in Oslo.

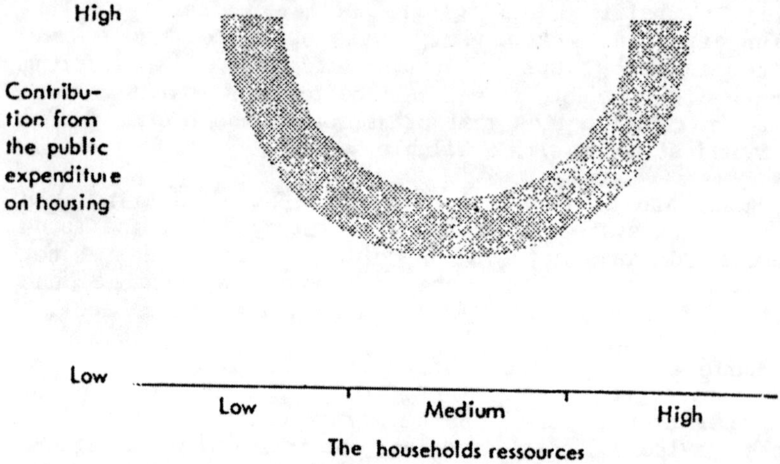

FURTHER WORKS ON MOVING CHAINS

A similar study of moving chains generated by new building in Trondheim, will support or weaken our data from Oslo. This new study is done in an area of a balanced housing market. In order to broaden the knowledge of the structure of the population's housing need, we are now also working on a study of chains generated by households moving out of Oslo, leaving vacant dwellings behind.

NOTES

Paper presented at the "European Meeting on Applied Urban Research", Erren. Oct. 2-4, 1981.

1 Bysveen, T., Foss, O. og Knutsen, S. : Flyttekjeder i Oslo-omradet. NIBR-rapportene 1981 : 5 og 1981 : 6.
2 Kristof, F.S. : Housing policy goals and the turnover of housing. **Journal of the American Institute of Planners**, vol. 31, 1965, nr. 3.
3 Lansing, J., Clifton, C.W. og Morgan, J.N. : New homes and poor people. A study of chains of moves. Publ. by University of Michigan, Institute for Social Research. Ann Arbor, Mich., 1972.
4 Watson, C.J. : Household movement in West Central

Scotland. Birmingham 1973. (University of Birmingham. Center for Urban and Regional Studies. Occasional paper 26).

5 Murie, A., Hillyard, P., Birrel, D. and Roche, D. : New Building and Housing Need. **Progress in planning**, vol. 6,p. 81-186, 1976 I.

6 Spohr, H. : Flyttekaeder pa boligmarkedet. Kbh. 1981. (Statens byggeforskninsinstitut. SBI-rapport 129).

7 Bysveen, T., Foss, O og Knutsen, S. : op. cit.

8 Murie, A., Hillyard, P., Birrel, D. and Roche, D. : Op. cit. p. 91.

9 Grigsby, W.G. : **Housing market and public policy.** Philad., Pa., Univ. of Pennsylvania Press. 1963.

10 White, H.C. : Multiplier, vacancy chains and filtering. **Journal of the American Institute of Planners**, vol. 37 (1971) nr. 3.

11 Sands, G. : Housing turnover : Assessing its relevance to public policy. **Journal of the American Institute of Planners.**, vol. 42 (1976) nr. 4.

12 Murie, A., Hillyard, P., Birrel, D. and Roche, D. : op.cit.

13 Moen, B., Reisz, B.A. og Strand, A. : Flyttemonster i Oslo-regionen. Oslo 1979. (NIBR-rapport 47).

EIGHTEEN

Glenn Yago

Housing Speculation Impacts on the Quality and Cost of Housing

SHELTER CRISIS AND RENTAL HOUSING IN THE U.S.

The affluence of the post-world war II housing market has been replaced in recent years by increasing scarcity, runaway inflation, and declining quality. Historic patterns of home ownership, affordability, and increased housing supply have been steadily reversed in recent years (Frieden and Solomon, 1977; LeGates and Murphy, 1981). A variety of federal actions affecting housing location, supply, financing, quality, standards, prices and residential segregation have exacerbated the impact of demographic and economic trends on housing shortages and the maldistribution of housing. As other housing researchers have noted, this jigsaw of state policies have been directed not towards resolving the housing crisis, but with accommodating private financial, construction, and real estate interests in the housing market (Marcuse, 1977 : 11; Starr and Esping-Andersen, 1979).

What are the sources of the housing crisis and how have they affected rental housing in U.S. cities? The demographic structure of the urban housing market has changed radically in recent years. The largest series of birth cohorts in U.S. population history are entering the housing market this decade; simultaneously, the rate of household formation is 50% higher than the rates from 1950-70 (Alonso, 1977). On the supply side of the housing market, strict monetary policies have severely constrained the availability of capital for housing investment and increased the financing component as proportion of total housing costs. Material costs have skyrocketed and may be related to rising economic concentration and monopoly pricing in the construction goods sector.[1]

These aspects of the housing crisis have had their most deleterious impact upon rental housing costs. In the rental market, unearned increment, during an inflationary period, does not offset long-term housing costs as in the case of homeownership. Thirty-five per cent of U.S. families are renters; the above mentioned demographic trends and excessive rise in homeownership costs are projected to push that figure higher (Annual Housing Surveys, U.S. Bureau of Census, 1973-78). A recent report by the U.S. Comptroller General (1979) noted that renters are most severely affected by housing cost increases and declining housing quality : (1) 25% of all renters live in overcrowded or substandard conditions; (2) over thirty per cent of all renters pay excessive parts of their income in rent; (3) renters are increasingly poorer than homeowners (between 1973-77, average renter income increased 5.6% annually compared to 9.6% for homeowners); and (4) average rents have risen 5% above the growth in real income of renter households. Condominium conversions, foreclosure, and abandonment have removed millions of rental units from the housing market over the past decade, further worsening housing costs. The U.S. Department of Housing and Urban Development (1979) considers vacancy rates of 5% a rental housing shortage; the current average vacancy rate is 5.2% and dropping. In major cities, the vacancy rate is between 1-3%.

While many of these trends are national in scope (demographic trends, mortgage credit rates, and economic concentration), they afford local housing market actors with the opportunity to structure the local rental market through disruptive inflationary practices which distort the housing production system—increasing concentration of local land ownership; growing practices of tie-in arrangements between builders, developers and real estate agents; condominium conversions, luxury home and apartment construction; rapid property turnover; and other speculative practices. Rising costs of financing; construction, land, maintenance, and utilities have increased the incentive of speculative activity by all housing investors since profits rely increasingly upon tax breaks and inflated resale prices (see also Downs, 1979).

RENTAL HOUSING, HOUSING SPECULATION, AND THE LOCAL STATE

State policy at the federal-level in the U.S. has done

little to alleviate rental housing shortages; policy interventions consist of creating conditions for profitable private investment. Public housing and rent subsidy programs have reached a minute number of eligible families and are non-existent in the Reagan budget; no programs to reduce housing costs for average income tenants exist. Meanwhile, monetary, tax, economic, and other federal policies have further accommodated and accelerated capital flight from rental housing.

The failure or neglect of federal housing policy has created increased pressure upon local governments to respond to accelerating housing crises. The mechanisms and impacts of local housing inflation are readily visible, and potentially regulable, at the local level. Thus, local sources of housing inflation, particularly the organization, location, type and rapidity of property investment practices become critical during a period of runaway shelter costs.

What is speculation? Traditional neo-classical economics abjures the use of the word--all investment occurs in the context of an uncertain future therefore, speculation is implicit in each investment act. This position defines the problem away. On the other hand, institutional economics, urban political economy, and most tenant organizations understand speculation differently, viz., as the practice of buying and selling residential property for a high profit without making substantial improvements on those properties, thereby creating artificial housing demand based not upon shelter needs, but speculative profits. From this perspective, not all housing investment is speculative--investors may positively contribute to managing and improving housing stock.

THE EFFECTS OF HOUSING SPECULATION : AN EXPLORATORY STUDY

The impetus for this study came from neighbourhood organizations, tenant groups and local government in Madison, Wisconsin concerned about rapidly rising rents and costs of homeownership. Inflation--particularly property investment practices motivated by the desire for excessive profits--also were important.

Study Design

In this context, the exploratory and descriptive research reported in this paper was done between 1978-79. Due to small local sample sizes in the National Annual Housing

Survey and the infrequency of national census counts, nationally aggregate trends are insensitive to detecting local and neighbourhood change in the housing market, especially during the current inflationary period. Local housing market data rarely used for analytic purposes, do however exist for urban policy research. Unfortunately, the organization and management require extensive data management. Data gathered by the City Assessor's and Building Inspector's offices were merged from five separate sources--a general property file, a current and historical sales file, a geographical data file, and a building inspection file.

Such data had not been used previously in the U.S. to analyze relations between property turnover and a variety of social, demographic, and economic variables. Since the initial study, the research results have been replicated for Santa Barbara (Applebaum and Glaser, 1981) and for Madison between 1979-80 (Applebaum, 1981)[2]. Ideally, larger cities might also consider utilizing such existent local data for policy analysis and planning purposes.

Additionally, sales histories from documents at the County Registry of Deeds Office and interviews with tenants and owners in a random sample of central city units were also analyzed. This strategy of merging quantitative and field research techniques proved useful in providing a broad overview of speculative patterns, their causes, and their consequences.[3]

The inflationary impacts of rapid property turnover (in this case, a valid, unforced sale in three years or less) are as follows : (1) if exorbitant profits are a problem in property transactions, they are most likely evident in quick turnaround transactions; (2) since realtor and closing costs involved in selling property amount to 8% of sales price, frequent sales of the same property result in a large inflationary push from transaction and refinancing costs associated with the sale; and (3) recently sold properties determine market value and new property assessments for all properties.

Findings

Rates and Distribution of Speculative Activity in Local Housing

From 1977-78, 24.3% of all property sales were rapid turnover. The highest concentration of rapid property turnovers was on the south side and near east side where properties were 50% more likely to turnover properties as a proportion of recently sold properties. The central city has the highest proportion of recent sales that are rapid turnover properties, followed by the near east side. The outlying areas on the east and west sides of the city have the lowest proportion of rapid turnover properties among recently sold properties.[4]

Fig. 18.1 : Rapid Turnover and Type of Property : 1977/78 City Wise Data

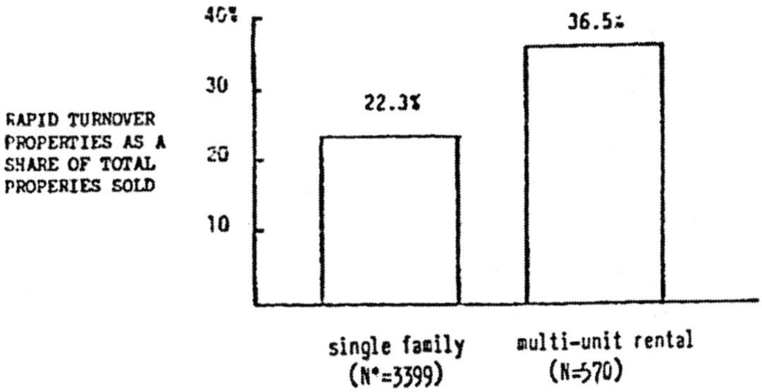

Fig. 18.2 : Rapid Turnover and Type of Property : Seven Isthmus Area Census Tracts. 1977/78 Data

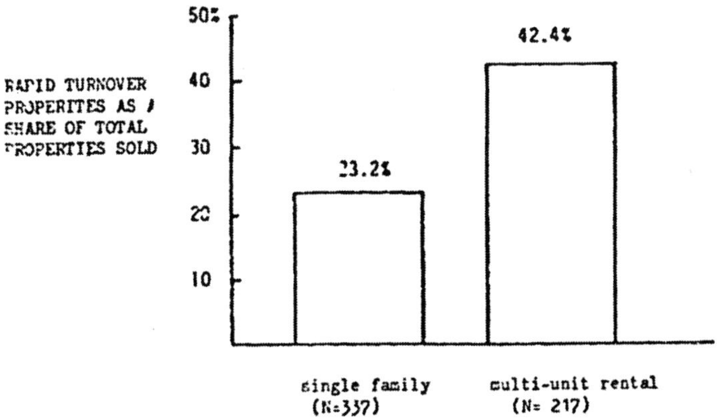

*N indicates sample size. For example, 3399 single family residence sales occurred between May of 1977 and June, 1978. Of those, 22.3 % were rapid turnover; that is, 22.3 % had been sold at least one additional time in the previous three years.

Not surprisingly, the highest rates of property assessment increases were in the areas of highest speculation. Multi-units, small apartment buildings are far more likely to have two or more sales in a three year period than are single family dwellings, especially in the Isthmus area. Turnover was greatest among absenteeowned rental properties.

Fig. 18.3 : Rapid Turnover and Type of Property : Seven Isthmus Area Census Tracts. 1976 DATA

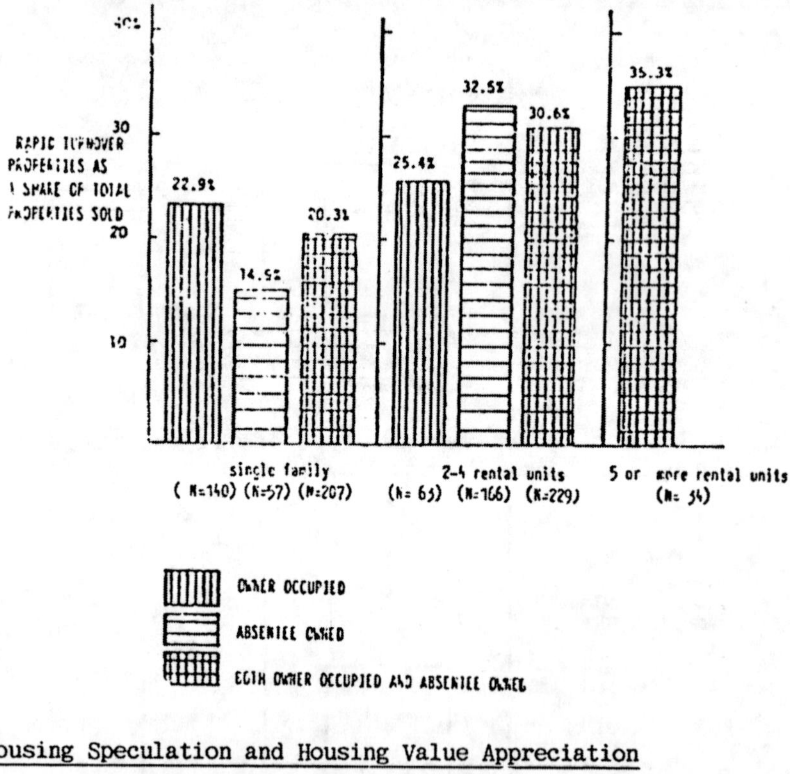

Housing Speculation and Housing Value Appreciation

Figure 18.4 indicates the average annual appreciation rates for properties twice in a twenty-five to forty-eight month period. The average appreciation rates for the more rapid turnover properties are twice as high as the rate for the slower turnover properties.

A slightly altered definition is employed of rapid turnover in the appreciation analysis. Because of the general inflation in the real estate market since 1973, it would be misleading to compare properties that sold twice in the 1973-76 period with properties that sold once in 1976 and once before 1973. Consequently, we compare sales over shorter intervals within the period of high market appreciation. We are in effect comparing very rapid turnover properties (1-24 months) with moderately rapid turnover properties (25-48 months).[5]

In every type of property the average annual rate of price increase is greater for the rapid turnover properties than the less frequently sold group. The annual rate of appreciation for rapid turnover properties was greatest for the seven census tract central city area (the Isthmus) (30.5% versus 22.5%). Real estate informants explained the higher appreciation rates for rapid turnover rental properties by the practice of buying properties, raising rents and thereby attracting an investor who is willing to pay a higher price because of increased revenue. Since demand for central city units rose during the years of the study, sales price for a rental property was based on rent levels. Investors would buy a property "below market rents" make cosmetic improvements, raise rents, then resell at a price calculated on the basis of the higher rents.

Housing Speculation and Housing Quality

Building code violations were used as the indicator of housing quality in this body. In order to conservatively estimate the relationship between speculative activity and code violations, we eliminated superficial maintenance violations (e.g., unmowed lawns, unshovelled sidewalks). Rapid turnover properties were twice as likely to have building code violations was higher in the central city than elsewhere. Almost a third of the rapid turnover rental properties have had at least one violation in the 1977-78 period. This trend is most pronounced in the central city area.

Historical Trends in the Seven-Census Tract Central City Area (Isthmus) : Housing Tenants and Owners

A random sample of rental properties located in the seven central city census tracts was extracted. Using the Registry of Deeds Office, sales data on each property going back to 1960 were compiled. This data was cross-checked with City Assessor data to determine whether a property was occupied by its owner in 1961 and 1978. Fig. 18.7 shows the decline in the share of owner occupied dwellings among the rental properties between 1961-1978. The sharpest decline occurred in the rapid turnover category where 41% of the sample properties were occupied by the owner in 1961 versus 10% in 1978. The rise in absentee ownership in central Madison was great in rapid turnover properties.

Fig. 18.4 : Rapid Turnover and Appreciation : Seven Isthmus Area Census Tracts. 1976 Sales Data

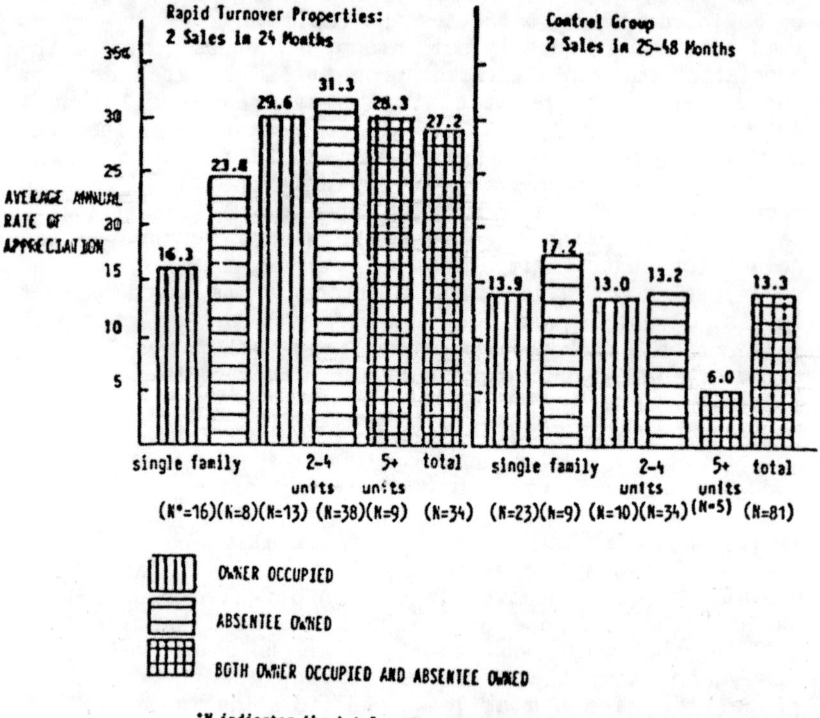

*N indicates the total number of paired sales. For example, a property that was sold in June, 1976 and in June, 1975 is one paired sale in our rapid turnover category.

Tenant and Owner Interviews

The principal aim of these interviews was to explore the differences between owners and tenants in rapid property turnover or other properties that have not been sold as often. Forty-seven tenant interviews were conducted in almost every sample rental property. The interviewer was instructed to find the tenant who had the longest tenure in the building. Ninety per cent of the tenants living in rapid turnover buildings replied that they had lived in the building only since 1978 compared to 65% of the tenants living in the control group.

Fig. 18.5 : Rapid Turnover and Rate of Appreciation : 1977/78 City Wide Data

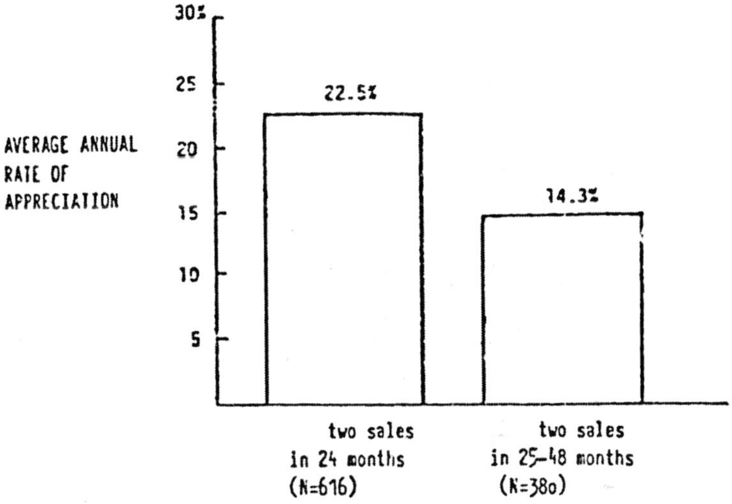

30.5%

Of the 33 sample rapid turnover properties, 29 owners were interviewed. Since we were interested to ask an owner why he/she bought and sold a property, we interviewed the next to most recent owner. The typical investor in a rapid turnover property entered the rental real estate market more recently and also was more likely to engage in real estate on a full or half time basis, in contrast to the owners of the other recent sale properties who typically engaged in real estate on an occasional basis. Second, the reasons that owners gave for buying and selling a property differed between the two groups : owners of the other recent sale properties cited reasons for buying and selling that relate to life cycle decisions like purchase of a property for retirement income and later selling it because they retire; investors in rapid turnover properties were more likely to give responses that reflect exigencies of the real estate market or federal tax laws.

Fig. 18.6 : Rapid Turnover and Rate of Appreciation : 1977/78 Isthmus Area Data

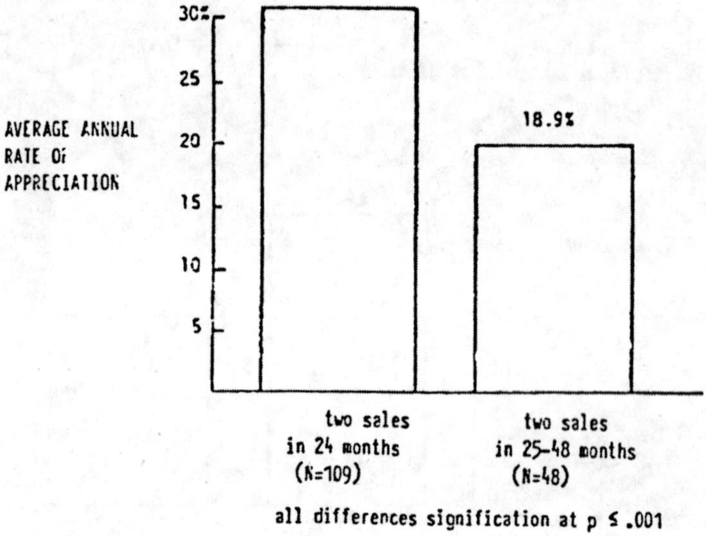

Fig. 18.7 : Owner Occupancy of Rental Properties, 1961-1978

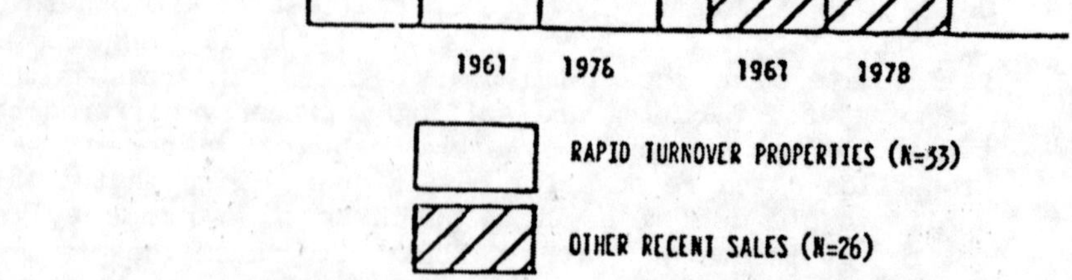

N is sample size. In each case, we used a random numbers table to generate the samples from an appropriate population.

Fig. 18.8 : Distribution of Rapid Turnover Properties as a Proportion of Residentia Residential Sales

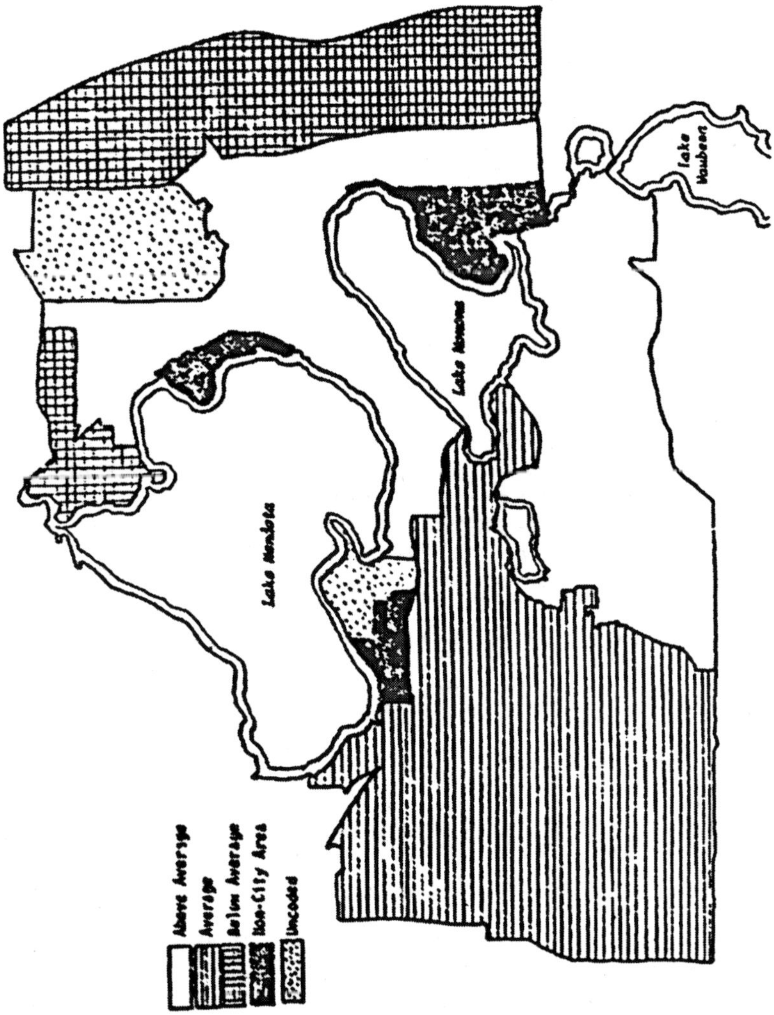

Summary and Discussions

Rapid turnover, the measure of housing speculation in this study, is associated with inflated housing costs, a high indidence of building code violations, high tenant transiency, and increased absentee-ownership. These problems affect not only the tenants in rapid turnover properties, but also other renters and homeowners whose housing costs and property tax assessments are inflated by the effect of speculative investment practices. Housing speculation also affects the neighborhoods in which it occurs. Poorly kept properties and highly transient tenants detract from the quality and stability of neighbourhood housing.

Rapid turnover properties inflate artificially the overall housing market since the assessment of unsold properties is largely derived from the sale prices of recently sold properties of similar type and location. Short-term ownership does not carry with it incentives to maintain properties, make quality improvements, or maintain good tenant and neighbourhood relations. Similarly, landlords who live in their property and other small-scale landlords are less likely to engage in rapid turnover practices than larger-scale real estate investors whose entry into the housing market appears to have exacerbated housing inflation and related problems in rental housing.

CONCLUSIONS

This study investigates the relationship between housing speculation, housing inflation, tenure, quality, and neighbourhood, stability. This exploratory research suggests the types of dislocations and market distortions that shifts investment behaviour toward the use of housing for speculative investment rather than its service or use value. Further study might well indicate the relationship between local speculative practices (which can vary beyond our limited treatment) and other local housing problems such as displacement (Le Gates and Hartman, 1981), condominium conversion (Advance Mortgage Corporation, 1979; Goetze, 1981), and the distortion of new production towards luxury housing (Le Gates and Murphy, 1981). The potential tenant and housing conflicts resulting from these relations requires further policy study and programmatic responses.

In order to identify housing problems, local governments might use existing city, real estate, and banking data to monitor the flow and location of housing investment. This information would allow for better targeting of local, state, and federal housing assistance programs. Also, it would insure that federally chartered banks were complying with their legal obligations to communities (e.g., under the Community Reinvestment Act) and that housing investors were not involved in discriminatory practices. Moreover, it would allow tenants, homeowners, and resident investors with better market information for residential and responsible investment decisions. This information would allow municipalities to develop proactive, rather than reactive regulatory responses—e.g., rent control, code enforcements, and windfall profits tax on housing speculation (such taxes were introduced in Germany federally in 1906). Finally, such policy and planning analysis of local conditions might justify creative local public/private investment strategies (in co-operative or conversion of commercial space to residential use) that would encourage affordable and accountable new housing production.[6] This kind of local state intervention might restructure the community housing market in such a way that further nationally caused housing inflation would result in new appreciation being captured by local community (e.g., neighbourhood development corporations), and/or joint public/private initiatives that could reinvest unearned increment into further production for shelter needs rather than speculative profit.

Acknowledgement

Assistance on the research from which this paper derives came from my co-investigators at Coact Research of Madison, Wisconsin, Jim Roseberry and E.G. Nadeau. Thanks also go to Barbara Forrest and Valerie Hodgson who prepared the graphic displays. I would also like to thank Kathy Naherny of the City Planning Department and Pat Schulte of the City Assessor's Office of the City of Madison for their cooperation in the study.

NOTES

Paper presented at the "European Meeting on Applied Urban Research", Erren. Oct. 2-4, 1981.

1 I am grateful to Jon Brown, chief economist of the Housing Task Force of Public Citizen, Washington, D.C. who pointed out to me Federal Trade Commission data indicating the relationship between recent concentration in building goods industry and evidence of adminstered pricing in building materials.

2 The Santa Barbara replication of the Madison speculation study reinforces our initial findings. In Santa Barbara, all properties apreciated at an annual rate about equal to the overall rate of inflation in income properties, while rapid turnover properties appreciated at an annual rate 10% higher than the overall rate. Rental property was the major focus of speculative activity; 18% of all rental structures had been purchased in the previous year, and 54% had turned over at least once during the previous four years. The turnover rate for rental property was therefore twice that of a single-family home. Owner-occupied rental properties experience the same low rates of turnover as single-family properties, suggesting the presence of large, professional investors in the speculative market. Additionally, the Santa Barbara study indicated that speculation was associated with increased property ownership concentration. Speculators use unearned increment, the profits acquired from the sale or refinancing of rapidly appreciating property, to acquire additional holdings. In Santa Barbara, 2.5% of the owners own at least 25% of the rental units based on incomplete data.

3 Neighbourhood level comparisons for three central city neighbourhoods within the 7-tract Isthmus area were also done (Coact, 1979 : 29-33). These findings were of use to neighbourhood planners from the City Planning Department, neighbourhood associations, and tenant groups who requested that level of analysis. There was little significant variation between these neighbourhoods, but the findings were useful for the formulation of neighbourhood responses.

4 The pattern of rapid turnover rates in different parts of the city should be discussed in reference to four processes : (1) the demand for rental units accelerated rental conversion of single family homes and other rental property sales primarily in the near east and central area of the city; (2) condominium conversion on the near east side; (3) some homeowners made a transition from smaller, older homes to larger, newer dwellings on the east, south, and outlying areas of the city; and (4) upper and middle income homeowners were transferred in and out of the city in a short period of time by their employers primarily in the outlying areas of the city.

5 Because these results are so dramatic and constitute a crucial finding in the study, we took a number of precautions in analyzing the appreciation data. 1976 was deliberately chosen as the base year for the analysis

because it was a year of low average appreciation. A study undertaken by John Matthews and Dean Wichern of the University of Wisconsin School of Business determined that the annual appreciation rate for sales of single family dwellings in Madison was 9.0% in 1973, 8.6% in 1974, 12.3% in 1975 and 8.2% in 1976. Since 1976 had the lowest average appreciation in this four year period, we avoid the bias of short term turnover properties having their appreciation rates inflated by different general market conditions between the first and second sale. A second important precaution was to determine whether there were any differences in appreciation rates between warranty deed sales and land contract sales. By analyzing the appreciation rates separately for warranty deed sales we were able to determine that warranty deed and land contract sales had very similar patterns of appreciation, and thus that the use of land contract sales was not a source of bias in the results. Finally, properties that sold two times in less than six months were treated as if the sales dates were six months apart. The effect of this treatment is to reduce the annualized appreciation rate on these properties. This avoids the appearance of astronomical appreciation rates for very rapid turnover properties, and, in fact, biases the data against an association between short term turnover and high appreciation. (For example, a property that was bought for $100,000 in March and resold for $105,000 in April has an annualized appreciation rate of 60%, however, we treat the annual appreciation as 10%).

6. The further dismantlement of federal housing initiatives and the promotion of speculation through tax and housing measures proposed by the Reagan Administration coincides with the peaking of the housing crisis. This coincidence of political, economic, and demographic trends will most certainly shift the focus of housing struggles from the national to the local potitical arena. In this context, local governments, no longer able to rely upon federal growth policies and housing renewal and subsidization, will be increasingly forced to monitor and effectively control local housing markets.

REFERENCES

Advance Mortgage Corporation, "Undocumented Boom : Conversions doubled in 1978," **U.S. Housing Markets**, 20. April, 1979.

Alonso, W., The Population Factor and Urban Structure. Cambridge, Mass. : Harvard University Center for Population Studies, Working Paper O. 102, 1977.

Appelbaum, Richard, P., **Housing For Whom : Housing on the South Coast.** Santa Barbara, Department of Sociology, University of California, Santa Barbara, 1980.

Appelbaum, R.P. and T. Glasser, "Housing Speculation in Santa Barbara, " Department of Sociology, University of California, Santa Barbara, 1981.

Coact Research, Residential Property Turnover Study : A Report to the City of Madison. Madison, Wisconsin : Coact, 1979.

Consumers Opposed to Inflation in Necessities. There are Alternatives. Washington, D.C. : COIN, 1979.

Downs, Anthony, **The Future of Rental Housing in America.** Washington, D.C. : The Brookings Institution, 1979.

Frieden, B. and Solomon, A., **The Nation's Housing, 1975-1985.** Cambridge, Mass. : MIT/ Harvard Joint Center for Urban Studies, April, 1977.

Goetze, Rolf, "The Housing Bubble", Working Papers for a New Society, (January/February) : 44-52, 1981.

Lauria, Mickey, "Marxian Rent Theory and Strategies for Neighborhood Redevelopment," paper presented at the conference on **New Perspective on the Urban Political Economy**, Department of Economics, American University, Washington, D.C., May, 1981.

LeGates, Richard and Chester Hartman, **Gentrification-caused Displacement**, Department of Urban Studies, San Francisco State University, San Francisco, California, 1981.

LeGates, Richard and K. Murphy, "Austerity, Shelter, and Social Conflict in the Unites States," **International Journal of Urban and Regional Research**, 5/2, June, 1981.

Marcuse, Peter, **The Political Economy of Rent Control : Theory and Strategy**, Papers in Planning, Department of City Planning, Columbia University, New York City, 1978.

Starr, Paul and Gosta Esping-Andersen, "Passive Intervention," Working Papers for a New Society, July, 15-25, 1979.

U.S. Bureau of Census, **Annual Housing Survey**, Washington, D.C. : Government Printing Office, 1973-78.

U.S. Comptroller General, **Rental Housing Report.** Washington, D.C. : Government Printing Office, 1979.

U.S. Department of Housing and Urban Development, **Home Mortgage Disclosure Act and Reinvestment Strategies.** Washington, D.C. : GPO, January, 1979.

NINETEEN

Yona Ginsberg and Arza Churchman

The Future of Housing Quality

Satisfaction with Living Quality in Multi-Story Housing

SOME CHARACTERISTICS OF THE ISRAELI HOUSING MARKET

IT SHOULD be pointed out that the housing market in Israel differs from many countries in several respects : (a) a large proportion of the housing construction has been carried out by the Ministry of Construction and Housing for specific population groups (young couples, new immigrants, the elderly, those living in substandard housing). 42% of the dwelling units completed in 1978 were built by the public sector; (b) most apartments are owner-occupied in some form of condominium arrangement. In 1961 60 per cent of the dwelling units were owner-occupied; by 1978 this had increased to 70 per cent; (c) most of the urban population of Israel lives in apartment buildings. In recent years, less than 5 per cent of the dwelling units in urban areas has been low density buildings, such as single-family and terraced houses. The typical building is that of four storeys with 8 to 16 flats.

In recent years high-rise housing has become a common phenomenon in Israel, and buildings of 8 to 20 storeys with up to 120 apartments have been constructed in the urban centres. However, despite the fact that many of these housing units are built by the urban sector, their impact has not been examined by policy-makers.

This paper is based mainly on a study on high-rise housing; with some references to two additonal studies[1]. The study on high-rise housing was carried out in 3 middle class neighbourhoos of Haifa, Israel. Individual, structured interviews were conducted with 344 randomly selected women.

The sample was drawn from high-rise buildings varying in height — 8,12,16 and 20 storeys high and included a control group from 4 storey buildings. In addition, the cleanliness and maintenance of the semi-public areas of the buildings were evaluated by an objective observer.

Most of the families in the sample were young (2/3 of the women were under 35); native Israelis or of European origin. 1/2 of the women had an academic education, 2/3 of them were gainfully employed, mainly in academic or clerical work. Most had 1 or 2 children and lived in 2-3 bedroom apartments. As is common in Israel, all were owners of their apartments. No difference were found between the building heights in these characteristics.

SUMMARY OF THE FINDINGS

Image and Satisfaction

Among the high-rise residents, there was a general consensus that the height of the buildings is an advantage in terms of the view, but a disadvantage in terms of overdependence on the elevator. There was no consensus as to children being too limited in their ability to go outside to play; as half of the respondents thought that children are limited in this respect. In terms of the relatively large number of residents in a high-rise building, the consensus was that this offers the advantages both of more anonymity and of a greater variety of adults and children from whom to choose friends.

The control group had a consistently more negative image of high-rise living than did those who live there. The fact that those who live in the high-rise buildings differentiate between various issues, indicates that their more positive image is based upon their experiences, and is not merely a dissonance-reducing phenomenon. In our study of many-entrance buidlings we found a similar pattern, i.e., that their residents had a more positive image of that building type than the control group.

There were no significant differences on various measures of satisfaction between the different size buildings, or between high-rise and low-rise residents. 69 per cent of the high-rise sample were satisfied with their building, 84 per cent with their apartment, and 88 per cent with the storey on which their apartment was located.

Despite the general picture of relatively high satisfaction, 74 per cent would prefer living in a building lower than their present one, and about half expressed the desire to move to another apartment. However, again, the low-rise control group did not differ in these regards, nor were there any significant differences between buidlings of different sizes. The main reason for residential mobility aspirations, among all groups, was that their apartment was too small.

Neighbor Relations

It is clear that respondents who wish to, are able to develop active ties with their neighbours. In contrast to the widespread image of high-rise housing, these residents were far from being isolated from their neighbours. Only 5 per cent of the sample (even in the tallest buildings), reported not knowing any other resident in her building. On the other hand, 26 per cent reported knowing a majority of the residents. As could be expected, however, the taller the buildings the smaller the proportion of neighbours known.

As for active neighbor relations, 70 per cent of the respondents reported exchanging help with their neighbours and visiting one another. No relationship was found between helping or visiting patterns, and the height of the building. Intensive ties with neighbours seem to be limited in most cases to a small number of families. Therefore, it does not make a difference what height the building is and how many people live there.

It seems that the stage in the life cycle is a more significant variable in explaining neighbor relations than the building itself. Families without children living at home tend to have fewer contracts with their neighbours than those with children. In general, women over the age of 45 reported having less helping and visiting relationships with their neighbours than younger ones. It is interesting to note that in contrast to other studies (Michelson 1977), we did not find any difference in neighbor relation between women working outside their homes and those who did not work.

Most of the sample were satisfied with the nature of their relations with the neighbours, and only a few complained that they had fewer ties than they would have liked. Furthermore, despite the large number of residents, there were few reported instances of arguments and conflicts between neighbours

It could be argued, as others did, (Gans, 1968) that the positive neighbor relations were due to the fact that the high-rise population was quite homogeneous in its demographic and social economic characteristics. Indeed, over half of the respondents perceived their neighbours as being similar to themselves in age, education, ethnic background and economic circumstances. Moreover, although no relationship was found between perceived similarity and helping behaviour, a positive association was found that the former (with the exception of ethnicity) and visiting pattern. Thus, it seems that a certain degree of perceived homogeneity is important, at least for more intimate neighbor relations. However, our study of many-entrance buildings suggests that a certain degree of heterogeneity, even in the same building, is not a problem so long as it is not extreme.

Crowding and Privacy

With regard to the residents' everyday experiences, building height per se was not related to the frequency with which they encounter other people in the semi-public areas of the building. It was, however, related to the frequency with which they encounter people whom they do not know. This was more likely to occur in the taller buildings than in the 8 or 12 storey ones. These experiences were not, however, related to subjective feelings of crowding.

There was no straightforward relationship between building height and feelings of crowding within the building. Residents of the two extremes, the 8 and 20 storey buildings, were significantly more likely to feel crowded than were residents of the 12 and 16 storey buildings. Feelings of crowding were negatively related to the satisfaction with the building and with the number of rooms of residents' apartments. There were no significant differences between high-rise and low-rise. For both groups the neighbourhood was rated as more crowded than the building.

90 per cent of the respondents said that they have privacy in the building. The problem of acoustic privacy in these buildings is more critical than that of visual privacy in the sense that a larger percentage can be heard than seen. About 50 per cent of the sample reported that it is possible to see into their apartment from the outside; and a majority (70 per cent) reported that one can hear from

apartment to apartment. We also found that where acoustic privacy was invaded, residents complained more of problems with their neighbours. However, on the whole, a somewhat larger percentage were disturbed by infringement of visual privacy, than that of acoustic privacy.

Children's Outdoor Play Opportunities

In popular writings the major problem associated with high-rise living is its general implications for children and specifically for the possibilities of unaccompanied outdoor play. In our sample, all children from the age of 6, and 52 per cent of those aged 4-5, were allowed to play outside alone. The critical factor was clearly age, although for ages 4-5 there was an increase in the percentage who cannot play outside alone with an increase in the height of the building. (From 33 per cent in 8 to 62 per cent in 16-20 storey buildings). The children were allowed this freedom even though 50 per cent of the mothers reported not being able to see or hear them when they were outside.

The taller buildings seem to be more problematic in this respect. More children who live in them play only inside the home. They are less likely to offer the possibility for contact from the apartment to the outside, and women who live there were more likely to agree that children in high-rise buildings are "stuck inside". However, in the comparison of the way children are raised in high-rise vs. low-rise buildings there were significant differences between neighborhoods rather than between building heights. This suggests that there are a number of relevant factors rather than the simple one of height. The situation was most difficult for families whose children were all under age 5, and this expressed itself both behaviorally and attitudinally.

Maintenance

This issue may be specific to Israel because maintenance is completely in the hands of the residents, and requires agreement amongst them. The usual legal arrangement is for each family to own its apartment, while the yard, stairs, elevator and other facilities of the building are common property. Maintenance of the structure in the semi-public areas is the responsibility of the residents and is usually arranged by a residents' committee. However, it is difficult for the residents' committee to take legal action against any apartment owner who refuses to pay his share of the expenses and to carry out an active policy of improvement and even maintenance.

One would assume that the larger the building, the more difficult it would be to reach a consensus among residents. However, it seems that residents of larger buildings are more likely to adopt the norms of organizing for maintenance. In each of the high-rise buildings in our sample, there was a residents' committee to take care of the maintenance, and the respondents expressed a high level of satisfaction with its functioning. In fact, satisfaction with the committee increased with building height. Subjective and objective evaluations of the cleanliness and maintenance were positively related, although not very highly. Subjective evaluations were more related to satisfaction with the building than were the objective evaluations.

CONCLUSIONS

As is evident, our findings do not confirm the negative image of high-rise housing. In our sample there were hardly any problems of isolation from neighbours, feelings of crowding or difficulties in organizing for maintaining the building. The only families with problems seem to be those whose children are all under the age of 5. Other than this aspect, our studies indicate that for Israeli middle-class families even with 2-3 children, this kind of housing does not pose particular problems. Thus it is clear that high-rise housing cannot be categorically considered good or bad. It may be more suitable for certain population groups than for others.

It should also be emphasized that most of the complaints voiced by our respondents related to design or planning problems not inherent to high-rise buildings. Thus, lack of acoustic privacy or lack of outdoor play facilities were complaints voiced equally by respondents in the study conducted by us in lower buildings. It would seem that public policy should be directed at improving those design and planning aspects.

The differences between our results and the negative image of such buildings in other countries may reflect the following contextual deferences : (a) differences in the socio-economic status of the residents and their family size; high-rise residents are mainly middle-class, medium-size families. (b) cultural differences in neighbor relations and the freedom of movement of children; it is customary and even expected that families with children will help each other and hence be in frequent contact. (c) the fact that Israeli apartments are owner-occupied rather than rented. (d) deferences in the size of the buildings and the number of families. (In Israel high-rise housing does not exceed 20 storeys and 120 families). (e) the difference in the housing alternatives to which comparison are made; in many countries the comparison is to one-family houses, while in Israel it is to smaller but still multi-family buildings.

NOTES

Paper presented at the "European Meeting on Applied Urban Research", Erren. Oct. 2-4, 1981.

1 The two other studies included the following housing types : (a) 4-storey row houses with 3 or 4 entrances, and sited differently in relation to the street (Churchman & Ginsberg, 1980); (b) 8-storey buildings with bridge entrances designed to cope with the hilly terrain (Ginsberg & Churchman, 1978).

REFERENCES

Churchman, A and Ginsberg, Y., **Many Entrance Buildings : Resident Attitudes and Behaviour Patterns.** Israel Ministry of Works and Housing, Jeruselem (Hebrew) 1980.

Gans, H., **People & Places.** Basic Books, New York 1968.

Ginsberg, Y. and Churchman, A., **Behaviour Patterns and Neighbour Relations in High-Rise Housing : A comparative Study.** Israel Ministry of Works & Housing, Jerusalem (Hebrew) 1978.

Jephcott, P., **Homes in High Flats.** Oliver & Boyd, Edinbugh 1971.

McCarthy, D. and Saegert, S., Residential Density, Social Overload and Social Withdrawal. **Human Ecology** 6, 1978 pp. 253-272.

Mackintosh, E., Olsen, R. and Wentworth W., The Middle Income Family's Experience in an Urban High-rise complex and the Suburban Single-Family Home. Graduate Center, City University of New York 1977.

Marcus, E. and Hogue, L., Design Guidelines for High Rise Housing. **Journal of Architectural Research** 5, 1976, pp. 34-49.

Michelson, W., **Environmental Choice, Human Behaviour and Residential Satisfaction.** Oxford University Press, New York 1977.

Stevenson, A., **High Living : A Study of Family Life in Flats.** Melbourne University Press, Melbourne 1967.

Werckele, G. and Hall, E., High-rise Living : Can the Same Design serve Young and Old? **Ekistics** 33, 1972 pp. 186-191.

TWENTY

Dieter Frick

Evaluation of the Quality of Usage of Urban Residential Quarters Through the Communicational Behaviour of Inhabitants

Approach to an Empirical Study

POSING THE PROBLEM

There is no lack of criticism concerning the social quality or quality of usage of urban residential quarters. On the one hand, it is directed at the increasing loss of this quality in the course of modernisation and sanitation measures, the intensification of traffic load and air pollution, predominantly in older, inner city localities, on the other hand it is directed at mainly peripheral quarters dating back to the last 2-3 decades in which such quality often did not even develop at all. Also in segregational processes which are concomitant with the outward drift from the city nucleus or with the phenomena of vandalism in the residential quarter, deficits in the quality of urban living conditions are to be found. All the same, the demands made upon the individual's physical and psychical reproduction have rather increased in view of the specific burdens which many people have to bear at their place of work.

The frequency and emphasis of such criticism denote an enhanced consciousness regarding the fact that the quality of the living conditions in the residential area consists of more than mere accommodation, technical comforts of living, status symbol or being equipped with all kinds of devices, and spatially it extends beyond the front door or the next street crossing. This 'extra factor'relates to social conditions in the immediate and more remote environment of the apartment, residential surroundings and quarter, as well as to urban design conditions, the manner the apartments or business premises, the buildings and other installations as well as their adjacent outdoor spaces are arranged in relation to each other. Accordingly, quality of usage, in the context of the project outlined here, is defined as those characteristics of urban design structures, which contribute positively to the creation of social conditions in the residential surroundings and in the quarter. Vice versa, conclusions are drawn from the specific nature and manifestation of the social conditions in the quarter with respect to the quality of usage of the urban design structure. However, how can the goal addressed in this context be defined and how can quality of usage be measured?

The few examples reflecting a cautious and resolute approach to existing quarters or an urban design conception for new quarters which favours their social quality have to make their way in the face of considerable opposition and are seldom realized. Nevertheless, one can conclude from such examples that the aim of preserving, improving or initiating quality of usage, can be realized in principle. In addition, numerous older quarters which have not yet been changed by recent planning show that a satisfactory quality of usage often came into existence rather 'accidentally' and almost always is the product of a development over a lenghty period of time. We have a number of quarters on hand with, as it were, an intuitively ascertainable, existing or lacking quality of usage, the measuring of which is a task to be taken in hand in order to attain criteria which are more easily objectifiable.

The theoretic approach to the project to be presented here proceeds from the fundamental assumption that the quality of usage of a residential quarter (or a spatial subunit thereof) is based on the possibility of territorial appropriation by the inhabitants. Territorial appropriation is advanced or hampered by certain social and physical structures in the quarter. We assume that they mainfest themselves in the presence or absence of certain individual and social modes of behaviour. The relation between such modes of behaviour and the social and physical structures in the quarter indicates quality of usage.

Communicational behaviour in the outdoor space is selected as a relevant section of such modes of behaviour. Communication in this context is defined as a presupposing and determining factor in respect to the territorial appropriation of semi-public and public spaces in that the usage of such spaces by different groups of inhabitants or adjoining inhabitants requires a concept of quality which to a certain extent is common to all. The communicative relations, relevant in this context, which extend beyond the apartment and which take place within a single quarter, manifest themselves in the outdoor space or are related thereto. The precondition for this is that the outdoor space is suitable for these purposes and is accepted. Otherwise the communication, which characteristically is semi-public or public, has to be limited to the apartment, which adversely affects the development of the exchange as well as the private sphere (Heil, 1971). In the outdoor space, different forms of territorial behaviour present themselves within the range between withdrawing and opening up, individual and social action, as well as between what is private and what is public (Zinn, 1978; Bahrdt, 1961).

The operationalization of the relation between physical structures and attitudes, perception and modes of behaviour (in the context of human territoriality) was tested with reference to the 'Defensible Space Theory'. With his investigation aimed at examining his theory, Newman (1972, 1973) made a significant step towards operationalization in researching the relation between physical structures and social behaviour - limited, however, to the contribution of physical conditions to crime restriction or its prevention. Taylor, Gottfredson and Brower (1978, 1979) criticize Newman's concept under certain aspects as inadequate and expand it by taking the socio-cultural context in quarters to be investigated into consideration and by considering not only the physical but also the social potential for appropriation[2]. Our approach proceeds from the usage or appropriation potential existent in the physical and social structures.

2. AIMS AND INVESTIGATION APPROACH

Against the background of the research results in hand, the following limitations are made for the investigation approach pursued here :

- By 'physical structure' in an area we understand the way the buildings and other facilities are arranged in relation to each other to form a building and accessibility system, which can be seen positively (as building structure) or negatively (as outdoor space structure). The investigation approach focuses on the outdoor space, inter alia because on an urban design level it makes the more comprehensive aspect feasible, morphologically it is continuous and functionally it is designated for multi-purposes, i.e., more flexible in terms of usage.

- For social strata whose living situation is characterised by a high degree of dependence, pressure to conform and material as well as social deprivation, the residential quarter-related outdoor space in its various forms (private, semi-private, semi-public, public) has a special function as a spatial reference quantity of social self-presentation and individual as well as collective self-realisation (Heil, 1971; Bostrom/Gunter, 1976 and others). The investigation approach is therefore aimed at residential quarters in which these social strata are dominant.

- The quality of usage of physical structures presupposes the territorial appropriation of these structures by the inhabitants. Territorial appropriation inter alia means a familiarising process and constant incorporation of the buildings and outdoor spaces or their elements in the everyday models of perception and modes of behaviour. The investigation approach is aimed at that section of the process which manifests itself in the communicational behaviour of the residents or the adjoining inhabitants.

- Communicational behaviour with regard to physical structure is to be interpreted in two ways : on the one hand, a high degree of social interlocking, communicational interaction and collective creative action can be seen as an expression of social functionality of outdoor space structures and single outdoor spaces. In this context, urban design concepts and measures are both assessable as supporting/impeding factors within the multilevel complex of 'social behaviour' and verifiable in their quality of usage. On the other hand, physical and social potentials relating to communicational behaviour in the outdoor space are described as accessible to the planning and could be further developed by making available appropriate urban design and social measures conducive to the creation of more human reproductive conditions in urban residential quarters.

The aims of this research project are :

1. Determining and assessing the significance of the effects of
   - specific characteristics of outdoor spaces (physical potential for territorial appropriation)
   - specific characteristics of adjoining inhabitants

and employees (social potential for territorial appropriation)
on the communicational behaviour of the users of the outdoor spaces.

2. Comparative evaluation of
   - the quality of usage of the outdoor spaces/outdoor space structures
   - the appropriation ability of the users

   in different quarters in the light of their communicational behaviour in the outdoor space on the basis of the ascertained effects (aim 1).

3. Determining the significance of the physical as opposed to the social potential in their effects on the communicational behaviour in the outdoor space of the examined quarters.

4. Formulating physical or social measures in order to
   - guarantee/improve the quality of usage of the examined outdoor spaces/outdoor space structures
   - stabilise/strengthen the appropriation ability of the users of the examined outdoor spaces/outdoor space structures

on the basis of the results of the comparative evaluation.

Following Taylor, Gottfredson and Brower (1978, 1979), a model based on an extended 'Defensible Space Theory' is used for the analytical part of the planned investigation (Fig. 20.1). They use 'criminal behaviour' as dependent variable which indicates a deficit in territorial appropriation. On the contrary, the approach pursued here uses 'communicational behaviour in the outdoor space' as dependent variable (H) which serves as an indicator of a certain degree of successful appropriation. Independent variables are : the 'physical potential for territorial appropriation' (D) and the 'social potential for territorial appropriation' (E). Their influence on the communicational behaviour in the outdoor space is to be measured. By the physical potential for territorial appropriation we understand the (physical) characteristics of an outdoor space which advance appropriation. By social potential for territorial appropriation we understand the (social) characteristics of the adjoining residents and users of the outdoor space which make appropriation possible. The mediating variables 'territorial behaviour' (F) and 'territorial cognition' (G) determine the relation between (D)/(E) and (H) to the extent that the physical potential of an outdoor space and the social potential of its adjoining residents and users only have an influence on the territorial appropriation or on the communicational behaviour in the outdoor space if they simultaneously support territorial behaviour and cognition in general (Taylor et al., 1978). As marginal conditions for comparative quarter investgations, we refer to certain physical and social structural characteristics (B)/(C) of potential areas of research which are decisive for selecting the residential quarters to be examined. It is assumed that there is an interrelation between these structural characteristics and the respective potential for territorial appropriation which exists in the quarter. The physical and social potentials for territorial appropriation are considered to be part of the structural characteristics of a quarter which promote appropriation or communicational behaviour in the outdoor space. The inclusion of the sociohistorical conditions in the quarter (A) which are contributory determinants of the existing physical and social structure, permits a causal verification and, if necessary, a more precise definition of the structural characteristics referred to. In addition, it is a precondition for the countrywide or intercultural comparison of investigation results.

Fig. 20.1 : Model of Analysis

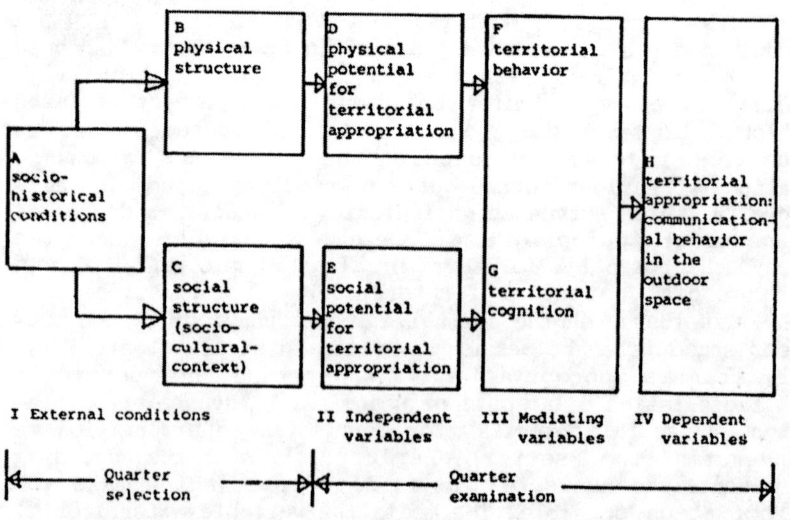

The result of the examination of a quarter or its outdoor space structure/its single outdoor spaces is the determining of the interrelation between the physical potential/the social potential for territorial appropriation and of the nature and degree of appropriation represented by communicational behaviour in the outdoor space - i.e., those characteristics of the physical and social structure of a quarter which hypothetically were adjudged a potential for territorial appropriation in advance, are examined as to the degree of their interrelation with characteristics of communicational behaviour in the outdoor space.

By means of a model of action (Chart 2) the relation between the analytical investigation results and their application is established : an evaluation of the quality of usage of the physical structure/of the appropriation ability of the users, formulation of the measures, changes in the structures of the quarter, changes in the appropriation potentials, improvement of the quality of usage/ strengthening the appropriation ability. The planned investigation extends to the step concerning evaluation (aims 1 to 3) which takes place on the basic of a comparison of the investigation results from several quarters. The evaluation is, however, carried out with a view to the formulation of urban design and social measures. The investigation is based on the following questions :

Fig. 20.2 : Model of Action

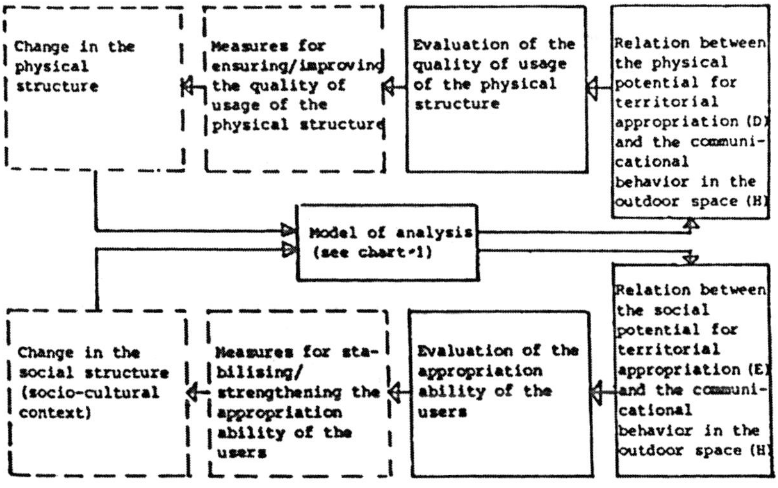

In respect of aim 1 :

- In the event of a given social potential, which

characteristics of the physical structure in a quarter (physical potential for territorial appropriation) hinder or promote communication in the outdoor space?

- In the event of a given social potential, to what extent is the physical potential of a single outdoor space dependent upon :

  - the nature of degree of closure of the limitation of space
  - the nature or degree of accessibility
  - the equipment with trees, benches, playing implements etc.
  - the degree of coincidence between the elements of traffic network and the outdoor space
  - the condition regarding the construction and maintenance of buildings and other facilities which border on the outdoor space
  - the equipment with installations of the public and private infrastructure

- In the event of a given social potential, to what extent is the physical potential of a quarter dependent upon :

  - the structuring of the outdoor space system (way the outdoor spaces are arranged in relation to each other)
  - the laying-out and structuring of the footway network (reciprocal attainability of the individual outdoor spaces in the quarter)
  - the equipment of the quarter with public and private infrastructure
  - the clear spatial differentiation between semi-private/ semi-public and public outdoor spaces

- In the event of a given physical potential, which characteristics or qualities of the social structure of a quarter (social potential for territorial appropriation) hinder or promote communication in the outdoor space?

- In the event of a given physical potential, to what extent is the social potential, relating to an outdoor space/a quarter, dependent upon :

  the neighbourhood solidarity amongst the in habitants

- . the socialisation experience of the inhabitants relating to the quarter
- . the proportion of inhabitants who are members ot local organisations
- . the use of local facilites of the social infrastructure.

In respect of aim 2 :

- In the event of comparable social potentials, to what extentis the (relative) quality of usage of the outdoor space structure in a quarter determined by the development and forms or mainfestation of the communicational behaviour in the outdoor space?

- In the event of comparable phsical potentials, to what extent is the (relative) appropriation ability of the inhabitants of a quarter determined by the development and forms of manifestation of the communicational behaviour in the outdoor space?

In respect of aim 3 :

- What degree of quality of usage of the individual outdoor spaces/the outdoor space structure is necessary to fully develop the appropriation ability of the inhabitants of a quarter?

- What degree of appropriation ability of the users is necessary so that the quality of usage of the outdoor spaces can have an effect favourable to territorial appropriadtion?

NOTES

Paper presented at the "European Meeting on Applied Urban Research", Erren. Oct. 2-4, 1981.

1. In cooperation with Karolus Heil, Dittmar Machule, Rudiger Schwencke, Michael Stein, Angelika Kowalev
2. For the state of the North-American discussion, see : Frick, 1979.

REFERENCES

Bahrdt, H.P., (1961). **Die moderne Grobstadt.** Reinbek/ Hamburg. Rowohlt.

Bostrom, J. R. Gunter, eds. (1976). **Arbeiterinitiativen im Ruhrgebiet.** Berlin (West). Verlag fur das Studium der Arbeiterbewegung.

Frick, D. (1979). Baulich-raumliche Strukturen and soziales Handeln in Stadtquartieren. In : **Archiv fur Kommunalwissenschaften.** 2. Halbjahresband 1979, pp. 241-262.

Heil, K. (1971). **Kommunikation und Entfremdung.** Stuttgart/ Bern. Karl Kramer.

Newman, O. (1972). **Defensible Space. Crime Prevention through Urban Design.** New York, N.Y. MacMillan.

Newman, O (1973). **Defensible Space. People and Design in the Violent City.** London. Architectural Press

Taylor, R.B., Gottfredson S.D., Brower, S., (1978). **Territoriality, Defensible Space, Informal Social control Mechanisms and Community Crime Prevention.** Baltimore, Md. The Johns Hopkins University, Center for Metropolitan Planning and Research

Taylor, R.B., Gottfredson, S.D.,Brower, S., (1979). **The Defensibility of Defensible Space : A Critical Review and a Synthetic Framework for Future Research.** Baltimore, Md. Center for Metropolitan Planning and Research, The Johns Hopkins University

Zinn, H. (1978). Raumgebundenes "territoriales" Handeln und Verhalten. Forschungskonzepte und empirische Ergebnisse. In : **Zusammenhang von gebauter Umwelt und sozialem Verhalten im Wohn- und Wohnumfeldbereich** (E. Mühlich et al., eds.) pp. 23-50. Bonn-Bad Godesberg. Bundesminister fur Raumordnung, Bauwesen und Stadtebau

TWENTY ONE

Helmut Kromrey

Evaluating the Quality of Residential Environments

1. SOME REQUIREMENTS TO RESEARCH INTO THE ASSESSMENT OF THE RESIDENTIAL ENVIRONMENT

Any research aiming at an empirical assessment of the quality of residential environments, or at results on the effects of residential surroundings on behaviour, cannot — according to the present standard of knowledge — be content with gathering questionnaire data. What is even more important : It is not sufficient to ascertain the information by asking direct questions concerning the subject to be examined.

On the one hand, if evaluations are investigated by asking residents in a direct way (e.g., "Are you satisfied with ...?"), the results often lead to nothing else than to the confirmation of existing attributes of the physical environments and of supply systems, thus helping to strengthen conservative ideas of planning and design. On the other hand it should be quite obvious that residential behaviour cannot at all be investigated validly merely by means of questionnaires. By asking questions you only gain statements on behaviour (the respondent's own behaviour or that of other persons).

In the latter case alternatives for gaining a more comprehensive account could for instance be : (a) the filling in of a standardized journal by the respondents, or (b) the research worker's direct observation of the behaviour modes in the residential areas.

In the case of the inhabitants' appraisals of the environmental quality some authors suggest indirect ways of investigation. A strategy often mentioned is the inhabitants' evaluations by reconstructing how the residents perceive their surroundings (see for instance Craik/Zube, 1976; Franke et. al., 1972, 1974, 1975) : Perception always includes evaluation at the same time.

In any case the analysis has to cope with problems of ascribing the findings (i.e., assessments or differences in behaviour) to the "objective" characteristics of the environment. To this purpose it is not sufficient for the study to represent heterogeneous residential areas (contrasting different types of living environments is a matter of course). In addition the analysis has to control for characteristics of the social context as well as for such individual attributes of the inhabitants that affect the personal view (or the behaviour) independent of the features of physical structures. Thus an empirical study on living conditions that wants to come up with results relevant for planning purposes, always has to be a complex one. Ideally, it should apply a mix of data-gathering instruments.

2. EVALUATING RESIDENTIAL ENVIRONMENTS : **SOME EMPIRICAL RESULTS**

The following remarks are based on an empirical study of my own. Its aim was to assess residential environments in the view of their inhabitants (Kromrey, 1981). The findings first of all confirm that the validity of perception-based indices, ascertained indirectly, is stronger, compared with the data gained by putting direct questions. Furthermore, it turned out for the perception/evaluation dimensions[1] that their refererence to the considered "objective" characteristics of the physical environment[2] varied in degree.

On the one hand there are two dimensions of perception that can be called "environmental quality"[3] and "modernity".[4] 54 resp. 64% of their variance can be accounted for by intercorrelations with the variables in the (linear) analysis model; and within this frame the variables representing the physical residential surroundings are predominant. It is therefore possible to say that these perception/evaluation dimensions tend to be rather descriptive, or at least include only inter-individualistic evaluations.

On the other hand there are three perception-based indices that can be termed "functional and social valency"[5] "valency of order"[6], and "emotional valency"[7]. With these indices, the ratios to which their variance can be accounted for by the variables considered, only amount to 29 resp. 27 resp. 17%. In addition individual features of the respondents as well as attributes of the social context become more significant. Thus, quite obviously, these indices seem to be dimensions of evaluation which are more individually coloured. In a more refined analysis, nowever, their reference to characteristics of the built environment can be shown, and so they, too, give evidence of the individually experienced quality of a residential quarter.

Without going into much detail, as a result of contrasting perceptions of the residents with features of the built environment three general tendencies can be pointed out :

(a) According to the residents' differentiating judgement urban life does by far not appear as negative as conventional research on housing aspirations and housing satisfaction seems to indicate. In the global responses and evaluations from the inhabitants of urban places, gathered by this kind of research, the negative consequences of disturbing traffic congestion and of uncontrolled mixture of city fuctions[8] dominate the advantages of urban living, which nevertheless are pointed out at the same time. Thus the refined analysis shows that (together with the dominating negative view evoked by the strongly experienced disadvantages mentioned above) the old urban environment is perceived as :

- familiar and "naturally" grown (i.e., not artificially planned),
- distinct and clearly arranged,
- not anonymous and not oppressing (in contrast to, for instance, densely built high-rise housing sites).

Thus suburban or exurban living does not seem to have a positive value of its own. It is rather the absence of troubles and annoyance, caused by the often deplored "destruction of the city" as a human habitat, that counts here.

(b) The alternative to multifunctional urban residential quarters therefore cannot be an escape into "pure" housing areas in the urban fringe : similar to the extreme intensity and extreme mix of land uses within the city the inhabitants also do not accept the monofunctional organization of space which is to be found in settlements planned exclusively for dwelling purposes. On the contrary, in addition to amenities like green plots and recreational space (as attributes of non-urban places) other, more urban characteristics are evaluated positively : a complete, household-oriented infrastructure as well as a (limited) mix of land uses with sites for various services and facilities.

(c) Rejected is finally any uniformity of buildings, configuration and design — be it the side-by-side arrangement of nearly identical one- or two-family houses, or the cramming of vast areas with multi-storey buildings with large, monotonous fronts. Positive assessments, on the other hand, are attributed to such elements of design as variation in height, concentration of buildings and service facilities in small centres, in brief : to a varied and multiplex built environment.

If we take into account all positively valued subjects of perception, we could combine them to a hypothetic image of an "ideal" residential quarter. This would lead to the hypothesis : A residential area that - at the same time - unites the advantages of urban quarters with those of "green" habitats and does not have the disadvantages of both, should look like this :

It is not a monofunctional dwelling place. It has shopping facilities, crafts and other private and public services, scattered all over the area. Yet the functional and land-use mix is limited in a way as not to disturb residential qualities appreciated by the inhabitants, such as outdoor activities. Concerning the dimensions and the design of the projected environment, large-scale multi-storey buildings have been avoided in this "ideal spot" as well as any uniform, straight lined one- or two-family houses. Instead the planner has strived for a variformed and multifarious residential quarter with some variation in height and density of buildings (concentrating towards a small centre), with some open space and green plots spread all over the area.

Not only this. The concept would - in addition - have to avoid the impression of being a drawing-board produced, artificially constructed, resident-alienated ensemble of "retort" buildings. The best concept thus appears to be one that the inhabitants do not at all perceive as being designed by an architect "for the purpose of dwelling".

Everyone will, of course, see that the planner and the architect will never be able to fulfil the task of creating a residential area that shows all these attributes at the same time. Nevertheless such findings point out, which elements of design and land use are - in the view of urban residents - compatible and which are not.

NOTES

Paper presented at the "European Meeting on Applied Urban Research", Erren. Oct. 2-4, 1981.

1 The dimensions were extracted by means of factor analysis from a battery of opinion statements (rating scales).

2 That is, spatial organization/configuration and design, quality of the built environment, its functional organization and context, services and facilities.

3 The index "environmental quality" points out the disadvantages of city areas (mainly noise, strain, numerous buildings densely crowded together, dirty backyards, feelings of insecurity, lack of nature) in contrast to the advantages of non-urban areas (such as well-kept surroundings, quietude, air quality, cleanliness, "human dimension", nature and amenity resources, familiarity, feeling of security).

4 The index "modernity" contrasts the impression of "modern" surroundings (i.e., progressive architecture, new, practical, matter-of-fact, but also "weighty"/ oppressing buildings) with the feeling of familiarity ("naturally grown", old and familiar, full of variety, not artificial and not oppressing).

5 The index "functional and social valency" accounts for the variety and vividness of the residential area (advantages of a multifunctional quarter such as variety, complexity, entertainment, homelike atmosphere; the environment being perceived neither as "cold" nor without human contact). The other end of the scale - disadvantages of monofunctional areas - entails evaluations like monotony, lack of human contact, boredom, "coldness", quietude.

6 "Valency of order" on the one hand means that the area is perceived as clearly organized, well-kept and attractive, including a "human dimension" (not oppressing or "weighty") as well as giving possibilities of orientation. The other pole of the scale stands for the feeling of a lack of order : disorderly, badly built, "crooked", dense and narrow, evoking feelings of insecurity.

7 "Emotional valency" means that feelings of familiarity,

harmony and being at home are established. The residential environment is experienced as neither cold nor repulsing, neither alien nor artificial, home-like, inviting, full of variety, promoting contact, clearly arranged and with "human dimension". Contrary evaluations correspond with the opposite side of the index.

8 Such as endangerment, noise, air pollution, broad "street gulfs" cutting through residential neighbourhoods, destruction of living space by concentration of commercial and administrative land use (in German : ungesteuerte Funktionsmischung).

REFERENCES

Craik, Kenneth H., Zube, E.H, (eds.) Perceiving Environmental Quality. Research and Applications, New York, London 1976.

Franke, Joachim et. al. (1972, 1974, 1975). Beitrage zur Anwendung der Psychologie auf den Stadtebau :

I : Voruberlegungen und erste Erkundungsuntersuchung der Beziehung zwischen Siedlungsgestaltung und Erleben der Wohnumgebung (Franke/Bortz). In : **Zeitschrift fur experimentelle und angewandte Psychologie**, 1972.

II : Erkundungsexperiment zur Beziehung zwischen Fassadengestaltung und ihrer Wirkung auf den Betrachter (Bortz). In : **Zeitschrift fur experimentelle und angewandte Psychologie**, 1972.

III : Allgemeine Strukturkomponenten des Images von Siedlungsgebieten (Franke/Hoffmann). In : Zeitschrift fur experimentelle und angewandte Psychologie, 1974.

IV : Zusammenhange zwischen baulichen Merkmalen und dem Image von Siedlungsgebieten (Franke/Rothgang). In : **Zeitschrift fur experimentelle und angewandte Psychologie**, 1975.

Kromrey, Helmut . **Die gebaute Umwelt.** Wohngebietsplanung im Bewohnerurteil, Opladen 1981.

Index